Agency, contingency and census process:

Observations of the 2006 Indigenous Enumeration Strategy in remote Aboriginal Australia

Frances Morphy (Editor)

ANU

THE AUSTRALIAN NATIONAL UNIVERSITY

E PRESS

Centre for Aboriginal Economic Policy Research
The Australian National University, Canberra

Research Monograph No. 28
2007

ANU

E PRESS

Published by ANU E Press
The Australian National University
Canberra ACT 0200, Australia
Email: anuepress@anu.edu.au
This title is also available online at: http://epress.anu.edu.au/c28_citation.html

---

National Library of Australia
Cataloguing-in-Publication entry

Title:	Agency, contingency and census process : observations of the 2006 Indigenous enumeration strategy in remote Aboriginal Australia / editor, Frances Morphy.
Publisher:	Acton, A.C.T. : ANU E Press, 2007.
ISBN:	9781921313585 (pbk.) 9781921313592 (online)
Series:	Research monograph (Australian National University. Centre for Aboriginal Economic Policy Research) ; no. 28
Subjects:	Indigenous Enumeration Strategy. Aboriginal Australians–Census. Aboriginal Australians–Population–Statistics. Census–Methodology. Australia–Census, 2006.
Other Authors:	Morphy, Frances, 1949- Australian National University. Centre for Aboriginal Economic Policy Research.
Dewey Number:	306.0899915

Cover design by Brendon McKinley.

Contents

List of Figures

List of Tables

Notes on the contributors

Frances Morphy

Frances Morphy is Fellow at the Centre for Aboriginal Economic Policy Research at The Australian National University. An anthropologist and linguist, she has conducted research in Aboriginal communities in the Northern Territory since 1974. She is co-author (with David Martin, Will Sanders and John Taylor) of *Making Sense of the Census: Observations of the 2001 Enumeration in Remote Aboriginal Australia* (CAEPR Research Monograph No. 22, CAEPR 2002 [ANU E Press 2004]) and author of 'Lost in translation? Remote Indigenous households and definitions of the family' (*Family Matters*, vol. 73, 2006) and 'Uncontained subjects: "population" and "household" in remote Aboriginal Australia' (*Journal of Population Research*, vol. 24, no. 2, 2007).

Will Sanders

Will Sanders is Senior Fellow at the Centre for Aboriginal Economic Policy Research at The Australian National University (ANU). He previously held positions at the ANU's North Australia Research Unit and the Urban Research Program, Department of Political Science. His interest in the adaptation of administrative systems to the circumstances of Indigenous people in north and central Australia extends also to the social security system and to electoral administration. He is co-editor (with Duncan Ivison and Paul Patton) of *Political Theory and the Rights of Indigenous People* (Cambridge University Press, 2000).

John Taylor

John Taylor is Senior Fellow and Deputy Director of the Centre for Aboriginal Economic Policy Research at The Australian National University. With a disciplinary background in geography and population studies, he has been researching issues related to the enumeration of Aboriginal people in remote areas since 1986. He is co-editor of *Population Mobility and Indigenous Peoples in Australasia and North America* (Routledge, 2004) and the author of numerous papers concerned with Indigenous social and economic policy development.

Kathryn Thorburn

Kathryn Thorburn is a PhD scholar at the Centre for Aboriginal Economic Policy Research, The Australian National University, under the Indigenous Community Governance Project. Her disciplinary background is in geography and politics. Her PhD will examine the governance practice of two Indigenous organisations in the Fitzroy Crossing area. As part of the doctoral process, she spent all of 2005 and some of 2006 living in and around Fitzroy Crossing, and working with communities associated with each organisation.

Abbreviations and acronyms

ABS	Australian Bureau of Statistics
AC	automatic coding
ALT	Aboriginal Lands Trust
ANU	The Australian National University
ARC	Australian Research Council
ASGC	Australian Standard Geographical Classification
BRACS	Broadcasting for Remote Aboriginal Communities Scheme
CAEPR	Centre for Aboriginal Economic Policy Research
CC	Community Coordinator
CD	Collection District
CDEP	Community Development Employment Project(s)
CEO	Chief Executive Officer
CFO	Census Field Officer
CHINS	Community Housing and Infrastructure Needs Survey
CI	collector-interviewer
CMU	Census Management Unit
COAG	Council of Australian Governments
CRB	Census Record Book
CRN	Census Record Number
DICD	Discrete Indigenous Communities Database
DOB	date of birth
DPC	Data Processing Centre
ERP	estimated resident population
FaCS	(Commonwealth Department of) Family and Community Services (now FaCSIA)
FaCSIA	(Commonwealth Department of) Families, Community Services and Indigenous Affairs
IDC	Interviewer Dwelling Checklist
FRP	first-release processing
IES	Indigenous Enumeration Strategy
IHF	Interviewer Household Form
IHO	Indigenous Housing Organisation
IPT	Indigenous Processing Team
MDC	Master Dwelling Checklist
MWW	Marra Worra Worra
NCATSIS	National Centre for Aboriginal and Torres Strait Islander Statistics

NGO	non-governmental organisation
NT	Northern Territory
PES	post-enumeration survey
PTA	person(s) temporarily absent
SIM	State Indigenous Manager
SRA	Shared Responsibility Agreement
SRP	second-release processing
STA	State Transit Authority
TRC	Thamarrurr Regional Council
WA	Western Australia

Preface

During the period leading up to and during the 2006 Census, a team of four researchers from the Centre for Aboriginal Economic Policy Research (CAEPR) at The Australian National University undertook an observation of the census enumeration in four remote locations. Three of these were in the Northern Territory—the Alice Springs town camps (Will Sanders), Wadeye (John Taylor) and a group of homelands in the Yolngu-speaking area of eastern Arnhem Land (Frances Morphy)—and one was in Western Australia, at Fitzroy Crossing (Kathryn Thorburn). One researcher (Frances Morphy) also spent time at the Australian Bureau of Statistics' (ABS) Northern Territory Census Management Unit (CMU) in Darwin and at the Data Processing Centre (DPC) in Melbourne, observing the training of the Northern Territory Census Field Officers (CFOs) and their assistants, the handling of the Northern Territory Interviewer Household Forms (IHF) in Darwin after the count and the coding of the data from the forms at the DPC. This research was undertaken as an Australian Research Council Linkage Grant, with the ABS as the collaborating institution. The researchers signed an Undertaking of Fidelity and Secrecy under the terms of the *Census and Statistics Act 1905*, and are thus bound by its conditions of confidentiality.

This work builds on previous research undertaken by CAEPR researchers on the 2001 Census, published as Martin et al. (2002 [2004]) (see also Morphy 2004, 2006; Sanders 2004). In 2001, only the count itself was observed. Morphy and Sanders were also members of the ABS's 2006 Census Indigenous Enumeration Strategy Working Group, which considered all aspects of the Indigenous Enumeration Strategy (IES), but particularly the design of the forms to be used in 2006, in the light of the 2001 experience. Morphy also participated in the field testing of the 2006 form (see Morphy 2003).

In 2006, Morphy and Sanders returned to the same areas they had covered in 2001, enabling a comparison between the two censuses in these two locations.[1] The other two sites were new study areas. The four sites chosen comprised a group of discrete Aboriginal communities in an urban location (Alice Springs), a smaller town where Aboriginal people lived in discrete communities and in 'mainstream' locations (Fitzroy Crossing), a large discrete Aboriginal commmunity (Wadeye) and a group of remote and scattered homeland communities (Arnhem Land). These sites were chosen so that the operation of the IES could be observed in a variety of situations, and also because, in each case, the researchers were working in areas where they had previously undertaken research and with which they were therefore familiar. Finally, the inclusion of Fitzroy Crossing

---

[1] Morphy's 2001 study was limited to a single homeland ('Community A'). Her 2006 study was more wide ranging.

enabled a comparison between the 'rolling count' strategy adopted in the Northern Territory with the 'standard count' strategy adopted in Western Australia.

One aspect of our 2006 observations that we would like to note is the way in which, as researchers, we were drawn almost inevitably into a role that was somewhat more than just that of observer. This relates to the difficulty of the census and the fact that everyone in the hierarchy of census administration represents a distinct interest and we, as researchers, had to win them over to cooperate with our research efforts. The obvious way to win people's cooperation is to offer them some help with their difficult task. At the very least therefore, we would end up offering our vehicles as an extra resource that could be used by Community Coordinators (CCs) and collector-interviewers (CIs). More substantially, some of us effectively became CCs and CIs for periods or, at other points in the process, someone's assistant on some task that needed to be done, but which they were finding difficult to resource. This could be seen as our failing as objective researchers, but we were winning the cooperation of others with our research by helping them with their difficult administrative tasks. In reality, this is probably the only way that this sort of research can proceed. Having the top of the ABS hierarchy give us the status of official observers was only the beginning of the job of persuading others to cooperate with our research and see something in it for themselves as they struggled with difficult tasks.

Our aim in this monograph is to provide a frank and objective assessment of the strengths and weaknesses of the IES as it applied in 2006. This project was based on the premise that the national census was a necessary instrument of the nation-state and that its purpose was, firstly, to count the population of the country and, secondly, to collect data that allowed broad-brush comparisons of different sectors of the population across a variety of basic demographic parameters. We acknowledge that this puts constraints on the design of the census. Our focus, then, will be on suggestions that will improve the ability of the IES to fulfil these purposes.

Frances Morphy
Will Sanders
John Taylor
Kathryn Thorburn
CAEPR, November 2007

Acknowledgements

This research was conducted with financial support from the Australian Research Council (ARC Linkage Project LP0668432), and with the Australian Bureau of Statistics (ABS) as an industry partner.

We would like to thank the Australian Bureau of Statistics (ABS) as an institution for being so open to this research, which we recognise is at times quite critical of their processes and procedures. We acknowledge that perhaps the best that can be hoped for—in the extremely complex exercise that is the national census—is constant administrative self-awareness and continuing evaluation of the task. We would like to think that we have aided the ABS in that sort of process. We would also like to thank the many individual ABS employees in the field and at the Census Management Unit in Darwin and the Data Processing Centre in Melbourne who assisted us in our research and allowed us to look over their shoulders as they worked. Finally, we thank the case-study communities and their organisations and the many individual community members who allowed us to observe the progress of the 2006 Census. We hope that our findings and recommendations will result in changes that will ultimately benefit them, as individuals, organisations and communities.

1. Producing powerful numbers

Frances Morphy, Will Sanders and John Taylor

Census statistics are powerful numbers. Governments frequently use them in the allocation of important resources, such as seats in parliament or shares of expenditure between jurisdictional areas. More indirectly, they can be used to characterise social and economic situations among groups of people, and through that to drive important public policy debates. Who gets what, when and how from governments is often informed—if not determined—by what census statistics reveal about existing and projected numbers of people and their socioeconomic characteristics.

As researchers studying the socioeconomic circumstances of Indigenous Australians and contributing to Indigenous affairs policy debates, we have relied heavily on Australian census statistics in the past. In doing so, however, we have often had cause to wonder about the processes through which these statistics have been produced and the adequacy, accuracy and appropriateness of some of them—particularly in relation to Indigenous people in remote Australia. If these statistics are not adequately capturing the numbers or socioeconomic characteristics of Indigenous people in these areas, what effect might this be having on policy debates and on the allocation of public resources?

The Australian Bureau of Statistics (ABS) devised an Indigenous Enumeration Strategy (IES) because it had cause to be concerned itself about these questions with respect to the Indigenous population of Australia. The IES has evolved through the past 35 years to become a highly complex, multi-staged, multi-sited and multifaceted organisational exercise that consumes varying degrees of ABS resources and personnel continually between censuses, though obviously with most effort expended around the pivotal process of the enumeration itself. Over time, the ABS has committed steadily expanding resources to these collective exercises. Since 1971, when special enumeration procedures were first introduced in the Northern Territory and Western Australia, the IES has gradually become a truly national strategy, while the tasks and the personnel required to feed into IES processes have multiplied (Taylor 2002). In 2001, the direct cost of enumerating remote-area Indigenous populations was about $2 million (or $26 per capita) compared with the direct costs of about $49 million (or $2.60 per capita) for the total population. In 2006, the equivalent figures were $2.5 million (or $35 per capita) for the IES compared with $63 million (about $3 per capita) for the census overall.

This book provides, for the first time, an independent view of all stages of the enumeration process in remote, discrete Indigenous communities—from the training of the field staff and pre-census preparation through to data processing. The chapters are ordered in sequence to reflect the building blocks of what eventually emerges as population and housing data in census output tables. In this introductory chapter, we set the scene for the 2006 enumeration and the research project and, in the concluding chapter, we draw on our observations of the 2006 enumeration to make some quite radical suggestions for change in 2011.

The 2006 research project

Background

In 2001 a team of CAEPR researchers observed the conduct of the census in three remote Aboriginal communities (Martin et al. 2002). While we were supportive of the interview and time extension adaptations of the 2001 IES, we observed that the two-form structure of a household form and separate individual forms then in use was very cumbersome and made large, somewhat unnecessary administrative demands on the local recruited census field staff—the Community Coordinators (CCs) and the collector-interviewers (CIs). In two of our observed 2001 locations—one in the Northern Territory and one in Queensland—the two-form structure was made to work largely by keeping household forms in the background and exposing interviewees only to the personal forms. In the third location observed in 2001, 12 days of very slow progress led to abandonment of the personal forms and a salvage operation that focused simply on the household forms. The two-form structure was just far too demanding on the interest and persistence of the interviewers, and their interviewees. CIs were becoming burnt out and falling by the wayside in the process of enumerating just a limited number of households.

Frances Morphy's work in 2001 (Morphy 2002) focused in addition on the highly inadequate construction of Indigenous households through particular census questions. She judged that the attempt to translate Indigenous kinship systems into Western terminology had been largely unsuccessful and that many of the Indigenous household descriptions in the census data were, as a consequence, of limited value. Morphy also focused on the 'legendary mobility' of Indigenous people in her observation area in north-east Arnhem Land and how, together with time extension of the collection process, this meant that a 'complete enumeration' was almost impossible. Double-counting and under-enumeration, she reasoned, were highly likely, but the extent of each would be difficult to assess.

An awareness of these Indigenous mobility issues had led the Northern Territory administration of the ABS, over some years, to attempt to count 'usual residents' of Indigenous communities, rather than following the standard census procedure of counting people present, with some provision for adding absent usual residents who might not be counted elsewhere. Morphy sympathetically considered the merits of counting usual residents, but ultimately argued against it on the grounds that a robust definition of 'usual resident' was hard to develop. Will Sanders' work on the Alice Springs town camps argued against the usual residents approach because it allowed people present—labelled 'visitors'—to slip through the enumeration process.

One final common theme in our 2001 observations was the limited social relevance to the circumstances of traditionally oriented Aboriginal people in remote Australia of many census questions and their pre-specified categorical answers—whether this was the difficulty of defining a dwelling and its associated household, of categorising an education level or course undertaken, or a question about religion or marriage, employment or looking for a job. Often this limited social relevance of questions and categorical answers would introduce humour to the collection process—for interviewers and interviewees. Lack of social relevance could, however, also lead to disinterest and disengagement.

On the basis of all these observations, in the final chapter of our monograph on the 2001 Census (Martin et al. 2002), we argued for essentially three reforms to the IES as we observed it operating in remote Australia. In opposition to some half-hearted moves in the Northern Territory towards enumerating usual residents, our first suggestion was to argue for a return to the general ABS approach of counting people present, with some facility for adding absent usual residents who might not be counted elsewhere. Our second suggestion was to argue for the reintegration of the special Indigenous personal and household forms into a single Indigenous household form designed to be administered by interview. Our third suggestion was for this form to be tailored more precisely to the circumstances of Indigenous people in remote Australia by the restriction of some questions asked and the development of more appropriate categorical answers.

The ABS formed an IES Working Group after the 2001 Census to consider ways of improving field design and methods. Sanders and Morphy were invited to be members of this group. It produced two key initiatives—one conceptual, the other practical—which corresponded with our first two ideas for reform. First, in 2006 there was to be a clear move back to the standard of enumerating people present in a dwelling at the time of the count, plus absent usual residents judged unlikely to be counted elsewhere.[1] Second, the previous multi-form schedule of census questions was to be integrated into a single matrix-style Interviewer Household Form (IHF). Our third idea for reform, however—attempting to restrict this new form to a lesser number of questions of greatest social relevance to the circumstances of Indigenous people in remote areas—proved almost impossible

---

[1] This standard approach produces what is sometimes referred to as a 'de facto' population. When people are placed back in their usual place of residence, the term 'de jure' population is sometimes used.

for the ABS to implement. While individual questions and categorical responses to them could be modified slightly, the idea of leaving out any questions always met resistance. Any question left out would become a statistic for which there would no longer be a national Indigenous/non-Indigenous comparison. This was understandably very hard for the ABS to contemplate.

Aims of the 2006 research project

A primary purpose of observations in 2006 was to test the workability and impact of the reforms discussed above. In addition, the opportunity was presented for the first time to assess the nature and effectiveness of pre-census preparations and post-census processing. Two of the locality studies revisit places observed in 2001, while two others cover places being observed for the first time. The monograph also contains three chapters that observe related administrative processes leading up to and following on from enumeration in localities; preparing and undertaking training for the enumeration in the Darwin Census Management Unit (CMU), checking forms in the Darwin CMU after the field enumeration and, finally, the processing of these forms at the Data Processing Centre (DPC) in Melbourne (see also Morphy 2007). Our study this time has therefore been widened to include observation of 'back-office' administrative processes before and after the event, as well as enumeration in the field.

During the course of the research our focus shifted—as a result of what we were observing—to the broader structures and processes of the IES. The question of who was being counted where loomed ever larger as we watched the struggles of the Census Field Officers (CFOs) and their inadequate numbers of recruited field staff to maintain control of the process, and an orderly count, in the context of a prolonged engagement with a highly mobile population. We came to see that the strategy as presently conceived is ill-equipped to deal with the agency of a population for whom the census is essentially an unfathomable state project. It does not engage adequately with the resources and local knowledge embodied by the organisations that straddle the interface between these populations and the state. Nor is it designed to cope realistically with the contingencies that arise in everyday life in these remote communities.

The Indigenous Enumeration Strategy in 2006: structures and processes

The case-study chapters (Chapters 3–6) describe what really happened on the ground during the count. In this section, we outline briefly the structures and processes of the count as envisaged and planned for by the ABS for the Northern Territory IES.[2]

The IES was extended in time well beyond the process of enumeration itself—before and after—beginning in November 2005 with training for State Indigenous Managers (SIMs). SIMs were employed and CMUs established within ABS regional offices in each State and Territory. They were responsible for coordination of ensuing field operations associated with the Community Housing and Infrastructure Needs Survey (CHINS) and the census, including the training of the CFOs, who were responsible for organising the collection of CHINS and then census data in the regions to which they were assigned.

As in previous years, the IES involved firstly the designation of the communities and areas in which the remote strategy was to be applied. These then became the responsibility of the CFOs, whereas the 'mainstream' count was the responsibility of the local area supervisors. The IES involved the use of a form—the IHF—which differed in its structure and in the content of some of its questions from the form used in the mainstream count. In particular, the IHF was designed to attempt to capture data on household structure, education, employment and socio-cultural factors such as religion, language use and ethnicity, using questions and options for responses framed to allow for the 'difference' of remote Indigenous populations.

As in the past, the IES attempted also to mitigate the effects of remoteness and low levels of literacy in English in the remote Indigenous population. The census forms were not dropped off at households; rather, local CIs, ideally managed by local CCs, took the IHFs to the individual households in the communities and filled them in with the help of the household members. The responsibility for training these local temporary staff rested with the CFO for the region.

In the Northern Territory, it was decided—as in past censuses—that such a process made it logistically impossible for the count to take place on a single night. Accordingly—as in the past—the IES in the Northern Territory employed a rolling count over an extended period. The time frame initially allowed for the count was six weeks, and it was the responsibility of the CFO to organise the count within this time frame in their designated region. In 2006, for the first time, in acknowledgement that in reality this was a very exacting task, the CFOs were assigned an Assistant—also trained at the regional office—to go with them into the field. In the Northern Territory, a couple of 'floating' CFOs were trained, who were not assigned particular regions; their job was to provide backup wherever and whenever it was deemed necessary. In Western Australia, it was

---

[2] The processes planned for Western Australia differed in some respects. These differences are discussed in the Fitzroy Crossing case study (Thorburn, Chapter 6).

felt that the IES could be completed in a week, being in effect a slightly extended version of the more usual census method of counting on a single night.

In the best-case scenario, as detailed and emphasised in the training delivered to the CFOs, the IES should have proceeded as follows. During the initial visit to each community during the CHINS exercise, the CFO would also complete a form for each community, to be entered onto a new Discrete Indigenous Communities Database (DICD), which was being compiled for the first time for the National Centre for Aboriginal and Torres Strait Islander Statistics (NCATSIS). These data and the initial population figures revealed by the CHINS—together with the population figures from the 2001 Census for the community—would help the CFO to determine how many CCs and CIs would be needed to achieve a timely and complete count in the area. During this initial visit, the CFO would also carry out an awareness-raising exercise about the impending census by liaising with local community organisations and potentially helpful individuals, such as the census volunteers who were being recruited locally (for the first time) to provide logistical backup and assistance. If they had time, they might visit the local school and so on, and they had posters and other publicity materials to distribute in the communities. The CFO would also begin the process—with the help of local organisations—of identifying and meeting potential CCs for the census process.

After returning to the State or Territory CMU for a week's training on the IES procedures, the CFO with their Assistant would then return to their designated region to begin work. Their task, in each of the communities in their region, would be to recruit and train the necessary CCs and CIs for each community, sign them up as temporary ABS employees and ensure that all the details necessary for their payment were relayed to the CMU.

The first task after training would be for the CFO and the CC (or CCs) to go around the community—which had been assigned the unique identifier code for its Collection District (CD)—and compile a Master Dwelling Checklist (MDC) that would include all private dwellings, temporary dwellings and non-private dwellings in the community. Each separate dwelling would be assigned a unique Census Record Number (CRN). Non-Indigenous households and non-private dwellings would be identified and special arrangements made for the delivery and collection of the forms relating to them. Indigenous households, once identified, would be divided among the available CIs, using the local knowledge of the CCs to distribute the workloads most appropriately. Each CI would then be given an Interviewer Dwelling Checklist (IDC), on which the CD and the CRNs of each dwelling to be visited by them was to be listed, along with the surname of the 'head' of the household. They were to complete the details on this checklist as they went along. Once a household had been counted, the dwelling would be ticked off the list and the numbers of males and females in the household recorded on the IDC.

The task of the CCs—aided initially by the CFO until they were confident that the CCs had fully understood their responsibilities—would be to manage the CIs by ensuring that they visited all the dwellings on their list, and reassigning workloads if unplanned-for contingencies arose. It would be their task to collect and store securely the completed forms and to transfer the details of people counted from the IDCs to the MDC, having first checked that the forms had been completed fully and that the numbers of people on the IHFs tallied with the totals listed on the IDC. One copy of the IDC would be kept by the CI as a record of the pay owing to them, one would stay with the CC and one would be forwarded to the CMU by the CFO to initiate the payment process. It was envisaged—and it would be necessary if the count for the CFO's region was to be completed in the time allowed—that a day or two after the beginning of the count, the CFO could leave the community to start the same process in another of the CDs in their region, leaving the Assistant CFO behind for a while if this was felt to be necessary.

After the count was completed in a CD, and all the IHFs were returned to the CCs, the CFO would return to the community and double-check with the help of the CCs that all dwellings had indeed been visited and accounted for, that the totals of males and females on the MDC and the IDCs tallied and that all forms had been completed correctly. The CFO would also use available administrative data and the figures from the CHINS exercise and the 2001 Census to determine whether or not the coverage was complete. They would be alert for large discrepancies in totals, and for under-counting of particular sectors of the population, such as young men, children and infants. If there were any such discrepancies, they would be documented, followed up in the field and accounted for.

The CFO would then return all the forms for a CD, boxed together, to the CMU. There, further checks would be made (see Chapter 7) before the forms were finally sent en masse to the DPC in Melbourne. The boxes containing the IHFs would contain—in addition to the forms themselves—copies of the MDC and the IDCs, the completed DICD forms and two checklists, one completed by the CFO before the forms left the CD and one completed at the CMU.

This very quick sketch of what is a very complicated administrative and logistical exercise is designed as a necessary background to the case-study chapters. It will become obvious that the reality fell far short of the ideal, in the face of the complex realities encountered by the CFOs and their teams on the ground.

One final important step in the process—which was new in 2006—was the extension of the Post Enumeration Survey (PES), designed to estimate census net under-count (ABS 2007) in remote areas and discrete Indigenous communities covered by the IES. This survey is conducted by the ABS a month after, but independent of, the census, and is used to estimate numbers of people missed or counted more than once in the census enumeration and then to adjust population estimates accordingly. In the past, the PES has not been carried out in remote Australia and discrete Indigenous communities and the rate of people missed or counted twice there has been estimated as roughly equivalent to elsewhere. This survey was not observed by the current research team because of its independence as a process from the census itself. John Taylor (2007b: 18) reports that, according to the ABS's data, 'In Western Australia around 24 per cent of the Indigenous population was estimated to have been overlooked by the census; in the Northern Territory the figure was 19 per cent.' This recognition of a larger than normal under-count has significant implications for the use of census statistics in matters concerning Indigenous affairs funding. Our observations also show that the data collected for many of the people who were counted were incomplete (see Chapter 7). Together, these two facts point to some very serious problems with the IES.

We conclude that, despite the best intentions, the census is failing to capture adequately the characteristics of remote Indigenous populations. In Chapter 9, we call for a substantial rethink of the way in which the ABS engages with Indigenous communities and their organisations.

2. Preparing for the 2006 enumeration at the Darwin Census Management Unit

Frances Morphy

Introduction

In broad organisational terms, a national census poses particular problems because of its scale and the five-year gap between census events. The Australian Bureau of Statistics (ABS) cannot keep on its permanent staff the thousands of people needed to coordinate the exercise on the ground and to distribute, collect and code the data from the forms. The 2006 Census exercise therefore involved the hiring of a temporary workforce of more than 42,000 people, who had to be trained adequately to carry out their allotted tasks. In such a context, the flow of information becomes vital—across time (so that the accumulated wisdom from previous census exercises is brought to bear on the organisation of the current one) and within the organisation itself, which is multi-sited and hierarchical.

One of the unique aspects of the research reported here is that it was itself multi-sited. This enabled us to observe aspects of the flow of information from the centre, the ABS headquarters in Canberra, to the periphery, the collector-interviewers (CIs) in four remote Aboriginal community settings, via the intermediate institution of the Census Management Unit (CMU) in Darwin, which was responsible for managing and planning the count in the Northern Territory, and its emissaries, the Census Field Officers (CFOs) and their Assistants, charged with responsibility for coordinating the count on the ground. We have also been able to observe the reverse flow after the count, from the ground back to Darwin and then back to the centre—in this case, the Data Processing Centre (DPC) in Melbourne.

This chapter is concerned primarily with the pre-enumeration flow of information from Canberra to Darwin and to the CFOs, and concentrates primarily on the pre-field training of the CFOs and on the information that was made available to them from Canberra and locally in Darwin.

The collection of census data from Indigenous people living in remote Australia is a dauntingly complex exercise. In recognition of this the ABS began, in the 1971 Census, to put in place a special Indigenous Enumeration Strategy (IES), which has subsequently been developed and finetuned with each successive census (see Taylor 2002). From the ABS's point of view, the remote count poses particular logistical problems because of the difficulty of access to the remotest small communities, the mobility of individuals within their regional networks, the low levels of English literacy of many Indigenous people and their relative unfamiliarity with and lack of understanding of the workings of the bureaucracy of the nation-state (instantiated in this case in the census exercise).

To ameliorate these problems, the IES uses CIs rather than expecting people to self-administer their forms. Ideally, the CIs are local people, so that advantage can be taken of their local knowledge, their knowledge of local languages and their familiarity with the interviewees. Ideally again, the CIs are selected and trained by the CFO in charge of the region with the help of local Community Coordinators (CCs). (The CCs might also act as CIs, but their main task is to help the CFO in coordinating the count in their community and managing the daily workloads of the CIs.)

In the Northern Territory—and in remote areas generally, such as parts of Western Australia—distance and remoteness, and the size of the areas that CFOs are responsible for, make it impossible to achieve a count in a single day. In the Northern Territory a time-extended 'rolling count' strategy is employed: notionally a CFO has between six and seven weeks to complete the count in their area of responsibility.

The CFOs, then, are a crucial link in the chain of information between the centre (the national guidelines of the census) and the periphery (the CIs on the ground). They are not permanent employees of the ABS, so must be trained from scratch. They have varying degrees of experience of working or living in remote Aboriginal localities and come from a variety of different working backgrounds. None of the 2006 CFOs in the Northern Territory had worked on a previous census. Their task is logistically complex and multifaceted, and the training they receive has a very direct bearing on the success or otherwise of the count—in terms of its completeness and of the quality of the resulting data.

The sociopolitical context of the census

In its instructions to the CFOs on how to frame the census to the Indigenous public, the ABS focuses on the census as a planning tool, used to 'identify the needs' for health or educational services, housing and so on in keeping with its view of itself as set out in its mission statement:

> We assist and encourage informed decision-making, research and discussion within governments and the community, by providing a high quality, objective and responsive national statistical service. (Quoted in ABS 2006b: 3)

Perhaps for most census events this characterisation of the role of the ABS serves its purpose, but the 2006 Census—at least in the Northern Territory—took place in a politically charged environment, for two main reasons. The first was the furore over the almost realised political consequences of the 2001 count: the potential loss of a Northern Territory seat in the Commonwealth House of Representatives (Wilson et al. 2005). The second was the turbulent and changing state of Commonwealth Indigenous affairs policy, which was experiencing an upheaval of a magnitude not seen since the early 1970s. This was impacting directly on Indigenous communities and their organisations in unprecedented ways. Both these factors had an influence on the way in which the ABS and the census were perceived on the ground, and this will be a recurring theme in the pages that follow.

The Community Housing and Infrastructure Needs Survey and the census

Before considering the training for the census, I make a brief digression to comment on the Community, Housing and Infrastructure Needs Survey (CHINS), which the ABS conducted again in 2006 on behalf of the Department of Family and Community Services (FaCS, now FaCSIA). This too was in the job remit of the CFOs. On the ABS website, the CHINS work is portrayed as complementary to—and possibly helpful to—the conduct of the census itself: 'To minimise disruption in communities, CHINS visits to communities will be combined with visits to consult on arrangements for the 2006 Census' (http://www.abs.gov.au, accessed 12 February 2006).

At the Darwin CMU, the CFOs were trained first to conduct the CHINS in their region, and one day of training on the census—concerned mainly with pre-census arrangements—was added at the end of that week. They then went out to conduct CHINS before returning to Darwin for the fully fledged census training. I attended the one-day census training day and the full census training.

The CHINS and census exercises are quite different, and arguably require different skill sets on the part of the CFOs (this opinion was put to me in retrospect by CMU staff)—at least under the current IES arrangements. In CHINS, the CFOs' major contact is with staff of Indigenous Housing Organisations (IHOs) rather than directly with community members, and their work is largely office based. For the census, on the other hand, the CFOs and their Assistants had the responsibility for recruiting, training and managing the CCs and CIs, as employees of the ABS.[1] This is a potential source of tension at the community level (see, in particular, Chapter 5).

---

[1] During their training, the CFOs had one session on the new initiative put in place by the Northern Territory government in partnership with the ABS, in which community volunteers—such as local teachers and health staff—were being trained and encouraged to provide logistical support to the CFOs and their teams. Some CFOs reported early teething troubles with the implementation of this initiative, in which some volunteers were exceeding the bounds of their duties and attempting to play a role in the recruiting of CIs and in organising the count. They also reported confusion at the community level between the roles of the volunteers and the CIs, with people believing that the CI role was to be an unpaid one. These facts, too, contributed to the feeling among the CFOs that the boundaries between ABS staff and others needed to be demarcated clearly. In the event, no volunteers were forthcoming in

On their return to Darwin after undertaking the CHINS, the CFOs' first day of the training for the census consisted of a debriefing on the CHINS exercise. The CFOs were generally of the opinion that, far from assisting with the census, the CHINS exercise got in the way of their attempts to prepare for the census count.

The Discrete Indigenous Communities Database

The problems caused by the CHINS were compounded by the request that was put to CFOs—and that had been covered only briefly at the end of the CHINS training—to fill in a detailed Indigenous Community Information form for each community they visited. It was the first time that a form of this type had been used.

In the debriefing, the CFOs commented that this was a big task that had been given to them at the last minute, and that the instructions about the status of the form were unclear. Some said it had interfered substantially with their ability to undertake census promotion activities. The form was time-consuming to fill in and CFOs had felt reluctant to take up more of people's time after doing the CHINS exercise. Some organisations were reluctant to cooperate, saying that this kind of information was already being collected and held by other agencies, and expressing distrust about the uses to which the information would be put. The CFOs had therefore mostly not completed them fully.

The information from these forms is to be fed into a Discrete Indigenous Communities Database (DICD) that will be maintained by the ABS's National Centre for Aboriginal and Torres Strait Islander Statistics (NCATSIS) section and will be for ABS internal use only. If properly maintained and updated, it will provide invaluable background information for subsequent surveys and censuses. The form and the necessity to fill it out for each community was mentioned in the written instructions to the CFOs about their roles and responsibilities, so possibly this indicates that—like the CCs and CIs—the CFOs did not make much reference to their written instructions. More charitably, given the amount of information and documentation that they have to absorb, more thought needs to be given in the training sessions to highlighting information that is considered crucial.

As noted above, this particular census took place in the context of considerable changes in the policy settings in Indigenous affairs, and many community organisations were under extreme pressure and were feeling somewhat distrustful of government intentions. In such a context, it appears to have been difficult for the CFOs to persuade them that the ABS, although a government agency,

the area where I made my observations (see Chapter 4), and I cannot report directly on the success or otherwise of the volunteer initiative. Some CFOs commented that the initiative had worked well in their communities.

was not government per se, and that much of the data it gathered was for internal purposes only.

The training of the Census Field Officers for the census

This section on the training received by the CFOs in Darwin must be read in context: the training is being evaluated with the benefit of hindsight. I will tend to focus on those aspects of the training that did not prepare the CFOs adequately for their task, in order to provide useful feedback to inform the training process for 2011. I want to stress at the outset that there were many positive aspects to the training, not least the amount of time and effort that went into preparing the training materials and the openness of the CMU staff to comments and suggestions from the CFOs and Assistant CFOs.

The value of local knowledge

None of the CMU staff involved in managing the conduct of the IES in 2006 had been a part of the CMU in 2001. They were therefore heavily reliant on the advice and training materials provided by the central office, and on gleaning information from those people at the CMU who had experience of the count in 2001.

It is my impression that the *practical* knowledge and experience gained on the ground in successive censuses is fed back to Canberra in the form of reports from the CFOs and CMU staff, and it then informs central planning for the next census. It appeared to me, however, that very little of that practical knowledge and experience had been preserved at the local level from 2001. In other words, there appeared to be little institutional memory at the local level for the CFOs to draw on. The information that comes from the centre is informed by past experience, but the reasoning behind decisions that have been made is opaque to those who then have to use that information locally. They are presented in the training with a plethora of procedures and forms, with little sense of the real-life contexts in which they are going to be using them.

For example, it would have been invaluable to the CFO in charge of the eastern Arnhem Land region (see Chapter 4) to have access to the journal—or an edited version of the journal—of the CFO who had been in charge of that same area in 2001. The CFO for 2006 would then have had the benefit of the local knowledge gained by his predecessor and also the opportunity to learn from his mistakes and build on his successes. This information, together with updated forms for each community from the DICD, would give the CFOs a much better 'feel' for the real-life contexts in which they would be operating, and would give them a context in which to understand the procedural details on which the training inevitably focused in an exercise as complex as the census.

Imparting information: instruction and practical application

In the first part of the training session for the census, the CMU staff asked for feedback from the CFOs on the CHINS training that they had received. The CFOs were quite critical, feeling that the training period had been too compressed and that there had been too much delivery of information in a lecture format and not enough practical scenarios. They felt there had been too much emphasis on procedural matters and not enough on the content of the survey instrument. For example, the ABS definition of 'temporary dwelling' differs from the one used by other agencies, and this caused some problems with IHOs because funding is dependent on such definitions.

The general tenor of these comments also applied to the census training itself. It too was very concentrated and the information was presented in a highly condensed way, with little opportunity for the CFOs to practice what they were being taught. Rather than concentrating the training into a solid block, it would have been more effective to have half-day or one-day sessions spread over several weeks, concentrating on one aspect of the exercise at a time. One of the regional managers delivering the training commented to me that if people had read all the documentation they had been provided with before the training, not so much time would have been spent on unimportant questions. The trouble was that there was an enormous amount of documentation. If the training had been broken up into smaller blocks it would have been possible to ask the CFOs to review the documentation for that topic alone before the training session, and then re-enforce and amplify the written materials. This would have been a more effective way of ensuring that they were familiar with those materials.

Breaking the training into blocks would also allow time for practical sessions in which the CFOs would have the opportunity to consolidate their understanding. Scenarios would have been particularly beneficial in the session on providing training to the CCs and CIs. Most of the CFOs were not trained 'trainers', as they commented themselves. Giving them practical experience—by asking them to practice delivering training to one another in a mock tutorial—would have been an effective way of building their practical experience, supplementing the information that they were given on different 'learning styles'.[2] This information, although interesting in itself, was not presented in such a way as to feed into the practical situation of a training session.

The focus throughout the training was on processes and administrative procedures. This was understandable, particularly in view of the complexities involved in some procedural matters—for example, the payment system for CCs

---

[2] Indeed, as I learned subsequently from a member of the CMU staff who had been involved in the 2001 IES in Darwin, this was how the 'training' training was delivered in 2001.

and CIs.[3] One overriding concern—that the count should be as accurate as possible and *be seen to be accurate*—dominated the discourse. The focus on this concern had two effects. The emphasis on the 'head count' aspect of the census meant that the details of the questions on the Interviewer Houshold Form (IHF) received relatively little emphasis. And the focus on checking the count against other data—such as the 2001 Census, the 2006 CHINS and any administrative data that the CFOs could access—in order to assess the accuracy of the count led to a de-emphasis on strategies for getting a complete count *in the first place*. As a consequence, certain issues that turned out to be of crucial importance on the ground received only cursory treatment in training. With the benefit of hindsight, I will focus on the most significant of these: the question of how to treat 'persons temporarily absent' (PTA).

Persons Temporarily Absent

The intention of the ABS in 2006 was to carry out—as far as possible—a de facto count of the people in dwellings in discrete Indigenous communities. From past experience, however, it was known that some exceptions would have to be made, to cover people who were absent temporarily and who might not be counted elsewhere. In the *Census Field Officer Manual* for the 2006 Census, the following instructions were given with regard to absent people and vacant dwellings:

9.7.3. Absent People

- Any people who usually live in the dwelling but are away at the time of the Census should be listed in the Table for Persons Temporarily Absent on page 3 of the Interviewer Household form, unless they are at a place where they are unlikely to be put on a Census form, such as the bush or fishing.

  To avoid either double-counting or missing individuals, the following rule is applied to people who were absent from the household at the time of the census:

- If they were at a place where they would have been counted on a different Census form, such as a town or another community, the person should only be included in the Table for Persons Temporarily Absent.
- If they were at a place where they would not have been counted, such as camping in the bush, travelling, or on other cultural or business activities, the person should be listed on page 4 with the people staying in the dwelling

---

[3] The payment system had received some close attention between 2001 and 2006 and the form-filling aspect of it was, in fact, more streamlined. It continues to be problematic, however—perhaps inevitably so. Radical simplification would entail a move away from the present centralised system of payment, and this, presumably, is not possible.

at the time of the Census, and all other questions in the form should be answered for the person as though they were there.

9.7.4. Vacant dwellings

If the Collector-Interviewer comes across any dwellings in their workload where no one is staying, they should complete the front page and questions 2–3 of the Interviewer Household Form. The rest of the form is left blank.

In the CFO training notes for the training of the collector-interviewers, a further distinction is made:

Counting an unoccupied dwelling

Explain: If you come across a dwelling that no one lives in (an empty place), you should fill in an Interviewer Household Form for that dwelling, answering questions 2 and 3 only. This includes dwellings that are unoccupied for cultural reasons.

Counting an occupied dwelling where no one is home

Explain: If you visit a dwelling where people usually live and find there is no one home, try to find out whether they will be back before the Census is finished. If they do come back, complete the forms. If no one returns during the Census time, the dwelling is counted as an unoccupied dwelling (empty place).

During their training, the CFOs flagged PTA and the rules for dealing with them as something that was worrying them. One of them said, 'This is the issue that has been jumping off the page for me', and they all wanted to spend more time on this topic. Their main concern was how one could know for sure that a PTA had been counted elsewhere, given the rolling nature of the count. They pointed out that the local knowledge of the CCs and CIs would be of little use here, since there was no way those people could know whether or not someone had been counted elsewhere. The general advice given was, if in doubt, include the person in the main part of the form as if they were present, and get as many details as possible for them. In the event, not a great deal of time was spent on the topic, because, in the absence of a detailed compendium of the kinds of scenarios that might occur, the discussion could not be framed in a useful way. There just seemed to be endless possible scenarios, each less clear-cut than the last.

The case-study chapters (3–6) show that the CFOs were right to be worried about this question. In the training of CCs and CIs that I observed in Arnhem Land, the CFO was not able to articulate a plan of action for the CCs and the CIs that was any clearer than the instructions he had received himself. As is argued in Appendix B, the design of the form itself tended to lead CCs and CIs to leave

PTAs out of the main body of the form, and the lack of training on how to make judgments to do otherwise certainly compounded this tendency. I return to the consequences in the discussion of the post-count phase at the CMU (Chapter 7).

Logistics

In talking to the CFOs about logistics, the CMU staff was constrained by the time frames that had been set by the ABS in Canberra. The CFOs were expected to have the CC and CI training, the count itself and the post-count checking completed and all the forms back to Darwin in six to seven weeks (10 July–28 August). After their CHINS experience, it was clear that most of them considered this to be unrealistic—and, as it turned out, they were right. The CMU staff was in a position in which they had to maintain the idea that everything could be done realistically within the time frame that had been set. It was clear, however, that they also had their doubts: it was said that the most important thing was to get as good a count as possible, and that if the worst came to the worst that took precedence over deadlines. They had also put into place 'emergency backup' provisions, with a 'floating' CFO who could be called in to help in areas where things were going slowly. The net effect was a tendency to curtail discussion about possible problems and to 'focus on the positives' to a somewhat sceptical audience of CFOs. I felt this situation is hard on the CMU staff and the CFOs, and that Canberra needs to take on board the fact that the IES—as it is presently organised—cannot be undertaken in the envisaged time frame.

Conclusion

This chapter concludes with some recommendations that would apply equally if the IES were to remain substantially the same as it is now, or, alternatively, if it were to be overhauled radically in the manner we recommend (see Chapter 9).

The way in which information about local conditions is preserved from census to census, and the availability of such information to those who most need it (the CFOs), could be vastly improved. One tool in the future armoury will be the DICD, but it will be useful only if it is updated constantly. This task should be decentralised to augmented Indigenous Liaison Units within the ABS regional offices in all States and Territories where the IES is implemented.

The detailed reports of the CFOs and CMU staff from the 2001 census should not only be analysed centrally in Canberra; they should be available, perhaps in edited form with commentary, to the CMU staff and CFOs employed for the subsequent census. Given that each region—or even community—has its own characteristics, substantive information about logistical problems and solutions, about the mobility patterns of regional populations and about cultural factors specific to particular regions would be of particular value. Such information would give the CFOs a 'feel' for the size of the task and for the local conditions they might encounter. This kind of information cannot be imparted formally and in abstract in the very compressed training time that is available.

The sheer number of different kinds of information that the CFOs have to master needs to be taken into account more fully in the training methods employed. It would be useful—and less daunting for the participants (CFOs and CMU staff)—to break the training up into more manageable chunks, allowing the CFOs the opportunity to focus on just one topic at a time. This would allow them to absorb the relevant written materials more effectively beforehand, and have that information reinforced during training. It would also give more scope for acting out scenarios, rather than just having the information delivered in lecture format. Such scenario-building, as well as giving people practical experience, is likely to throw up omissions or lack of clarity in the written materials. These can then be addressed before people go out into the field, lessening the likelihood of ad hoc and possibly inconsistent solutions being implemented on the run out in the field.

In the training that was delivered to the CFOs in 2006, there was a great deal of emphasis—necessarily so—on procedural matters and on the 'head count' aspect of the census. For the latter, however, there was an inadequate anticipation of the scale and complexity of the PTA problem and of the difficulties likely to be caused by the time-extended and rolling nature of the count (see following chapters). Documentation of the PTA phenomena encountered and how they were dealt with in 2006 should be analysed carefully at central and State/Territory levels, so that future training on this question can be better informed.

Matters of content and definition received relatively little emphasis in training. In particular, the IHF—the collection instrument—is itself a complex document that needs careful and detailed explication. It must be remembered that census questions are framed in terms of categories devised by the ABS, which in turn reflect the planning and policy concerns of the nation-state and its agencies. These concerns and categories are not necessarily transparent to the CFOs, let alone to the CCs, CIs and individual respondents.[4] In order for the CFOs to train the CCs and CIs in an informed manner, it is necessary for them to understand the content and structure of the questions, and the nature of the information they are intended to elicit. In the future, if the CC role is augmented in the

---

[4] For example, one CFO questioned the utility of Questions 30 and 31, which ask whether the person's mother/father is in the dwelling, and also ask for the parents' 'person numbers' (see Appendix A). He thought these questions were redundant in view of the fact that information about relationships between household members and Person 1 had been elicited earlier in the form. In fact, these questions had been added to the form in order to elicit a finer-grained account of the internal structures of households, replacing a much less successful question on the 2001 form concerning an individual to whom the person was 'more closely related' than they were to Person 1. Once this was explained, the CFO saw the point of the questions and the value of asking them.

manner in which we have suggested in the concluding chapter, it will be possible also to train the CCs to this level of understanding.

3. A vast improvement: the 2006 enumeration in the Alice Springs town camps

Will Sanders

Introduction

The conduct of the 2006 Census in the Alice Springs town camps was a vast improvement on 2001. Later I will suggest some reasons for this, as well as identifying some remaining issues. I will begin, however, by recalling some of the major problems of the 2001 collection process and identifying developments since. I will then tell the story of the 2006 collection in the Alice Springs town camps, as I observed it. This should lay some foundations for understanding more analytically in the later sections of the chapter how and why the 2006 Census collection process in the Alice Springs town camps was such a vast improvement on 2001.

2001 remembered and developments since

My analysis of the collection of the 2001 Census in the 19 Alice Springs town camps pointed to the overwhelming demands of the task (Sanders 2002). The household plus personal form structure used in 2001 was extremely cumbersome and quickly wore out interviewers and interviewees. About 25 collector-interviewers (CIs) were employed during a four to five-week period in 2001, with many lasting only a day or two, or a camp or two, before quietly slipping away. The Community Coordinators (CCs) in 2001 had to salvage the situation by giving up on the personal forms about 12 days into the collection process. From then on they focused just on the household forms, augmented slightly with a few hand-ruled columns.

Another inadequacy in 2001 was that visitors in the camps were not being counted. The assumption was that they would be counted elsewhere as absent usual residents. As an observer, I was dubious of this idea. As well as short-term visitors who might possibly be counted elsewhere, the term 'visitor' seemed to cover some quite long-term residents of town camps who were still distinguished from the recognised tenants of houses or owners of camps. I judged that the likelihood of these long-term visitors being counted elsewhere was very slight. In addition, not counting visitors did nothing to demonstrate the demands these people placed on town camp services, which was an important issue for the town camp servicing organisation, Tangentyere Council. Any attempt to count visitors in the town camps in 2001 would, however, have only added to the overwhelming demands of the census task, so it was perhaps just as well that this was not attempted.

The results of the 2001 Census, released in 2003, showed the Alice Springs town camps had 973 residents in 189 dwellings or households (Sanders 2004). Tangentyere was dissatisfied with these figures because they did not include visitors but also because they thought this was a significant under-count of residents. It was partly this dissatisfaction with the 2001 Census that spurred Tangentyere to develop its own population and mobility study in 2004 and 2005 (Foster et al. 2005). This study surveyed the town camps four times from mid 2004 to mid 2005, finding at various times between 906 people in 151 dwellings and 1341 people in 195 dwellings (see Table 3.1). These surveys demonstrated that between 16 and 21 per cent of the people counted in the town camps at these various time were visitors. They also led to the compilation of a cumulative list of 2326 named people counted in 255 dwellings in the 19 camps during the course of the year. This study was therefore beginning to show how Tangentyere had a significantly larger service population in the town camps over a year than the resident population at any one time, including visitors.

Table 3.1 Results of Tangentyere population and mobility surveys

	Dwellings surveyed	People counted	Proportion visitors
June 2004	151	906	0.21
Oct 2004	202	1205	0.20
Apr 2005	177	1111	0.16
June 2005	195	1341	0.17

Through these and other research efforts, Tangentyere had by 2005 developed a strong research unit of its own. In late 2005, the Tangentyere research unit was asked by the Australian Bureau of Statistics (ABS) to conduct a trial of the new Interviewer Household Form (IHF) for the 2006 Census in one of the town camps. This they did with a combination of enthusiasm and trepidation. The Tangentyere researchers were interested in the census, but were reminded through the trial of the size of the census task and its demanding nature. They were also beginning to realise how the census might potentially crowd out their own research opportunities. I will return to this later, but will conclude here by arguing that in 2006 Tangentyere was far better prepared and positioned for the coming of the census than in 2001.

Collecting in 2006

Planning and negotiations between the ABS and Tangentyere for the collection of the 2006 Census in the town camps began quite early in the year. The ABS opened an Alice Springs office in March—compared with somewhat later in 2001. By the time I visited in May, there had already been discussions and developments regarding the ABS supplying cars so collectors could move between Tangentyere's central office complex and the camps scattered across Alice Springs (see Figure 3.1). There had also been negotiations about working and being paid in teams of two, as was the practice in the Tangentyere population and mobility surveys.

Fig. 3.1 The Alice Springs town camps (Community Living Areas)

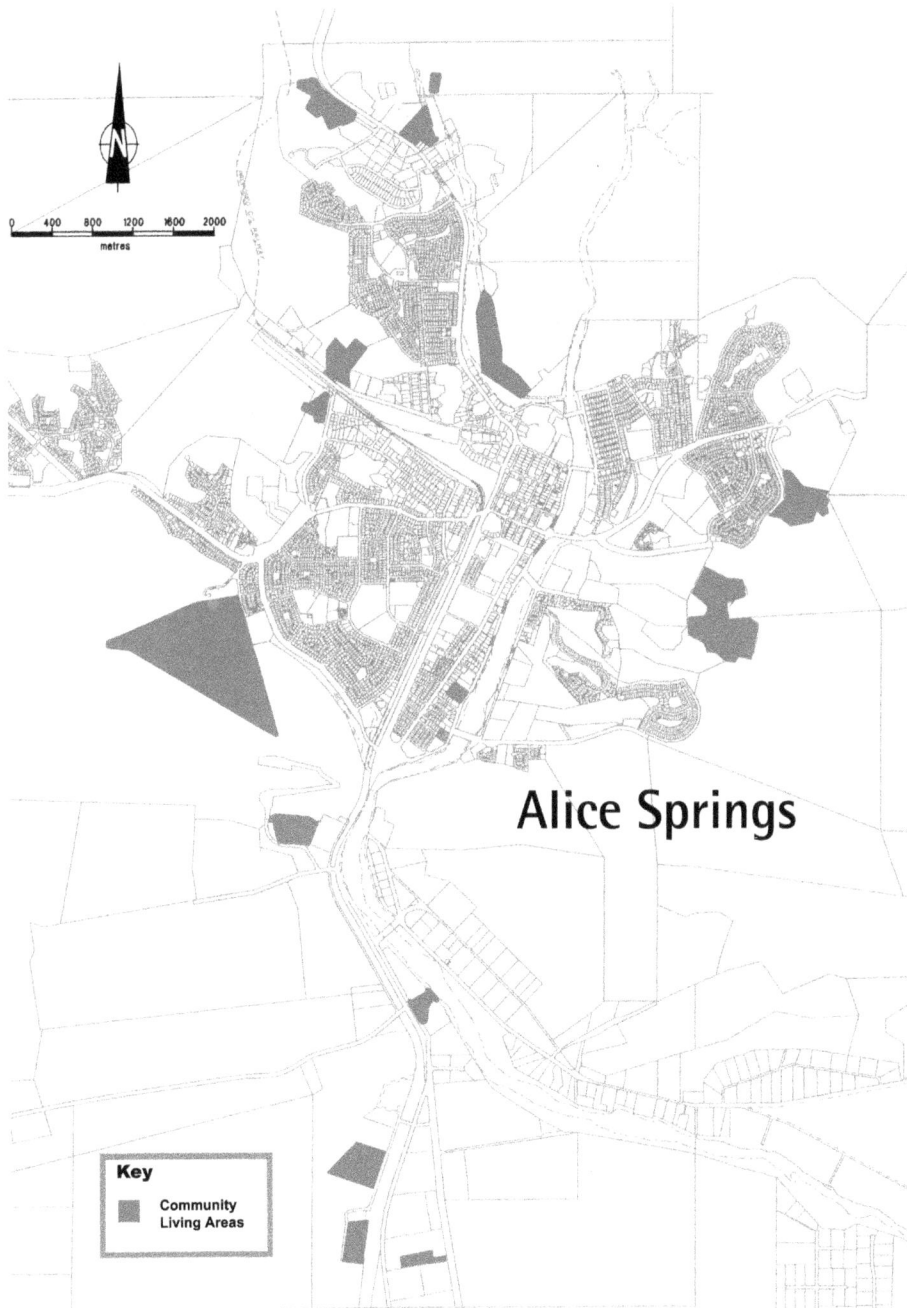

By the time I returned on Monday 17 July—three weeks and one day out from the general census night on Tuesday 8 August—the Census Field Officer (CFO) had conducted training of eight CIs late the previous week and the first day of collecting in the town camps was under way. All the CIs were Aboriginal women, some of whom lived in the town camps themselves, but most of whom lived in other housing around town. In the next day or so, another two or three CIs were added, still all women, though there was some consciousness at the time of trying to recruit some men. The new CIs who had missed the formal training of the previous week were effectively trained by giving them a DVD to watch and by pairing them with established CIs, who by then had a day or two's experience. One or two CIs pulled back after their first encounter with the hard reality of collection. Most, however, stayed with the task, while also clearly realising that it was not always going to be easy. There were also a few teething troubles in those first few days over the numbering of dwellings in the camps on the green Interviewer Dwelling Checklist (IDC). There was an initial attempt to use a different dwelling numbering system to Tangentyere's existing house-numbering system. It soon became evident, however, that it was clearer to use the existing Tangentyere system and then to add as necessary any other occupied dwellings, such as tin sheds or community facilities.

The collection process settled during its first week into a pattern of about eight women CIs assembling at the Tangentyere research unit office about 8.30am and, under the supervision of the CFO, dividing into two or three car-loads of teams. A car-load of collectors would focus on one of the 11 groupings of town camps that corresponded with an ABS Collection District (CD). Generally, two such CDs of camps were being worked on at a time by different teams of CIs. Out in the camps, the women approached a dwelling and asked for the 'house boss'. If the house boss was available, the interview generally took place then and there; if not, an attempt was made to identify a time to come back. Occasionally, someone present was identified who was not the house boss but who had sufficient knowledge and authority within the household group to answer on their behalf. Another possibility was to meet the house boss elsewhere—for example, at their work. Local knowledge proved important here, since most of the CIs seemed to know most of the house bosses, even if only vaguely, and when and where they might be found if they were not home on the first visit.

Interviews could take anywhere between 40 minutes and an hour, depending largely on the number of people in the household. Teams of two CIs could generally complete between three and four household interviews in a morning, depending on whether they stuck together closely as a team of two or split up as opportunities for interviews developed. Teams of CIs would regroup at the Tangentyere research office for lunch and to transfer details from the pink IHFs to their green IDC. Dwellings were being dealt with at a rate of about 12 a morning and then, in the afternoon, through follow-up, at a rate of perhaps another three or four. Mornings were therefore the main work period, followed by a considerably less concerted work period after lunch.

Within interviews, the first half of the 40 to 60-minute process would be spent answering the opening questions about the dwelling and listing people who were either living in or staying in the dwelling now (Question 12; see Appendix A) or who lived there most of the time but were away (Questions 10 and 11). These questions also covered the basic age and gender characteristics of each person listed, and also whether they were a visitor, or their location if they were away. Once this listing of people's names, ages and genders was complete, interviews settled into a somewhat more routine mode of answering questions about the people listed in Question 12 as living or staying there now. Interviewers generally answered each question for each person listed before moving on to the next question. This 'vertical' working method had been anticipated during form design as the likely dominant mode of collector operation and certainly this proved to be the case in the Alice Springs town camps.

This process of enumeration of about 12 to 15 dwellings a day continued from Monday to Thursday in the first week of the collection process under the supervision of the CFO. Friday was seen as a day off, as is commonly the case in Aboriginal communities, particularly where employment is through the Community Development Employment Projects (CDEP) scheme. During this first week it also gradually became understood more clearly that in the second week, the CFO would be attending to collection processes out of Alice Springs and hence would not be around. The CIs, one of whom was also now designated as the CC, would therefore be a little more on their own. It was also understood, however, that with the absence of the CFO the District Manager and her Assistant would endeavour to provide daily support, at least at the Tangentyere research office if not out in the camps. Perhaps their most important form of daily support was providing lunches, which were proving a useful social and administrative focus for the group of CIs as they returned to the Tangentyere research unit office after their morning's work.

The second week of the collection process proceeded, in fact, much like the first. The group of women CIs seemed to have developed a fairly good camaraderie and, apart from some occasional absences to attend to other life matters, the team of eight or so CIs hung together well. By the end of the second week, at least a first attempt had been made to carry out the collection in eight of the 11 town camp Collection Districts. Three of perhaps the largest and most difficult town camps remained to be tackled, as well as many follow-ups of dwellings in the other town camps in which the house boss had not been available for interview at the first or even second visit. Progress with the count was, however, generally seen to be good and two of the women CIs decided to take opportunities to accompany CFOs to the bush the next week as Assistant CFOs.

The third week of the census collection process in the town camps therefore began with a slightly reduced team. As well as the two CIs now out bush, another CI pulled back because she had lost her working partner and a fourth, reportedly, pulled back due to concerns that earning too much might adversely effect her Centrelink entitlements. One or two of the other CIs told me that this was not a concern for them as they were on CDEP, which had more relaxed and generous provisions for earning additional income than Centrelink payments. Therefore, only about five or six CIs were left for this third week, and there was a sense in which the collection process in the town camps was now winding down. There were, however, still two quite large camps to count, which had been left to last in part because they were seen as perhaps the most difficult and possibly disrupted by large numbers of current visitors or other recent events—including some 'sorry business' and fighting. In the event, four male Tangentyere housing workers were coopted to assist the women in approaching dwellings in the last three camps. Although I did not directly observe the difference this made, it was reported by those involved as making a significant contribution to a difficult final task. By the end of this third week, the task of collecting the 2006 Census in the Alice Springs town camps was seen as essentially done. Most of the women collectors had had enough and were happy to finish, however, the woman who had been doing some CC tasks stayed on for a couple of days, crosschecking IHFs with IDCs and Master Dwelling Checklists (MDCs).

This crosschecking of forms showed that roughly 1200 people had been counted as present in the town camps in about 190 households. Hence, what had taken four or five weeks with 25 CIs in 2001, resulting in a salvage operation and no counting of visitors, had been achieved in 2006 in three weeks in a planned and orderly fashion with eight to 10 CIs and included visitors. So why, one might ask, was there such a vast improvement?

Reasons for improvement

The single most important reason for the improvement, it seems to me, was the new IHF. Although physically a little cumbersome, as an administrative system for enumerating people associated with a dwelling, the new form worked well. It was far less cumbersome and demanding than the previous system of household and personal forms. Under the old system, the collection task had only just begun at the point where people associated with a dwelling had been listed. A vast task of attempting to fill in personal forms for each person listed then still lay ahead. With the new IHF, once the people associated with a dwelling had been listed at Questions 10–12, together with their gender and age, the collection task was about half complete. What lay ahead was a more routine process of answering substantive questions about the people listed predominantly by putting marks in boxes and occasionally doing a bit of writing. This was far less demanding than the daunting task of separate personal forms required in 2001.

Another reason for improvement—specific to the Alice Springs town camps in 2006—was that Tangentyere was far better tied into the ABS than in 2001. The research unit in Tangentyere provided a focus for forward planning and negotiation for the ABS, which had not been there in 2001. Issues such as the need for cars, working in pairs and being paid in pairs were negotiated well in advance. This laid the foundations for an orderly collection process that, although still demanding for CIs, was realistic and achievable. That the CIs could use the Tangentyere research unit office as their operational and social base was also particularly important, even though, in the end, the group of CIs recruited included only three people who had been involved directly in the Tangentyere population and mobility study. There were also two employees of the Tangentyere research unit operating in the background who had been involved in the population and mobility study and who were supporting the CIs and the CC, even though they were not themselves employed directly by the ABS. In a number of different ways therefore the Tangentyere research unit provided an enormous base of strength and support for the 2006 Census collection process and personnel.

A third reason for improvement was that the ABS committed more of its staff time to the Alice Springs town camps in 2006 compared with 2001. In 2001, the District Manager had acted effectively as CFO for the town camps, squeezing his involvement between other commitments. In 2006, the town camp collection process had the full-time attention of a CFO for a week and a half in order to get training done and the count substantially under way, before he went off to do similar work out bush. After the CFO had moved on, the District Manager and her Assistant took a continuing monitoring and support role for the next two weeks. I would say that, compared with 2001, the level of ABS staff attention and support for Tangentyere and the town camp collection process was probably about double.

A fourth minor reason for improvement was possibly also the greater engagement of the Northern Territory government in 2006. This was partly because the Territory had almost lost a House of Representatives seat in 2003 on the basis of the 2001 Census count (Joint Standing Committee on Electoral Matters 2003). It was also because the recommendations of the Commonwealth Grants Commission for general revenue sharing relied heavily on population numbers and the Northern Territory government believed it might be missing out here as well. Indeed, in the lead-up to the 2006 Census, the government ran a newspaper advertising campaign under the slogan 'We're counting on you', in which Chief Minister, Clare Martin, explicitly made the link between the numbers of 'Territorians counted' and 'the amount of money we receive from the

Australian government' (see, for example, *Centralian Advocate* 2006). The Northern Territory government also directed its employees to be as helpful as they could to the census process. At the regional office level, this led to the ABS's temporary administration in Alice Springs being co-located with the Territory government's Department of Local Government, Housing and Sport, which through its field staff could provide intelligence on situations and service personnel in various Aboriginal communities. My intuition is that these intergovernmental links probably contributed more to improving the census collection process in outlying areas than in the Alice Springs town camps, where the ABS had well-established, direct relations with Tangentyere and did not need to rely on government connections and intelligence.

Remaining issues

There are some issues remaining with the design and content of the IHF; these are addressed in Appendix B. One final issue relates to visitors. The Tangentyere research unit found in its population and mobility study that it was hard to distinguish between residents and visitors. They had a 'long discussion' about the issue when designing their survey, including the possibility of defining visitors by 'how long they had been staying there' (Foster et al. 2005: 16). In the end, the Tangentyere research unit decided to let the 'house boss' for each dwelling tell them who was a resident and who was a visitor. They found that there were a significant number of visitors who had been staying at dwellings for longer than six weeks, or even longer than three months. They commented, after noting this, that 'it seemed that who is a visitor is related to the right to be at [a] particular camp or dwelling' (Foster et al. 2005: 16).

This finding bears out emphatically the inadequacy of the 2001 approach of leaving visitors in the town camps to be counted elsewhere, and the correctness of the 2006 Census approach of trying to count visitors. When such long-term residents are referred to as visitors, however, the question arises as to whether very short-term visitors are also being captured by this terminology. This issue can also be approached by reflecting on another finding of the Tangentyere population and mobility study.

The third survey in the Tangentyere study in April 2005 was carried out during two weeks straddling a major weekend football carnival. The Tangentyere research unit expected that this might lead to higher numbers of visitors in the camps than in their first two surveys; however, with a line of questioning that focused explicitly on who stayed in a dwelling 'last night' they still did not seem to be able to capture this short-term visitation. They commented of their third survey: 'The football visitors were not at the camps after the weekend, and there was not a significantly higher number of visitors. It seemed that most of the football visitors came in for the weekend only and went back to their communities straight away' (Foster et al. 2005: 19).

With Tangentyere unable to capture this expected short-term visitation in its survey, it is perhaps to be expected that the census might have similar problems. Question 12 on the IHF did not go quite so far as saying that everyone should be listed who stayed at a dwelling last night; rather it opted for the slightly more general terminology of people 'who are living or staying here now'. It is possible therefore that the census collectors in 2006 missed overnight visitors to town camps in much the same way as the football visitors were missed by the Tangentyere research unit survey in April 2005. This is not a problem for the census as a whole, since such short-term visitors to the town camps are reasonably likely to be counted elsewhere. It simply means that the visitor count at Tangentyere, while capturing longer-term visitors, might still not capture fully very short-term visitors.

Tangentyere's list

One final interesting aspect of the 2006 Census collection process in the Alice Springs town camps was some discussion that occurred between Tangentyere and the ABS about the possible use of Tangentyere's list of 2326 named people present in town camps between June 2004 and June 2005. There was some suggestion that this list might help collectors locate people or act as a form of validation of those counted; however, in the end, the list was not used during the collection process.

Tangentyere's interest in using the list was partly also a wish to update it, as it was by census time more than a year out of date. Tangentyere saw the census as occupying some of its available research time and opportunity in the camps, and hoped that the ABS might see its way clear to allow them to use the census to update their list as a quid pro quo. As it became clear that the ABS could not under any circumstance allow personal information collected in the census to be transferred to some other database, Tangentyere became somewhat less interested in making their list of names available to the ABS.

In the past, there have often been suggestions that existing lists generated by administration of other processes could in some way lessen the demands of the census on Aboriginal communities and increase its reliability (for example, Martin and Taylor 1996). I have never been as convinced of this argument as some others, feeling that lists are generated for particular purposes at particular times and are often of limited use beyond those particular purposes and times. One issue raised by this example of the non-use of Tangentyere's list is that the owners of those lists will often want something in return for their use and the ABS has extreme difficulty offering anything. I do not believe that the use of the Tangentyere list would have greatly changed the collection of the 2006 Census in the Alice Springs town camps. I suspect that the majority of the 1200 people enumerated as present in the town camps in July and August 2006 were on Tangentyere's list of 2326 named people from 2004 and 2005. The people who were present in the town camps did in the end seem to be able to be identified reasonably readily. What the list would have added would have been as many names again of people who could have been asked about. Most of these people would probably have been identified as not currently living in the camps. A few might have then been remembered as living there but were away, or even living there but forgotten—which could have increased the count a little. To pick up this last category of genuinely missed people, it would have been quite a lot of work to go through more than 1300 additional names.

Ten months on, the ABS compared the census counts in four camps with Tangentyere's survey of 4 August 2005 to see whether there were any significant differences in numbers of people enumerated by age structure or number of dwellings. This was a very modest validation exercise in contrast with some of the early ideas for the use of Tangentyere's list.

The vast improvement of the 2006 Census on the 2001 Census in the Alice Springs town camps lay in the fact that it reduced the collection task to a reasonably simple and manageable administrative procedure. Any attempt to use Tangentyere's list as an adjunct to the collection process would, in my judgment, have added to the complexity of the task without greatly enhancing the ability of the CIs to find people. The CIs were successful because they had a familiarity with the town camp environment and were well supported by Tangentyere and the ABS. What Tangentyere's list could have added to this success was marginal at best.

Conclusion

In conclusion, I would simply return to and reiterate three of the reasons for improvement from the 2001 Census identified above. The first of these was the redesign of the household and personal forms into the single, integrated IHF. Although still not perfect—and still quite demanding on interviewers and interviewees—this new form did at least give CIs a task that was possible. This was not the case in 2001.

Beyond this general improvement, the second factor was a specific improvement in relations between the town camp servicing organisation, Tangentyere Council, and the ABS. Tangentyere's own research capacity had grown significantly since 2001, partly as a result of its dissatisfaction with the results of the 2001 Census. Because of this, Tangentyere was more interested in the census in 2006 and more assertive in its relationship with the ABS. Tangentyere could now draw on its own experience of doing surveys in the town camps and knew the difficulties and the requirements of doing so. For the ABS—perhaps somewhat unusually—Tangentyere was now a highly engaged and quite experienced Indigenous partner organisation. This was no doubt at times somewhat challenging and uncomfortable for the ABS, but it laid the basis for an orderly and achievable census collection procedure in the town camps in 2006. Tangentyere negotiated with the ABS about committing resources adequate to the task—in personnel and in other costs such as cars—and the ABS responded. This level of commitment of ABS resources was the third factor behind the vast improvement from 2001. To what extent this level of commitment of ABS resources was different from, and possibly even at the expense of, other Indigenous communities with less-engaged service organisations could throw some light on the rather less orderly accounts of the 2006 Census collection process that my colleagues report (Chapters 4–6). While the Alice Springs town camps were seen by some within the ABS in 2001 as possibly a 'worst-case scenario' (Sanders 2002: 88), in 2006, they might well come to be seen as more of an example of best practice, which the ABS will aim to repeat in the future and emulate elsewhere.

4. Mobility and its consequences: the 2006 enumeration in the north-east Arnhem Land region

Frances Morphy

Introduction

This case study is constructed from an anthropological perspective. An anthropological analysis has a particular kind of contribution to make in a situation such as a census enumeration, in which members of an encapsulated cultural minority are interacting with the institutions of the encapsulating state. I want to convey how the census enumeration appears to the Yolngu—particularly the Community Coordinators (CCs) and collector-interviewers (CIs)—in order to understand some of the problems that arise and what their possible solutions might be.

The census, being a dwelling-based count, is founded on assumptions about the characteristics of populations that fit sedentary settler societies such as mainstream Australia, but which do not fit populations such as the Yolngu, who, as I have argued elsewhere (Morphy 2007), behave in 'radically uncontained' ways. I am concerned to explore the consequences of this for the Indigenous Enumeration Strategy (IES) in general, and its impact on the role of the Census Field Officer (CFO) in particular.

I have also chosen to structure the major part of this case study as a chronological narrative of the count in four phases, to convey a sense of just how difficult a task it is to 'capture' this mobile population, and as a background to what might sometimes appear to be critical comments about how the 2006 enumeration was managed. There is no self-evident and easy strategy; however, in the way in which it is currently constituted, the CFO's job is all but impossible. I am not asserting necessarily that the current collection methodology results in a significant over or under-count, rather that the expectations put on the CFO are unrealistic and unattainable, and this makes the job unnecessarily stressful.

I also want to demonstrate that the mobility of the population, although radical, is not random; it takes place within particular parameters. Once these are understood, it becomes easier to devise more efficient enumeration strategies. I will argue that such strategies will depend crucially on making best use of local knowledge, not only of the CCs and CIs, but of the staff—Indigenous and non-Indigenous—of local organisations whose primary task it is to provide local populations with services and infrastructure. The patterns of mobility that I describe below are peculiar to this particular region and cannot necessarily be generalised to others. In each region, however, there are organisations that are repositories of knowledge about the characteristics of local population mobility. I will be suggesting that the Australian Bureau of Statistics (ABS) needs to engage in long-term relationships with these organisations and help them build their capacity to better understand the local dynamics of mobility. This in turn will deliver to the ABS, come census time, key individuals who will be in a position to help in significant ways with the organisation of the census enumeration.

Localities

In order to comply with confidentiality requirements, I use letters of the alphabet to designate the major hub settlements in the Yolngu-speaking area, and for the homeland communities I use the letter of the hub settlement to which they are attached, followed by a number. To further disguise the area of the case study, I have assigned a number of homelands to hub settlements that differ from the one that, in reality, is their service centre.

The Yolngu-speaking area contains roughly 6000 Aboriginal people—most of whom are speakers of one of the Yolngu languages—and also the mining town of Nhulunbuy. There are six hub settlements in the area, ranging in size from more than 1000 people (Galiwin'ku/Elcho Island) to just more than 200 people (Gunyangara/Ski Beach). These have been assigned the letters A–F. There are two other settlements—G and H—outside the Yolngu area proper that will also figure in this account.

The homelands that form the focus of this case study are A1–12 and C1–5—that is, 17 of the estimated 76 inhabited homelands in the Yolngu-speaking area.[1] The CFO for the Yolngu-speaking area was responsible for the enumeration at all of the Yolngu settlements and homelands, as well as Groote Eylandt and Numbulwar and its homelands. There are, in total, more than 10,000 Aboriginal people scattered throughout this remote area of 37,000 square kilometres.

The CFO had hoped to cover settlements A and C and all their attached homelands in the first week of the enumeration, starting on 6 July. He had decided that the best strategy was to try to complete the count in one subregion at a time, so that he and/or the Assistant CFO could be present for most of the count, leaving to start the CC and CI training in the next subregion only when the count was nearly complete. Unfortunately, things did not go to plan; the count in communities A and C and their attached homelands was still incomplete many weeks later. In theory, the CFO's initial strategy was a sensible one in terms of logistics and efficient use of time. In practice, it proved completely unworkable.

---

[1] This estimate is taken from the list that the CFO was given for reference at the beginning of the 2006 count.

Funerals: a major cause of mobility

No Yolngu funeral is a perfunctory affair.[2] Despite the fact that most Yolngu choose 'Uniting Church' over 'Traditional beliefs' in response to the census question on religion, funerals are a major focus of a rich ceremonial system founded on traditional beliefs. In the pre-mission past, primary burial—interment or placement on a platform—was a swift affair. The more major ceremony after death was secondary reburial when the bones were retrieved and, after a period of being carried around by close relatives in a bark container, were placed in a hollow-log coffin. These secondary ceremonies were often much longer than the first, involved regional gatherings and took place at times of year when resources permitted the concentration of large numbers of people. They took place only after negotiations among all the relevant kin about the form of the ceremony and the final placement of the hollow-log coffin.

Missionisation, beginning in the mid 1930s, led to the discontinuation of secondary reburial, so that the ceremonial focus began to move to the primary burial. These ceremonies began to be more lengthy affairs, although still not overly so until the introduction of a new technology—the portable morgue. Beginning in the mid 1970s, Yolngu funerals have become exponentially longer and more elaborate affairs. Politics surrounding control of the ceremony and the final resting place of the deceased have intensified, in part because, unlike the organisation of a secondary reburial in the past, negotiations are contingent on the circumstances and time of the death and are compressed in time. Funerals have become the site of community politics par excellence.

The funeral of an important and senior person can attract up to 400 people from a wide region, and take several months. Although the 400 will not be present all of that time, funerals are a major cause of continual intra-regional mobility on a massive scale. In some years—and 2006 was a case in point—funerals are a continual presence. There might be several going on at the same time, although one is often delayed until after another is finished so that they follow one another almost without pause.

It is logistically impossible and inappropriate to undertake an enumeration at a place where a funeral is happening. During the course of a funeral, close relatives of the deceased person will camp at the site of the funeral for the duration. Others will come and go, usually making sure that they attend certain important points of the ceremony, particularly the last few days leading up to the burial itself. It is fair to say that the organisation of and attendance at funerals takes precedence over everything else, particularly for senior ceremonial leaders and certain categories of relatives of the deceased person.

---

[2] For a detailed ethnography of a Yolngu funeral (for a small child), see Morphy (1984).

The count, phase one: 6 July to 3 August

When the CFO arrived at Settlement A, there were four funerals under way in the immediate region: one at A itself, one at homeland A10 and two at other large predominantly non-Yolngu settlements in the wider region (G and H). The CFO had difficulty recruiting local CIs for A and C. Using lists of people supplied to him by the council offices of A and C, he found and trained one CC for Community A and two for Community C, and two potential CCs for the homelands attached to Community A. He and the CCs tried and failed to recruit CIs for the training. It had been estimated back at the Census Management Unit (CMU) that eight CCs and 21 CIs would be needed for the count in these two communities and their associated homelands, so this was not an auspicious start.

Having got the count under way in sections of the main settlements that were not affected directly by the funeral, the CFO set off down the track—accompanied by myself and the Assistant CFO—to survey the situation in some of the homelands. We drove into A7 (a three-dwelling homeland) towards evening. It was empty—everyone was at the funeral at A. The next day we called in at A8, which has a usual resident population of about 80. It too was deserted—everyone was at the large funeral happening at nearby A10.[3]

It was decided to return to these communities after the funerals were over and people had returned. The CFO had been warned before leaving A—by staff of local organisations and by the CCs he had recruited—that these homelands would be empty, or nearly so. Because people know how everyone is related to everyone else, they can predict with a fair degree of certainty which people will be attending which funerals. At this stage, the CFO—who had not previously worked in the Yolngu area, apart from undertaking the Community Housing and Infrastructure Needs Survey (CHINS)—had not fully appreciated the potential impact of funerals on population movement, and wanted to see for himself.

We then called in at A9. Not many people were there—some were at the funerals at A and A10. The daughter of the community leader was seriously ill in hospital and her parents had just returned from seeing her there. Nevertheless, the community leader and his wife were happy to be recruited as the CC and CI for A9 and to conduct the count once everyone had returned from the funerals. They also volunteered to enumerate A10 once the funeral there was finished. The CFO arranged to come back in a few days to conduct the training, and we set off further down the track in an optimistic frame of mind.

---

[3] At its height, this funeral of a senior man, which was politically contentious, attracted more than 400 people from a region the size of Wales. In turn, however, members of the host community were themselves absent—at yet another funeral in the wider region at E2.

We drove on to the largest homeland in the area, C3, where the usual resident population is in the region of 160. The plan was to recruit another CC and some CIs here to cover C3, C4 and C5 (another large homeland), since these three are close to each other and their inhabitants are closely interrelated. The CFO was successful in recruiting two CCs (one of whom had been a CI during the 2001 Census) and three CIs. After their training, however, as the CCs and CIs began going from house to house, it became evident that at least one-third of the population of C3 was away, at four different funerals (the ones at A, G, H and A10), or visiting relatives, predominantly at A, and several people were about to leave for the final part of the funeral at A10. In two cases, the entire household was away and their dwellings stood empty. It was decided to do a first count here, go on to C4 and C5, then return to C3, hopefully to catch people as they returned from the various funerals. In the meantime, all those who were away were put down as 'persons temporarily absent' (PTA), including on the forms for the empty dwellings. There were at least 20 'visitors' present—people visiting their kin from other communities (predominantly C2, C4, C5 and the settlements of A, C, B and G).[4] These were counted as visitors in the main section of the form. The C3 team was about to go to C4 and C5, and there was a possibility that some of the visitors would be returning to these communities at the same time, but the CFO and the C3 team were confident that no double-counting would result because everyone would be able to keep track of who had already been counted as visitors at C3.

I stayed with the C3 team, and drove them on to C4 and C5 when they had finished their first pass at C3. The CFO and his Assistant returned to A to try to get the count going in the other A and C homelands, and to offer support to the single remaining CC at A, who at this point was endeavouring to enumerate this sizeable community on her own. Back at A, the CFO discovered that the entire populations of A3 and A4 were at A for the funeral there. They were enumerated at A 'as if' they were in their dwellings in A3 and A4. I will return to the reason why this happened below.

The burdens of literacy

In the meantime, the two CCs recruited and trained to cover the other A and C homelands had gone to the final phases of the funeral at A10. They were under a heavy obligation to attend, as close relatives of the deceased, and this took precedence over their duties to the census. This brings me to a separate but

---

[4] The pattern of mobility captured here in snapshot was very similar to that observed at the same homeland during the 2001 Census (see Morphy 2002).

equally important theme: the drop-out rate of Indigenous CCs and CIs is often a cause for comment, but it is necessary to understand why they drop out.[5]

Most Yolngu do not keep diaries. They might sign up in good faith to be a CC or CI, for example, only to be reminded a few days later that they have a medical appointment with a specialist who is paying one of their periodic visits to the area. For a homelands person, this means a plane ride into A. One of the CIs at C3 found himself in this situation. There are, however, more systemic reasons why people are likely to fall by the wayside during the count.

The people who are most likely to be recruited as CCs and CIs in a region such as this are the rare individuals with the requisite levels of literacy in English. They are 'better educated' in a Western sense, and this means:

- they might already have a job
- because they tend to be among the most able, intelligent and competent people, they are in demand for local events (such as funerals) and their status in their own community is judged by their commitment to participating in such events
- at the same time, they are expected—by their relatives and by local non-Indigenous staff of organisations—to represent the interests of the community at the interface between the Yolngu world and the encapsulating society
- they often have a sense of 'civic duty' that impels them to take part in the non-local event that is the census, despite competing demands on their time, because they have an understanding of the local consequences of more global processes.

People like this are in constant danger of burn-out. Aboriginal communities are conceived of popularly as places where people sit around on 'sit-down' Community Development Employment Projects (CDEP) money and do nothing much. The situation of the general population is the subject of a different study—in which this view would be disputed. The situation of the most able and the most Western-educated—and therefore most literate—is, however, as stressful as any in mainstream society in terms of competing and conflicting demands on their time.

As with the CFOs, I would argue, the current operation of the IES puts many local CCs and CIs in a no-win situation. The enumeration process necessitates a sustained and intensive effort, and, since it often proves impossible to recruit sufficient numbers of people for the size of the population, it can involve a very heavy workload.

---

[5] For example, during the training of the CFOs, it was recommended that they try to recruit more CCs and CIs than they really needed, so that if some people dropped out there would be others to fill their places.

In the way in which the IES is organised at present, this is an intractable problem. Competing demands often force CCs and CIs to abandon their census work—temporarily or permanently—and this in turn places heavier demands on the remaining CCs and CIs, and also on the CFO, who must then somehow recruit and train replacements. If he or she has already moved on to another subregion, clearly there is the potential for the census effort to stall completely. This is what happened in the case-study area and, as a result, the count in the A and C homelands—with the exception of the area covered by the C3 team—was a prolonged and tortuous affair. The relative smoothness of phase one was a bit of a false dawn. I conclude this section with two short case studies that illustrate the conflicting demands on people acting as CIs and CCs. Some details have been changed to protect their anonymity.

Case one[6]

One of the CCs recruited originally for the A and C homelands was back at Community A after the completion of the funeral at A10. He was ready and willing to restart work as a CC/CI. The CFO had in the meantime gone to start the count in a different region, leaving the Assistant CFO at A. She was very pleased to see the CC again, as his help was sorely needed at A and in some of the A and C homelands, where the count had temporarily ceased. We made plans to leave for A2—another homeland that had been visited once and found to be empty of inhabitants (they too had been at the funeral at A10, but were now known to have returned home). We had heard that the previous evening there had been a death, but the identity of the person who had died had not been confirmed. Just as we were preparing to leave for A2, two policemen arrived at the CC's house, asking him to identify the body. An hour later, he returned with the news that the dead person was one of his clansmen, a close 'father' of his. Although visibly upset, he insisted that he would carry on work because he realised that his help was badly needed. We were just about to leave when a group of senior clan leaders called him over. They were anxious to begin planning the funeral, which was to take place at A8, and wanted him to be a part of the discussion. (Most of the inhabitants of A8 were back home now after the end of the funeral at A10, and this meant precision planning was now needed for the count there because once the funeral ceremony began it would not be possible to go there.) It was impossible for the CC to refuse, so the count at A2 was postponed yet again.

Case two

The attrition rate among the CCs at A and C, who had never been numerous in the first place, had necessitated the ad hoc training of extra people, whenever

---

[6] In all these examples details have been changed to protect the identity of the specific individuals concerned.

they could be found. One person who already had a part-time job volunteered to work on her days off. She was assigned a workload in A, which she completed conscientiously and efficiently. It was then decided to use her as the CI for some of the remaining A and C homelands. With her help, the count at A6 was completed. (One entire A6 household was still away at A12, where the funeral had just ended. This household was not followed up until the forms had been returned to the CMU in Darwin, when it was realised that they had been missed.) The CFO and his Assistant were pleased and relieved that the homelands count was getting under way again. Then, unfortunately, the daughter of the leader of the A9 community died in hospital. This particular CI and her family were related to the dead woman in such a way as to make it imperative that they become involved in organising her funeral, which included arranging for the body to be flown back from Darwin. The family at A9 wanted a short funeral and they needed to arrange it quickly because the girl's mother was herself due to go to Darwin for an operation. The CI tried valiantly to continue her census work, but after a couple of days it all became too much. The family was relying on her, as a literate person, to complete the bureaucratic arrangements and she still had her part-time job on top of that. And, despite the family's desire for a quick and uncomplicated funeral, 'Yolngu politics' about where the funeral should take place began to manifest themselves. On one occasion, when this CI was helping someone to fill in the form for their household, she was reproached for doing this work when she should be attending to funeral matters. She asked to be relieved of her obligations to the census until after the arrangements for the funeral had been completed. After the funeral was over, she came back to work as a CI.

The count, phase two: 3–7 August

On 3 August, nearly a month after the beginning of the census count in this area, my field notes revealed the state of play to be as follows.

The CFO had just left to organise the count at H, leaving the Assistant CFO behind to continue supervising the work in the A/C area.

C3 had been done—in two stages; one household was still away, and was discovered later to have been counted at A as usual residents of a household there (see Case three); a few other individuals were still away at G. C4 had been done, but one house was empty, as people were at the funeral at A10. C5 had been done, but some people were away at the funeral at A10; others were visiting relatives at B. The residents of A3 and A4 had been counted at A because they were attending a funeral there, but were counted 'as if' they were at home. A6 had been done, but one household was absent at the A10 funeral. A5 had been done, although it was later discovered that some A5 people had been counted twice—as usual residents—at both A and A5.

Community A was, apparently, nearly done. There were still a few houses to do, but the CC who had done most of the work on her own was completely burnt out, and besides, as a schoolteacher, her normal employment was about to resume.

C1 had been established as empty—its residents had been counted as 'usual residents' in a house at A.

A1 was still to be done; it was geographically closer to F than to A, and the CFO intended to organise the count from F. In the event, A1 was nearly overlooked (see Chapter 8). A2's residents were apparently still not home and were proving elusive. Some residents of A7, which had been empty when first visited, were still at the funeral at A10, while the whereabouts of others was unknown. All the residents of A8 were still at the A10 funeral. A girl's funeral was now taking place in A9; there was a major funeral at A10; the usual residents of A11 were at funerals at A9 and A10; and A12 had not yet been visited. A CI who was resident at A but whose family belonged to C2 had been recruited to count C2, but so far had not produced anything and was proving elusive. C6, a large homeland, had not yet been visited.

The current workforce was: the C3 team, but their work was finished and the logistics of using them elsewhere were complicated by distance; the CC who had almost single-handedly counted A was burnt out; two CCs, who were finishing C and who were then going to do C6; and two other CCs, and one CI, all of whom were unavoidably involved at the funerals at A9 and A10, but who would probably become involved again once the funerals were over. The CI who was allegedly looking after C2 was an unknown quantity.

I recorded 'this week's new problems' as: a suicide at A (leading to the closing of part of the community), the funeral at A9 and the Garma Festival, which was potentially another source of major population movement in the Yolngu-speaking region, and which also attracted substantial numbers of people from H.

Within the wider area of his responsibility, the CFO had not yet visited, let alone begun work at, any of the following settlements and their associated homeland communities: B, D, E, F and G. It was clear that he was not going to be able to devote much more time or energy to the A/C area.

After a couple of days of enforced inactivity, during which the Assistant CFO caught up on her paperwork, she and I visited the man who was regarded as the leader of the community at A12. He had a job that kept him at A during the week, and he was counted at A as a usual resident there. We learned from him that the other residents of A12—his two sons and their families—were on their way into A to shop, so we waited until they arrived and the Assistant CFO filled in their forms with them, counting them as usual residents of their two households at A12 rather than as 'visitors' to the house at A where they would be staying for the next day or so.

A couple of days later, the funeral at A10 finally wound up and the much shorter funeral at A9 also finished. One CC had remained at A10, but the other CC and the CI who had been at these funerals came back to A. Phase three was about to begin. Before I describe the events of this phase, I will touch on an issue hinted at in the preceding paragraph: in this context, who is a usual resident and who is a visitor?

Problems of definition: 'usual resident' and 'visitor'

Some Yolngu people who have jobs in the main settlements but who have a strong attachment to a clan homeland—a situation that is likely to become more and more common—find it hard to categorise themselves as a 'usual resident' of one place rather than the other.[7] This must be a dilemma for certain people in the mainstream as well, but in the Yolngu case the attachment to their clan lands is more than just one of sentiment; it is the foundation of their social and spiritual identity. For Yolngu, the distinction 'my country/not my country' is more salient than the distinction 'resident/visitor'. This is also a factor in many other Indigenous societies, and it can affect how people categorise themselves on their census forms (see also Chapter 8).

People do not necessarily think of themselves as either 'residents' or 'visitors' in the places where they happen to be at census time, and for those who are highly mobile it is difficult for them and for others who might be answering the census questions on their behalf to decide how they should be categorised. At one end of the spectrum are the *dhukarrpuyngu* ('people of the track'): young men (and increasingly young women) who are highly mobile, and who cannot really be classified as residents anywhere. They are not, however, homeless in the mainstream sense of the term. Wherever they go in their travels they will be staying in the households of more sedentary relatives.

Dhukarrpuyngu have the potential to either be missed completely or double-counted—forgotten because their movements during a rolling count mean that they are not present in any community at the time that it is counted, or double-counted because they are present in more than one place during the count, and are included in the households where they are staying, either as a 'resident' or as a 'visitor'. Some children are also highly mobile. There are the children of young and/or 'bad' (a Yolngu judgment) mothers, who circulate between the dwellings of other relatives, typically of the grandparental generation. Others are children who just 'love to travel and visit their family', and do so when an opportunity presents itself. Children as young as five or six

---

[7] The Howard government's intention is clearly to put pressure on working-age adults leaving clan homelands to take up jobs in major settlements and towns. This intention became evident first in 2005, with changes to the CDEP program to focus much more on training for 'real' jobs and exiting participants into non-CDEP employment (DEWR 2005a, 2005b). In July 2007, as part of the current National Emergency Response, the government announced the abolition of the CDEP program.

have considerable autonomy, and parents have no anxiety about them as long as they are with trusted family members. In the enumerations I observed, I was able to pick up several instances where *dhukarrpuyngu* and mobile children were double-counted or not counted at all.

While it is possible, with a bit of local knowledge and a bird's-eye view, to track down instances of double-counting, it is far harder to pick up on people who have not been counted at all. To do so requires having a mental map of an entire community or region, and to notice absence rather than presence. No one involved in the census counts, from the CIs to the CMU, is in a position in which they have an overview of an entire regional population and simultaneously have the knowledge to pick up on absences. The CIs and the CCs have the local knowledge but not the overview, and the CFO and the CMU have the overview but lack the knowledge.

At the other end of the spectrum are individuals who are permanent residents either at a homeland or at a settlement. On the homelands, these tend to be the senior men of the community and their close families. Although their residency status tends to be unambiguous, this does not mean lack of mobility, for it is precisely such people who tend also to have responsibility for the organisation and conduct of ceremonies, and they are often away from home. In addition, only one of the A/C homelands has its own store, so even the most sedentary are often away from home shopping 'in town'. This often entails an overnight stop, and sometimes a more prolonged stay if the money runs out or the vehicle breaks down. During the count at C3, for example, an average of three small plane-loads of people came and/or went shopping each day, and vehicles were coming and going constantly.

In between the two extremes are a large number of people who, for a variety of reasons to do with their family affiliations, personal circumstances or personal preferences are hard to categorise as residents of any one particular place. I give two rather different examples in the short case studies below.

Case three

At C3 there is one household where the father of the family has a job at A. The rest of the family resides at C3, and he joins them at weekends. At the time of the count, the house was empty—the entire family had gone to A 'for a holiday' because it was the school holidays. The CCs and CIs at C3 considered the whole family, including the father, to be residents of their house at C3, so the household form was filled in with the help of relatives. They were first put down as PTA, but then it was decided that they might not be counted at A since they had gone from there to the funeral at A10. They were moved 'inside the form'—that is, they were counted as if they had been at C3 during the count. On double-checking the form completed at the house at A where the father of the family usually stayed, I found that they had all been counted there as well—as residents—before leaving for A10. Their Yolngu names had been used on the C3 form but their English given names had been used on the form at A, and their ages had been estimated at C3 while their dates of birth were entered at A. In a final twist, the parents—but not the rest of the family—appeared on a form completed at A10, once the funeral was finally over. By this time, the family in question had gone back to A. This form had been filled in by someone who was normally resident in the house at A, but who was still at A10. The CI had given her the form to fill in herself. She treated the form as the household form for her house in A, rather than counting herself as a 'visitor' at A10, and included the C3 husband and wife as usual residents of that household. In effect, then, the house at A ended up with two forms, and these forms had different but overlapping sets of 'usual residents'.

Case four

When it was possible, eventually, to do the count at A10 there were still many 'visitors' there who had not yet returned home after the funeral. It was decided that these people should be counted, just in case they were not caught later when they went home (the count had already been completed at some of the places, such as A, where they were usual residents). Only those who stated that they had definitely been counted elsewhere were excluded. There was one middle-aged man there from B1, a homeland that was not in the remit of the CCs and CIs who were covering the A/C homelands. B1 was not, however, his clan homeland, and he was often also to be found at the settlement of B. Later, at the CMU in Darwin, I looked at the forms from B1 and from B and found that this man had been *triple*-counted. As well as featuring as a visitor at A10, he had been counted as a PTA ('visiting B1 and then at funeral at A9') on a form at B and moved 'inside the form' on the grounds that he had not been at B1, but at the funeral at A9 when the count was done there. Finally, he had been counted as a PTA at B1 ('at funeral at A10') and moved back inside the form on the grounds that he would not be counted at A10. He was identified by his English given name on one form, by one of his Yolngu names on another form and by another of his Yolngu names on the third form. At A10, he had himself given his date of birth, but on the B and B1 forms his age had been estimated. The estimates differed by a decade, and neither of these imputed ages coincided with his real year of birth.

During the course of the count—a period of about four weeks—this man's real movements had been: B to B1, B1 to A10, A10 to B, B to B1, B1 to A9, and finally A9 to A10. Such a pattern of movement is commonplace for senior Yolngu men with ceremonial responsibilities.

The wider political context

As noted earlier, the 2006 Census took place at a time of considerable change in Indigenous affairs. In particular, the 'sustainability' of small homelands was being questioned and they were being portrayed in some circles as 'cultural museums' where the CDEP program had created a culture of dependency and fostered a 'recreational' lifestyle. Some commentators—and politicians—were advocating forms of social engineering that would 'encourage' people to leave the homelands and remote communities for 'real' jobs in the towns. The CDEP program was in the process of being refashioned, with less of an emphasis on 'community development' and an increasing emphasis on 'training for real jobs'. Yolngu were aware of these developments and many were very worried about their implications. Many of their community organisations were under severe pressure as they attempted to adjust to the new demands that were being placed on them, particularly by the changes to the CDEP program.

Yolngu had been among the first people to embrace the homelands movement of the early 1970s—indeed, they were active instigators of it. They began the move back to the homelands from the missions before the time when, under the Whitlam government, the movement began to receive government support under the rubric of 'self-determination'. Most homelands Yolngu want to continue living on their homelands. Many of them have been talking for some time about their desire to build local economies so that their young people will have jobs. Recent developments had shown them that they could no longer rely on government to 'look after' them, and had at the same time highlighted their vulnerability to externally imposed change.

For better or worse, most Yolngu perceived the census as an instrument of government, so the count took place in a politically charged atmosphere. I observed much more questioning of its purpose than in 2001, and more cynicism about the uses to which the data might be put. There was occasional resistance or politically motivated responses to some of the questions, particularly those concerning residence, and, interestingly, the ability to speak English. In 2001, Yolngu were not seeing fluency in English as a political issue—they tended to estimate their own and other people's abilities using objective criteria and, from an English speaker's point of view, they tended to overestimate people's ability. In 2006, I heard the leader of one homeland, whose spoken English is reasonably fluent, exhorting the CIs—loudly, so that many people could hear him, in English:

> Don't put me down as [speaking English] 'well', put me down as 'not well', and the same for everyone. It's time this government learnt the truth about their education system. We need better education for us and our children so we can start our own businesses and they can get real jobs right here, in this community.

The politicisation of the 'residence' issue was manifested in two ways. Some people questioned the notion of a single place of residence. One man commented, for example: 'I live in both places [A and A12]. Sometimes at one, sometimes at the other, because of my job here [at A]. I can't say which is "most of the time". I should put both.'

More significantly, the political climate led to several homelands being enumerated 'as if' their residents were at the homeland rather than where they really were when they were filling out the form. People reasoned that they were only temporarily absent, for funerals or other reasons, but that if they allowed themselves to be enumerated as 'visitors' at A, where they really were at the time, the 'government will say that we're not really living at our home, they will say it's empty'. Some of those who were included as residents of these homelands were indeed people who spent most of their time there, but others were people who went backwards and forwards between A and the homeland, much like the family from C3 discussed earlier. There was therefore potential for double-counting.

In most cases, the 'as if' practice did not lead to double-counting because these were small communities, all of the members of which were at A at the time of the count. They had made a joint and conscious decision to be counted as if they were at home, so they were not also counted as visitors at A. In one case (A11), however, there is a household whose 'usual residents' commute between A11 and the community of B because one of them has a job in the store at B. They were at B when the other usual residents of A11 decided to count themselves 'as if' they were at A11. The people at A also filled in a form for the B household. A crosscheck of the forms from B later at the CMU in Darwin revealed that this family had been double-counted: at A as residents of A11, and at B as residents of B.

Such an 'as if' count is not, however, the same as counting people at a place. Instead, it represents people's *idea* of who would have been there had the count really happened there. In such circumstances, certain categories of people tend to be forgotten—most significantly children. I was able to satisfy myself that the children of at least one couple failed to gain a mention in one of these 'as if' counts—I do not know whether they were counted elsewhere.

The count, phase three: 8–14 August

With the funeral at A10 finally over, the Assistant CFO decided that we should do the count there before the CFO returned from H. We set off from A on 8 August, with the CC who had just come back from the funeral there, hoping to meet up with the second CC, who was still there. When we arrived there were still many 'visitors' in a total of 22 tents, as well as most of the 'usual residents' in five dwellings. As the Assistant CFO and the two CCs began work, it quickly became evident why counting people at a funeral is not only inappropriate but also inadvisable. At the house nearest to the airstrip there were three clusters of two, three and five tents (see Figure 4.1). The first cluster, of two tents, contained the household from A previously mentioned in Case Three. The 'Person 1' for this family decided, as we have seen, to count the household 'as if' they were back at A. The second cluster, of three tents, contained most of the family that we had missed at C4. Since they had definitely not been counted there, the tents were designated as a 'temporary dwelling' and the occupants were enumerated as 'visitors'. The largest cluster, of five tents, contained mostly people who were from A (and the man from B1 mentioned in Case Four) and who had not yet returned there. It was assumed that they had not yet been counted and they were enumerated as 'visitors' to the dwelling (making this a 25-person household form).

Fig. 4.1 The 'tent city' at A10, August 2006

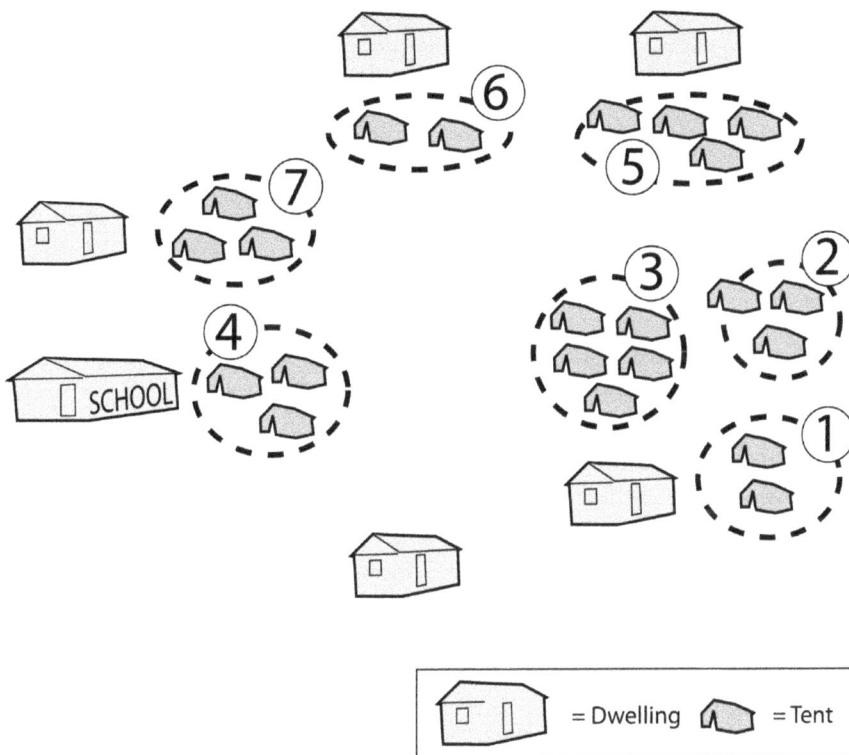

Notes: 1) Household from A counted 'as if' at A; 2) visitors from C4, counted as a 'temporary dwelling'; 3) visitors from A and B3, counted as visitors to adjoining A10 dwelling; 4) visitors from A8; 5) and 6) occupants said to have been counted at A, therefore not counted at A10; 7) status unknown.

The 18 occupants of three tents pitched near the school building turned out to be people from a single household at A8, the large nearby homeland that had been empty when we first visited it back in early July. The other residents of A8 had already left for home because, we were told, the personal effects of a person who had died elsewhere were about to arrive there, signalling the beginning of another funeral ceremony. The school tent-dwellers were about to return to A8, which had not yet been counted, but the Assistant CFO decided to play it safe and enumerate them there and then. She pondered whether they could be counted as 'visitors' in a 'temporary dwelling', or be counted 'as if' they were at home. In the end, they were counted as visitors.

The occupants of two other tent complexes (six tents in all) said they had been counted at A before coming to the funeral at A12. The Assistant CFO and the CCs, who were feeling a little overwhelmed at this point, were happy to take their word for it. There remained one tent cluster, the status of which I did not ascertain. They were either not counted or were counted as visitors to the nearby house.

In all, more than 90 people were counted at A12, the majority of them visitors. Somewhere between 20 and 40 were not counted, on the assumption that they had already been counted elsewhere. This was the most chaotic of the counts that I observed. No attempt was made to draw up a list of the dwellings and temporary tent dwellings (I made my own sketch map; see Figure 4.1). It was clear that the Assistant CFO and CCs were confused about who should and should not be counted. One CC thought only 'locals' should be counted, on the grounds that everyone who was there as a visitor should have been put 'inside the form' at their place of usual residence—that is, counted as if they were at home because of being at a place (the funeral) where they were unlikely to be counted. Strictly speaking, he was correct, because these were the instructions he had received in his training, and he was acting on the assumption that every CC and CI in the area had followed those instructions to the letter—which they had not. The situation was not, however, clear-cut because of the rolling nature of the count. There were in fact several kinds of 'visitors' present: those who had been counted elsewhere, either as residents or visitors; those whose home communities had already been counted in their absence and who might or might not have been put inside the form, depending on the proclivities of the CIs and CCs who had conducted the count there; and those whose communities had yet to be counted.

The count at A10 highlighted for me the full complexities of attempting a de facto count with principled exceptions (the instruction to count PTA as present if they were not likely to be counted elsewhere). Such an instruction, in the context of a rolling count and a population that evinces high mobility across a wide area, calls constantly for judgments to be made on the basis of insufficient information. An individual CI might be able to keep track of the people they have already counted, but they cannot know whether some of the people they have counted have or have not been counted elsewhere by other CIs. I will return to the PTA question in Chapter 7 (see also Appendix B).

The next day (9 August), the CFO returned to A, in order to pick up the Assistant CFO so that they could move on to start proceedings at Community E. We sat down to review progress and decide what should be done in their absence. The CFO was reasonably happy with the way the count was proceeding at H, having enlisted the services of a 'floating' CFO whose task was to act as a backup in areas where extra help was needed. The floating CFO was still at H and would stay there until the count was over.

The places that had still not been accounted for were: A1, A2, A7, A8, A11, C2 and C6. It had already been decided that A1 would be covered during the count of F and its associated homelands. It was decided that if I could find a willing CC or CI I would take them to do the count at A2. There were now said to be people back at A7, but they were possibly going on to A8, which was in full funeral mode. The latest local estimate for when this funeral would finish was 17 August, so it was decided to leave these two communities until the CFO and/or Assistant CFO returned to A. The CFO would, before he left, find the CCs who were supposed to be doing A11, C2 and C6 to check on progress.

In the event, the CFO could not find the CCs responsible for A11 and C2, and I also failed to locate them in the days that followed. One of them was the person I was hoping to take to A2. Nothing more happened in the A/C homelands count—with the exception of the count at C6—until 13 August, when I learned that the CI who had been instrumental in organising the girl's funeral at A9 was now back at A. She willingly agreed to come with me to A2, which was located on her clan country, and we went the next day.

When we arrived, there was a young woman and some small children at one house, but otherwise the whole community was out hunting. Fortunately—and somewhat atypically—everyone had gone to the same place and it was not too far away, although getting there involved a somewhat hair-raising drive along the beach. The count proceeded in a relaxed and amiable manner, to the accompaniment of feasting on fish, crab, stingray and shellfish. All in all, there were about 30 'locals' there and also a visiting family who stated positively that they had been counted at C by a named CC.

This count was an example of the IES working at its best. The CI, despite having been able to work only intermittently, was an efficient interviewer and understood the form well. She was well known to everyone present and her status as an owner of the land gave her a certain additional authority (as we were leaving, she saw a group of girls returning laden with fish, and was able to claim as of right a substantial proportion for herself). Doing the count at the hunting site was also a bonus: counts at homelands communities are frequently curtailed or hurried because people are anxious to go hunting, whereas this count could be fitted around the hunting activities of the group. The fact that the community members had returned, and that it was therefore worthwhile making the journey to count them, had been gleaned from people at A who were related to them. Finally, any non-local who had arrived to find that everyone had gone out hunting would not have known where to go to find them, or might have been hesitant to do so, whereas locating them was unproblematic for this CI.

At this point, it was time for me to return for a while to Darwin. I returned to A in the second half of September, for the fourth and final phase of the count.

A Darwin interlude

Once in Darwin, I began my work at the CMU (reported on in Chapter 7). From time to time, I heard from the CFO about progress in the rest of his region. He was beginning to sound pretty discouraged. In a phone call on 29 August, he told me he had returned briefly to A and C and had been unable to find any of the CCs or CIs who still had forms outstanding. There had also been problems with the non-Indigenous count at A, where he had entrusted some of the forms to a staff member of a local organisation for distribution to some of the local employees. This had not happened.

The count at H was complete, but it was five houses short. The floating CFO was now supervising the count at G, but progress was slow. The CFO had left his Assistant to finish up the count at D and F and things were not 'going real well'. He was going to B, the final community in his region, where the count had not yet started. He thought he would be back in Darwin the next week.

He said he was finding the same problem everywhere: not enough qualified and committed people to undertake the work—'Checking the forms takes forever. You really have to push them, people aren't enthused.'

On 9 September I was at the CMU when the CFO called in to his line manager to say that he was not coming to Darwin immediately. His manager reported that he 'sounded very flat'. He had trained 17 people at B, but only one was left, and they had counted only eight houses so far.

The CFO did come to Darwin later, for the debriefing of the CFOs. I discuss my observations of that debriefing in the first part of Chapter 7. He then went back into the field. He subsequently had some conversations with the CMU about my possible role in the final phase of the count in the A/C homelands. He envisaged that I would go to A8 with whoever was available in the way of CIs and supervise the count there. His line manager at the CMU decided, in consultation with Canberra, that what he was proposing necessitated my being signed up as a CC, rather than being classified as an impartial observer. I agreed to this on the condition that my status as CC applied only to this particular phase of the count.

I had mixed feelings about this development. The boundary between participant and observer, for an anthropologist, is *the* fulcrum of the anthropological approach to fieldwork and to the analysis of social and cultural processes. The anthropological project is to become part of a process—to 'see it from inside'—while simultaneously preserving a sense of distance that allows for objective analysis. From an anthropological perspective, the 'observer's paradox'—the fact that the observer's presence has an effect on what is observed—is part of the data. Thus far my active role had been mainly to act as a driver, to enable CCs and CIs to undertake the count in communities other than their own, but, at least in the case of the count at A2, force of circumstance had meant that it was I rather than the absent CFO and Assistant CFO who had selected the CI for the job. In practice, it is a short step from there to being a CC. My worry was that drawing a line in the sand at a particular point in this process of incorporation—although clearly necessary from an administrative point of view—would also affect the way in which my findings would be viewed.

The count, phase four: 20 September

The CFO's difficulties in making contact with the CCs had necessitated the introduction of backup forces. On 20 September, I flew in to A8 in the company of the CI who had conducted the count at A2 and a non-local Indigenous Assistant who had previously been helping to finish off the count at F. The funeral there had finished, but there were still several 'visitors' in tents who had stayed on for a while.[8] Meanwhile, the CFO was attempting to deal with all the other outstanding lacunae in the A/C area.

We counted nearly 90 people at A8. One household consisted of people who had been counted previously at A10. I had suspected that we would bump into them again and so had brought the A10 form with me, reasoning that if they were at home it would be better for them to be counted there and removed from the form at A10. I was also interested to see whether they would say that they had already been counted, and also whether the details on the two forms would differ. The Indigenous Assistant was assigned to their household. They did not say that they had already been counted, for the simple reason that they did not know they had been. At A10, the form that listed them had been filled in by a local CC, and only one person from the household helped with the form. The rest of the household had been out hunting at the time the form was filled in. Now, at A8, most of the household was present, but the person who had been interviewed at A10 was out hunting! Since I was officially a CC this time, I crossed all those present at A8 off the form that had been completed at A10. Four people were still at A10, so they were left as 'visitors' there.

---

[8] There were now two new funerals under way in the region, at C4 and C6, and there had been another funeral at A6 in my absence.

The details supplied for certain individuals on the two forms did indeed differ. Because the Indigenous Assistant was not a Yolngu speaker, people gave him their English names, while at A10 their Yolngu names had been given. Estimates of people's ages differed wildly. One child was put down as a three-year-old at A10 and as a seven-year-old at A8. The ages of several of the adults differed by a decade. It seems highly probable that had I not been the CC in this instance, the members of this large household would have been double-counted. Because of the differences between the two forms, this double-counting would have been undetectable once the forms were back at the CMU in Darwin.

Since I was a CC this time, I took the opportunity to act as the CI for one household at A10. I wanted to experience for myself the CI's task. I chose a large household with several visitors who had not yet returned to A. There were 21 people in all, necessitating the use of two forms. Bearing in mind that I am a highly literate English speaker with some competence in the Yolngu languages and a fairly detailed knowledge of the community, I still found the task pretty gruelling. It took two full hours and keeping the interviewees focused on the task was difficult, when so much of the time I was simply ticking boxes rather than engaging with them.

I also had to make some tricky judgments about who to put on the form. There was a woman from A and some of her family who said they had not been counted at A, so I added them as visitors. This woman's brother and his family had also been at the funeral and had left only that morning. The sister said she thought her brother's family had not yet been counted. On balance, this was probable, because the man had a medical condition that necessitated him staying for prolonged periods in Darwin, and he and his family were often in transit between Darwin and A. It was possible that they had been at A on census night, and had missed being counted in Darwin. It was equally possible that they had been in Darwin when the count took place at A. I decided therefore to put them on the form as visitors and crosscheck the household form from A when I got back to the CMU. It transpired that they had, in fact, been counted at A. I do not know whether they were also counted in Darwin.

This was yet another instance of the complicating effect of the rolling count combined with mobility. I was in a unique position, with access to knowledge at the local level where the CIs were operating and at the more regional level, because of my observation of the entire process in the A/C region and my access to the CMU in Darwin. I found myself in the same position as everyone else at the moment of the count: forced to make a more or less educated guess about whether or not to include someone on a form.

On our return to A, I found that the CFO was about to board a plane to Darwin. He had spent a nearly fruitless day looking for people. He was exhausted and feeling very unwell and was clearly unable to continue. He had contacted the

CMU and a replacement team was on its way: a member of the CMU staff and one of the other CFOs. They had been at F, tying up the loose ends there. They arrived just before he left and he handed over his paperwork to them. I was leaving for Darwin the next day, so I spent the evening with the new team and the Indigenous Assistant, who had stayed on to help. We reviewed what still needed to be done or checked. On 20 September, therefore, more than 10 weeks after the count had started, it was still not fully completed.

The role of local organisations: a missed opportunity

The communities of A and C are host to three organisations that could potentially have been engaged more fully in the census exercise. These are the community councils of A and C, and the homelands resource organisation, based at A, which services the satellite homelands communities. All three were at the time Indigenous Housing Organisations (IHOs), so had been visited by the CFO during the CHINS exercise. The two community council organisations had originally provided the CFO with a list of potential CCs and CIs for the census. At the initial training session at Community A, in a meeting room at A's community council office, one employee of C's community council came along to be trained as a CC. The homelands resource agency had originally agreed that one of its Yolngu employees would be available to act as a CC, but in the event he was away at a course in Darwin when the CFO first arrived and because the CFO did not follow him up he never became engaged in census activities. The resource agency did provide an outside space in which the CFO could sit and do paperwork and also gave him access to the health database, which he attempted to use, unsuccessfully, to check missing date-of-birth information for homelands residents.

It is fair to say that these local organisations were busy, under-resourced and understaffed, and that they therefore did not volunteer proactively to play a more substantial role in the census exercise. For his part, the CFO was content to make use of the facilities they did provide, but he did not seek to involve them further. In failing to get them further involved, he deprived himself of two things that might have made his task much more manageable: the Yolngu and non-Yolngu staff of the homelands resource agency, in particular, were repositories of local knowledge and intelligence about people's whereabouts on a day-to-day basis; and, had he engaged them more proactively during the CHINS exercise in the business of recruiting potential CCs and CIs, he might not have found himself as shorthanded as he was.

Having said that, neither the CFO nor the organisations are to blame for this lack of mutual engagement. There is a structural problem to be addressed before a more fruitful relationship is possible. We return to address this issue in Chapter 9.

5. Whose census? Institutional constraints on the Indigenous Enumeration Strategy at Wadeye

John Taylor

The 2006 Census enumeration in the Thamarrurr region provides an example of the logistical and cross-cultural issues associated with implementation of the Indigenous Enumeration Strategy (IES) in a large Aboriginal town (Wadeye) and surrounding outstations (Figure 5.1). In the past 30 years, many former mission and government settlements across northern Australia that were established for the purposes of administering Aboriginal welfare polices have grown steadily in size and complexity, with several now achieving the status of 'urban centre' (more than 1000 people) within the Australian Standard Geographical Classification (ASGC). Among those with populations that now exceed this number are: Wadeye, Maningrida, Nguiu, Galiwinku, Milingimbi and Ngukurr (in the Northern Territory) and Aurukun, Palm Island, Yarrabah, Doomadgee, Mornington Island, Woorabinda and Cherbourg (in Queensland). The population trajectory for these towns is for continued growth while many more such 'urban' places are expected to emerge in time. Consequently, the observations made in respect of census operations at Wadeye are representative of a category of Aboriginal settlement that will be of increasing relevance for the IES and to Indigenous affairs policy in the future.

There are other ways in which Wadeye is representative of an emergent type. As a polyglot, overcrowded, under-resourced and growing settlement that has drawn disparate social groups from surrounding country (Taylor and Stanley 2005), Wadeye presents a set of social, economic and governance difficulties that are increasingly evident across remote Australia (Ah Kit 2002; Dillon 2007; Westbury and Dillon 2006) and that provide an essential backdrop to any assessment of the conduct of census operations and their effectiveness. Among these, at Wadeye, is a scale of anomie, especially among youth, that has led at times to outbreaks of civil disorder. For example, in April and May 2006, just two months before the planned census date, many of the town's residents—anecdotal estimates of up to 500 were cited locally—had fled to set up temporary residence across the immediate region and beyond because of relentless inter-family feuding and destruction of property (a similar situation had occurred at the time of the previous census in 2001). Part of the fallout was a delay in conducting a ballot for the Thamarrurr Regional Council (TRC), with the elected body in abeyance for a period until new elections could be arranged in mid July. This not only complicated communication with community representatives regarding census preparations, it also meant that the council and the people were preoccupied with electoral matters in the crucial weeks leading up to census day.

Fig. 5.1 Settlement geography of the Thamarrurr region

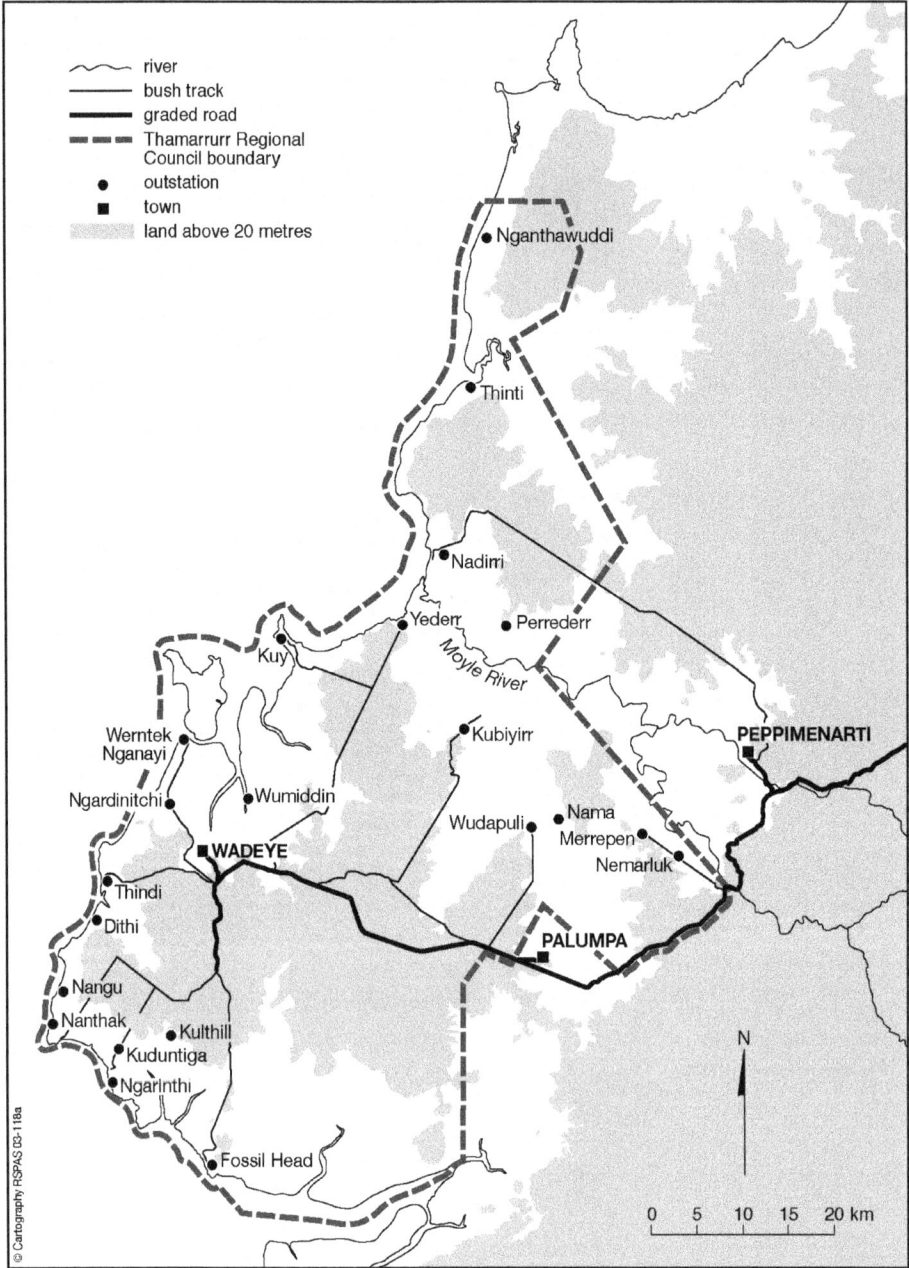

Needless to say, these were not ideal conditions in which to plan and conduct a census enumeration, and they underline the fact that the IES does not operate on a blank canvas. In order to be successful as a strategy, it is—or at least it should be—as much about having the capacity to anticipate and successfully negotiate these sorts of contingencies as anything else. One of the key questions posed by the research team was whether the strategy adopted for the enumeration of remote Indigenous communities was suitably adapted to meet the cultural and contingent situations encountered. By force of circumstances such as those above, the focus of census observation at Wadeye was concerned substantially with this question.

Along the way, two weeks spent at Wadeye and its outstations observing the census training and most of the census enumeration between 24 July and 6 August, together with subsequent follow-up, also provided a unique opportunity to witness at close hand the process of translation between two cultures: the local Indigenous community and the nation-state. This was manifest in several arenas: in the handling of interactions with community leadership, in the strategies adopted to engage, train and supervise an Indigenous census workforce, in the logistics deployed to connect with a mobile and scattered population and in the categorisations and interpretations associated with the questions on the census questionnaire. Other, more specific, issues concerning innovations in the structure of the Interviewer Household Form (IHF) were considered secondary to these more generic concerns, not because they were less important, but because they turned out to be of less consequence. They are discussed in Appendix B.

Census preparation: the relationship between the community and the Australian Bureau of Statistics

As noted, the IES does not unfold in a vacuum. In each Indigenous settlement there will be particular cultural and governance dynamics that can substantially influence the conduct of field operations. This is because—in stark contrast with the mainstream census—the interview format of the IES in remote settlements creates an encounter not just with individuals and their households, but with a social collective and related representative and administrative structures. This creates an institutional arrangement whereby councils and other local organisations can act as the interface between populations to be counted and the state (instantiated in this case by the Australian Bureau of Statistics [ABS] and its census).

In terms of the collective, the population of the Thamarrurr region is embedded in dense social networks across some 40 extended paternal family groups with affiliations to 20 locally defined and recognised clans. While members of all of these social units are present in the town of Wadeye, country and family ties beyond the town produce a population that is widely and variously scattered at any one time at local outstations and in neighbouring communities and towns across an area from as far south as Kununurra and Timber Creek through the Daly region and north to the Cox Peninsula and Darwin. This is especially so in the dry season around census time and within this network there is considerable short-term mobility. This configuration immediately raises a set of questions regarding what properly constitutes the population of the Thamarrurr region and how best this might be counted. In 2006, the ABS adopted a de facto enumeration to address this question—that is, assigning people to the place where they were found at census time rather than to the place where they usually lived—but issues still arose regarding the impact of frequent mobility and the consequent adequacy of de facto and usual resident counts. These are dealt with later.

As for representative and administrative structures, a significant development at Wadeye was the formation in 2003 of the TRC as a local government body built around representation from the 20 clans. At the same time, the TRC entered into a Shared Responsibility Agreement (SRA) with the Commonwealth and Northern Territory governments as one of several Council of Australian Governments (COAG) trial sites for Indigenous Communities Coordination Pilot projects aimed at effecting whole-of-government cooperative approaches to service delivery. These were based on the idea of streamlining government processes and supporting some restoration to local Indigenous populations of responsibility for, and control over, decision-making regarding service delivery and general planning for social and economic development. Within this arrangement, the TRC gained a substantial local profile and presence and it is fair to say that the council assumed its new responsibilities with some vigour. One activity it conducted under the auspices of the COAG trial was its own census of usual residents in 2003, and again in 2005. These activities were undertaken for the explicit reason that previous census counts conducted by the ABS were felt by the TRC to have been deficient given their own estimation of numbers in the region. A number of salient points flow from all of this.

In the period leading up to the census, the TRC had established itself as a prominent institution heavily involved with government in a partnership approach to regional social planning with strong interests in census-taking. As part of these and related survey activities—including by the ABS, for example, in the 2002 National Aboriginal and Torres Strait Islander Survey—a small cadre of experienced local enumerators had been developed and the council was keen to nurture this expertise. By 2006, however, after almost three years of participation in the COAG trial, the experiment in whole-of-government approaches to service delivery had all but collapsed, with very few beneficial outcomes and a loss of confidence at Wadeye in the COAG process (Commonwealth of Australia 2006: 27–33). It was into this environment of initial local optimism and then despair at the state's intentions that the ABS Census Management Unit (CMU) based in Darwin was about to step.

That is not to say that community–government relations were never propitious. In line with its pursuit of regional planning and cognisant of the approaching 2006 Census, the TRC and the ABS began in late 2005 to explore ways to ensure that people in the region were well prepared to participate optimally in the enumeration. Discussions with census officials were held at Wadeye and in Darwin, and an attempt was made to arrange for a workshop at Wadeye to explain the census questions and for this to be communicated in Murrinh-patha in line with council practice. The fact that this workshop failed to eventuate meant that by the time the enumeration finally began in late July, the council—and through it, the community—felt little ownership of or familiarity with the census content and process. By then, some council members expressed the view that the ABS alone had carriage and responsibility for the census. This was a far cry from the partnership approach to regional planning that had prevailed earlier and it meant that, for the most part, the census was going to be an encounter directly between the ABS and individual householders—a far more difficult task than working in effective collaboration with the council (see Sanders, Chapter 3 for the benefits of working in partnership with representative structures).

Consequently, communications regarding final census logistics between the ABS and the interface with the population to be counted became somewhat perfunctory. Almost inevitably, given the Census Field Officer's (CFO) myriad responsibilities in preparing for the census across a vast area from Lajamanu to the Tiwi Islands, these communications were compressed in time and content. For example, before and during the conduct of the Community Housing and Infrastructure Needs Survey (CHINS) at Wadeye (at the end of April), a request was made to the TRC for assistance in mustering a census workforce of 20–30 local people. The limited opportunity for effective follow-up (just one visit in early July) meant, however, that by the time census training began in late July the task of mustering an interview team was still to be done. At an earlier visit, an approach was made to the Thamarrurr Regional School to obtain assistance with census workers, but to no avail, given staff commitments. As for advertising the census, the usual publicity packs were distributed via the council and the school, while a brief explanation of the purpose of the census was broadcast by a member of the TRC on Broadcasting for Remote Aboriginal Communities Scheme (BRACS) radio. Other attempts to pursue logistics were made by the CFO via phone and email in the lead up to census day, either from Darwin or on the road in other communities. Not surprisingly, such communication from a distance proved ineffective in terms of preparing a census workforce. According to the CFO, the TRC administration was keen to assist, but any prospective workers were already fully occupied in their normal jobs. In the meantime, the TRC provided a map of all dwellings in Wadeye and at outstations, but it was reluctant to supply a copy of the Thamarrurr population database, as requested, as it regarded this as confidential.

In practical terms, what eventuated from all of these interactions, on the very eve of planned commencement of the census, was the deployment of two TRC staff—one local Aboriginal person as a collector-interviewer (CI) and one recently arrived non-Aboriginal person as a Community Coordinator (CC)—a council vehicle for travel around town and to outstations and council assistance on the first day of interviewer and CC training in driving around the community to mobilise potential interviewers. The TRC also provided exclusive access to a training room, and later an office, to serve as a base for the duration of census operations, which turned out to be more than a calendar month.

Interestingly, at the same time that these arrangements had been established, another Commonwealth agency, Centrelink, had also assembled teams of six Commonwealth officers to conduct a survey in Wadeye and across the region asking householders many of the same questions as the ABS regarding resident population, family composition, income and employment. While no observation of the possible impact of this on the conduct of the census was possible, to the extent that any repetition involved might have confused or irritated residents, at the very least it suggests a lack of coordination between Commonwealth agencies.

By the time the census enumeration began in Wadeye on 26 July, the impression obtained from discussion with key informants was of a regional population that was largely ignorant of the imminent census activities, that was administratively detached from the process and that was otherwise diverted by issues of more pressing concern including elections and Centrelink processing. One important practical consequence, as we shall see, was a failure to engage the small cadre of experienced interviewers who had been used for a variety of previous local surveys and potential local CCs who had some standing in the community and knowledge of the population, because by census time they were all fully engaged in other work. It also meant that the time available for CC and CI training was highly restricted.

Census preparation: engaging a local census team

As noted, in the lead-up to the census at Wadeye, the CFO had assessed that an interview team of 20–30 people would be required for the task, assisted by four CCs. This estimate was based on a calculation involving the idea that the CFO and Assistant CFO would be back in Darwin by 8 August for the start of the mainstream census, and that the Wadeye enumeration would be completed fully by then—a proposed enumeration time of eight working days. Against this schedule, given the estimated number of people to be counted and the estimated time required to administer the 55-question IHF, this workforce target was not unreasonable. It was, however, unrealistic under the circumstances.

On the morning of 24 July, the CFO arrived in Wadeye and the TRC Housing Office training room was made available to begin the census process. The first activity scheduled was for the CFO and his Assistant to explain the nature of the task to potential census interviewers, then to provide a day of training on how to administer the census form. Simultaneously, the newly recruited CCs—the seconded TRC employee and a non-Indigenous male who had been resident at Wadeye for a year and employed variously as a casual worker—were to be instructed in their roles. As the CFO's plan was to be in Palumpa, Peppimenarti and Daly River by 27 July to begin the same procedures there, three days were set aside in order to assemble this workforce, sign them up as ABS casual labour, train them and satisfactorily deploy them to be left in the capable hands of the CCs. This turned out to be an ambitious timetable and one that was dictated more by the pressures on the CFO to administer such a vast census area than by any proper consideration of real training needs.

Almost inevitably, it was nearly midday on day one before a group of interested people finally assembled in the training room. By the time lunch was provided, there were 13 potential CIs present (nine women and four men), but by the time lunch was over only seven people (five women and two men) remained for the training. This manoeuvring continued throughout the next day, leading to substantial turnover during training, involving 22 individuals out of whom only six (four women and two men) finally signed up as census interviewers, although in effect only four participated in enumeration since one of these served as an interpreter for one of the CCs and one withdrew early on. One consequence of this substantial shortfall in labour was that the CCs spent most of their time operating as census interviewers and less time on coordinating and assisting the activities of interviewers. This was unfortunate as the interviewers were deployed singly, and not in pairs, while CC support was physically limited. As a result, any errors or omissions on IHFs had to be discussed and dealt with back at the training room at the end of each day rather than addressed in situ.

Training

Training in the application of the IHF began after lunch on the first day. Taking into account technical glitches and a short break, it lasted for just one and a half hours. It was constructed around a viewing of the census DVD—which was delayed owing to technical difficulties and the fact that many of those present before lunch failed to return—with breaks for discussion. Views on the content and effectiveness of this training were sought from participants afterwards and the following is a precis. The DVD presentation was set in the New South Wales South Coast community of Wreck Bay. One view offered by the local participants was that this setting was too mainstream for the Wadeye context, with interviews conducted indoors in unfamiliar settings (well-furnished lounge and kitchen areas) among small social units. Most participants would also have preferred the presentation and discussion of census content and process to have been conducted in Murrinh-patha rather than English. Although the CFO halted the presentation occasionally to solicit any questions, all this produced was a blanket silence as opposed to the robust discussion in language that one often hears at Wadeye. People had questions, they just didn't ask them.

As noted, the basic instruction method was to halt the DVD periodically and attempt a discussion of the issues presented. In effect, what this provided was an opportunity for the CFO to establish certain standards in answering particular census questions. For example, it was suggested by one participant that $40 a dwelling should be indicated on the IHF in answer to Question 5 about rent. The Assistant CFO checked this subsequently with the TRC and the idea that each adult paid $10 a week was tabled. The general outcome observed during enumeration was some confusion about the real amounts inserted. This was partly because of the location of the rent question on the census form (at Question 5), which preceded the lengthy business of establishing the real occupants of dwellings including adults (Question 12), from which a retrospective calculation of rent could be derived. Similar conformity was sought for Question 13 on family relationships, though how this was to be achieved remained unresolved. The main advice was that CIs should think in terms of 'whitefella' categories, not local ones, and that if individuals were not clear they should defer to the CCs. The problem here was that the CCs had no idea how to translate local family relationships into 'whitefella' categories. Instances of such efforts observed during enumeration revealed that individual interviewers worked through the nuances themselves, so any notion that a common understanding prevailed can be discounted.

For Question 12, one of the CCs suggested using TRC administrative data on dates of birth (DOB) in the event that people did not know these—which turned out to be very common. This suggestion was, however, overruled by the CFO as too complex an arrangement, with a preference expressed for acquiring DOB information from the interview. On income (Question 40), the CFO offered to find out standard rates regarding how much people received from various allowances and pensions as well as from the Community Development Employment Projects (CDEP) each fortnight. Although this was never established, the amounts tended to be standardised anyway, with CIs acting intuitively in the field, aided by the grouped nature of income categories on the census form. For Question 46 about the person's employer, the instruction was to classify any activities associated with the TRC as 'community services' even though these could include a diverse range of industry types. Strangely, the DVD content then jumped from Question 25 to 40, so no discussion of the intervening questions was held. Along the way, an ad hoc list of common spellings was compiled for use in the field, although this was rarely utilised in practice.

At the end of the first day, the prevailing view of the training session among local participants was that far too much information was provided in too short a time, with the added difficulty that none of this was in Murrinh-patha. This referred not just to the census content, but to the many administrative details related to interviewer pay and conditions. While in practical terms the effect was high attrition during training, a fair degree of confusion was also evident among those who remained. This all left the CFO and his Assistant somewhat anxious given the time pressure on them to instigate the process and move on to the next community. They were hopeful, however, that a more hands-on approach on day two, with individuals practising by interviewing each other, would help to progress matters. This did, in fact, turn out to be more effective in generating understanding among the six interviewers who persisted through day two. As a precaution, however, the CFO had organised a team of ABS officers to stand by in Darwin to assist with the census if necessary, and arrangements had been made with the TRC to reserve accommodation for them.

A small workforce and its consequences

One important consequence of ending up with a much smaller workforce than hoped for was a lack of representation from across the local socio-cultural spectrum. Of the four effective interviewers and the translator, all were Murrinh-patha speakers but only one had affiliation with the large Marri Ngarr language group, and none with the other large language group, Marritjevin. Together, affiliation with the latter two language groups encompasses about two-thirds of the population of the Thamarrurr region. While the use of Murrinh-patha as a lingua franca in the region reduced the impact of this shortcoming at the level of communication, the fact that language and clan affiliation often graft on to social groupings and residential location meant that interviewing in certain parts of Wadeye became problematic, if not impossible, for most of the team—especially in light of recent communal animosities. While it is not clear how this affected the population count, it was apparent that interviewers were focused mostly on their 'own' areas of town, leaving certain other areas—and therefore particular social groupings—to be covered largely by the non-Indigenous CCs.

Of course, the ultimate consequence of a small workforce was that the count took much longer than was planned for. In fact, rather than taking the eight working days originally hoped for, the enumeration was pursued over 33 working days—from 26 July to 9 September, excluding weekends and two public holidays. Not surprisingly, perhaps, during this extended period the local enumeration team experienced gradual attrition with the final stages of enumeration conducted by just one of the CCs, and ultimately by the CFO and his Assistant. There were a number of reasons for this outcome.

First, the limited training provided for what was an inexperienced team meant that systems were learnt mostly on the job by working through the interview schedule—with mixed results. An important rider here is that none of the interviewers, when questioned, indicated that they had read the *Interviewer Household Form Guide* or the *Working for the Census* booklet that were provided with the census bag. The outcome was that while some of the CIs struggled throughout with form completion and administration, others learnt quickly, although all found the task arduous. Part of the issue here was the sheer length of the form with its 55 questions and the need to extract data for every household member. This meant that interviewing was often lengthy, with one dwelling observed taking a whole morning to interview. It should be emphasised, however, that the new, compact, single-form structure of the IHF compared with the two forms previously used did prove highly practical to administer—even in simple ways such as when questioning people under trees or on verandahs in the often blustery conditions of the Top End dry season.

Second, at the end of each day, the process of checking and reconciling the many data items from the front of the IHF with the Interviewer Dwelling Checklist (IDC) and the Master Dwelling Checklist (MDC) was at times chaotic as essential details had not always been completed in the field and forms were sometimes mixed up on return to the Housing Office training room. Third, as they proceeded through the census, most interviewers became enmeshed in social demands from their own family members—such as child minding, card games, shopping, providing meals, visits to the clinic and so on—and the combined effect was a variable rate of progress. The fact that lunch was not provided to interviewers also meant that they tended to stray in the middle of the day and it was difficult for the CCs to gain a regular sense of overall progress.

Finally, conscious of the fact that they were being paid piecemeal rates—$3.29 for each person enumerated—some of the CIs could see that their commitment to the process, over what was turning out to be a longer and more arduous period than expected, was providing diminishing returns to effort, not least because of delays in receiving payment from Darwin, and enthusiasm waned accordingly. On this last point, issues regarding payment for services were something of a running sore from day one. Some of the interviewers had been removed from their standard payroll in order to participate in the census and while ideas were floated early on about the TRC possibly paying them and then invoicing the ABS, the fact is some individuals experienced considerable delay in being recompensed. This led to the unusual situation in which one of the CCs was paying amounts personally out of pocket to be reimbursed later on a visit to the CMU in Darwin.

Counting a mobile population

As mentioned, the population usually resident in the Thamarrurr region is distributed at any one time across a wide area from the east Kimberley and Victoria River valley through to Darwin, though with most found within the region at Wadeye and surrounding outstations. The settlement geography of the Thamarrurr region is shown in Figure 5.1. Most people live in the town of Wadeye but there are some 20 other localities—all outstations—where families also reside, either permanently or occasionally. Most of these have some housing and basic infrastructure, while some have none. As the map indicates, these outstations are located either at coastal sites or on slightly elevated ground above floodplains. Aside from the relative lack of housing and basic services, a major factor that restricts more full-time use of these sites is the poor condition of regional roads and bush tracks, although in August at census time all localities are accessible. Indeed, this is the time of maximum population dispersal across the Top End because of the relative ease of travel. The people of the neighbouring communities of Palumpa and Peppimenarti also have strong social ties with people at Wadeye, and the overwhelming feature of interaction between all of the settlements shown in Figure 5.1 is the constant daily movement of individuals and families between them, as well as beyond the region. For a census that is dwelling-focused, rather than population-focused, this makes counting people a difficult process.

The emphasis in the conduct of the census was to ensure that every dwelling in the region had at least one completed IHF, either with the details of people present or to the effect that the dwelling was unoccupied. This was precisely in line with instructions in the *Community Coordinator Manual* and the *Working for the Census Guide for Interviewers*. Accordingly, there was a clear sense in which the count would be considered accomplished at the point when all known dwellings had been processed. Leaving aside some checking of forms by the CFO and CCs to ensure that all questions had been completed, no mechanism was deployed in the field to establish the population coverage of the count in the sense advocated by Martin and Taylor (1996)—again, apparently in line with census instructions, although some confusion reigns here. According to an internal ABS discussion paper on the 2006 IES, before the census forms were to leave communities, CFOs were to check all forms against community lists where possible. This was to help verify counts and coverage, and if insufficient coverage or errors were identified these were to be corrected before returning the forms to the CMU—in this case, in Darwin. This did not occur at Wadeye. Instead, on Saturday 5 August—13 days after arriving in the town—the CFO left for Darwin with all the forms that had been completed up to that point and quality checking was then done at the CMU (see Chapter 7).

One thing that was clear, however, was that the checklist procedure at Wadeye did not work well. As a result, it was difficult in the final stages of the enumeration to know precisely which dwellings had been covered. The basic problem was that CIs often went to dwellings that were different to their allocation off the MDC. By the time the CFO left with all existing completed forms on 5 August, an unknown number of dwellings in town remained to be enumerated (although a figure of up to 20 was mentioned), while several outstations—including Nama, Wudapuli, Table Hill and Fossil Head—had still to be visited. Accordingly, some census forms were left behind with the CCs to continue with the enumeration while assessment of coverage was continued in Darwin by painstakingly matching the existing forms with known dwellings. Instructions for continued census follow-up were subsequently communicated to the CCs, and one of them continued to fill out census forms until the end of August. Final mopping up, however, did not occur until 9 September, when the CFO returned to Wadeye to collect the last of the forms.

On this issue of dwelling coverage, time and again the need for constant local intelligence from outside the census team on the whereabouts of families was underscored. Ideally, this should have been a primary role of the CCs, but their lack of detailed knowledge of the community prevented this. Almost immediately on day one, empty dwellings were encountered because people were away at funerals, had travelled to outstations or the dwelling was due for repair, and it was apparent that tracking occupants in line with the allocation of particular families to dwellings on the MDC was going to be a challenge. In order to gain a sense of the scale of this issue, a quick drive around Wadeye with a key informant on day two revealed that 15 dwellings were empty because their occupants were away from town.

The idea that all dwellings have a single family name associated with them—as per the IDC and the MDC—or the more conceptual notion that individuals necessarily 'belong' to particular dwellings was flawed given the prevalence of extended and multi-family or multi-dwelling social groupings involving considerable intra-community mobility. A degree of procedural confusion was also observed here with some interviewers holding the impression that if a person could not be allocated to a lot number they couldn't be counted. In a number of instances observed, however, it clearly helped that interviewers were sensitive to the prospect of joint family living arrangements and efforts were made to allocate individuals accordingly. Also, what might be thought of as a particular family dwelling did not always turn out to be so. A random comparison of the distribution of families by dwelling between the 2005 Thamarrurr community census results and the 2006 ABS Census indicated that a substantial redistribution within town and away from town had occurred in the intervening months. While some of this occurs anyway for various reasons, the destruction of many dwellings during community violence in 2006 produced considerable upheaval, with a chain reaction of redistribution occurring as families regrouped into safer social clusters and locations.

Persons temporarily absent

Sometimes, dwellings that CIs and CCs thought were deserted turned out to be otherwise, but only because someone at the TRC chanced to point this out. Likewise, late in the count, no one in the census team seemed aware that a whole (and large) family group had been overlooked because the dwelling they were usually associated with was in disrepair. It transpired—when the team was informed again by the council—that these people were camping in nearby bush and hurried arrangements were made to track them down. While not reflective of mobility, a similar oversight occurred towards the end of the enumeration with regard to aged pensioners at the respite centre who were also overlooked until a casual remark by the housing manager brought this to light.

The extended timing of the census compounds the complications caused by this residential mosaic. Because people travel into and out of Wadeye to outstations and elsewhere on a regular, sometimes daily, basis, the question of whether individuals were either overlooked or picked up twice—or even more times—as the enumeration rolled out, was very real. Of course, ABS checking procedures should have dealt with any of the latter cases, but no procedures were deployed to address the former. One classic example of this dilemma was played out around the public holiday weekend of the Royal Darwin Show, beginning on Friday 27 July. Because of anticipated lack of activity in town, the CFO decided to swing through some of the region's northern outstations during the holiday period and conduct the enumeration there. On the previous afternoon, after a large funeral for a young girl, numerous vehicles had turned up in Wadeye from outlying areas to stock up at the store for the long weekend. Among those moving in were many members of a large family group from one of the northern outstations that had a population in 2005 of about 80 people. By this time, the census at Wadeye had more or less wound down and was resumed again (slowly) only on the Monday. On that same day, the CFO was back in town to report that not many people were found at the outstations and that some dwellings were vacated for a funeral ceremony. Almost simultaneously, most of the same aforementioned family group members were beginning their circuitous route back home. This raised the prospect that these people were not counted, although it should be noted that the CFO's trip also uncovered people at outstations who had already been counted in town.

Likewise, a group of older people who had been at Tchindi Outstation—which wasn't visited by the census team on the assumption that no one was there—eventually turned up in town and were enumerated at a previously listed vacant dwelling, but only because one of the CCs was informed of their arrival by a council employee. Elsewhere, two dwellings at Wudapuli Outstation—which was not visited until the middle of August—were found empty because the occupants had moved temporarily to Warmun in the east Kimberley for ceremonial business. Interestingly, an attempt was made by the CMU in Darwin to extract information on this group from ABS colleagues in Western Australia, but to no avail. It is also likely that the lack of people at Kuduntiga Outstation as reported by one of the CCs was due to their absence at ceremonial business in Elliot. These types of oversight and failures to track people seem inevitable when following a dwelling-focused census methodology that is extended over time among a mobile population. While at one level the extended nature of the census count can assist by allowing time for people to move (literally) into scope, the main lesson from Wadeye is that this is likely to assist their enumeration only if constant input of local intelligence on the whereabouts of people forms part of the process.

Confusion of this sort was not aided by an at times somewhat culturally inflected interpretation of the wording to Questions 10 and 11 on the part of interviewers and respondents. Question 10 asks, 'Are there any persons who live here most of the time but are away?' Given that high levels of temporary mobility are known to exist among the regional population, it was curious to the observer that affirmative answers to this question were very few, yet in a number of households where individuals were known to the observer to be away in other locations—in the sense that the ABS meant—their absence was not recorded. On quizzing interviewers about this issue, the fact that they were 'away'—and in cases could have been so for some days—did not register as an absence. This was not because respondents made a judgment that they were likely to be counted elsewhere—as per the instruction for Question 11, the 'Persons Temporarily Absent' (PTA) table (see Appendix A)—rather it was because they were still considered to be part of the present household and therefore not away. In any case, the idea that respondents, or CIs, could assess whether absent people might be counted elsewhere was highly presumptuous and generally avoided, at least in those instances observed.

This 'not absent' response was all well and good if such people subsequently appeared in answer to Question 12. A sometimes literal interpretation of 'people who are living or staying here *now*' (my emphasis, meaning 'at this moment'), however, meant that in some cases (admittedly only three observed) people who were absent at the shops, or were out bush for the day, were omitted. In an interesting variation on this, an instance was observed of a new-born child who was omitted from a household count because it had just left with its mother for the day to Palumpa and no one knew its name. Some confusion also arose over whom to indicate as Person 1 in Question 12 if the head of the household was listed as a PTA in Question 11. One final aberration surrounded the category 'visitor'. Though few people seemed to nominate this, where it was used the individuals referred to were fairly long-term residents and the term 'visitor' was clearly being used as a social category as much as a residential one.

As mentioned, a common characteristic of the Wadeye Aboriginal population—and of Aboriginal populations across the Northern Territory for that matter—is their temporary movement into regional centres such as Darwin for a wide variety of reasons ranging from service access and recreation to funerals. This movement is heightened in the dry season, and was augmented in 2006 by civil disorder and by the fact that the official start of counting at Wadeye (26 July) coincided with public holiday weekends, first for the Royal Darwin Show (27–29 July). The Darwin Cup (5–7 August) presented an additional attraction at that time for Wadeye residents. According to local informants, other places where usual residents of the Thamarrurr region were to be found during August 2006—aside from those already mentioned—included Palumpa, Peppimenarti, Daly River, Belyuen, the Tiwi Islands, Milingimbi, Wyndham, Kununurra and the greater Darwin area.

When visiting Darwin, Wadeye people locate themselves in various residential settings including in conventional housing with relatives in town or in motels, at town camps such as Railway Dam, Knuckey's Lagoon and Palmerston, at the Bagot Community and at various camping spots near the Catholic Mission headquarters in Stuart Park, by the Murin air terminal, the Airport Hotel, Lim's Hotel, Nightcliff Oval, the Catholic Mission hostel at Berrimah and along Rapid Creek. Given the likely numbers involved—estimated anecdotally in August 2006 at about 200 people—a key issue for the usual residence count of the Wadeye population was whether these people were captured by the census in Darwin and, if so, how the various forms used were filled out.

For example, those in conventional housing or in motels should have been captured as visitors on the standard mainstream form in answer to Question 2, but to be part of the Wadeye usual residence count they would need to have indicated 'Wadeye' in answer to Question 8 on usual residence. Those in town camps faced a similar combination of questions and issues, in Questions 12 and 15, on the IHF. For those camping out in urban areas, the general strategy employed by the ABS in the Northern Territory was to use the standard Special Short Form designed for homeless people. According to the CMU, this was deployed for two days from 9 August at known regular camping sites around the Darwin urban area. The particular feature of this form and its application that has importance for census counts is that it contains no question on usual residence. Information was primarily obtained through interview or self enumeration as the first preference, or by observation when circumstances prevented this. For Wadeye residents who were camping out in Darwin—and in any other urban area in the Northern Territory—the ABS, however, adopted a different approach in recognition of the large-scale dispersal of Wadeye residents that occurred due to community tensions just before the census. The procedure for this group was to use abridged mainstream forms (household and personal) rather than the Special Short Form, therefore activating the usual place of residence question. While this was well intentioned, it turned out that only a small number of 'homeless' Wadeye people were enumerated successfully using this approach, so any individuals enumerated in other camping locations using the standard Special Short Form method would have been lost to the Wadeye usual resident count.

Conclusion

Observation of the 2006 IES in the large Aboriginal town of Wadeye and its hinterland uncovered a range of structural issues concerning ABS interactions with community representatives, the strategies adopted to engage, train and supervise an Indigenous census workforce, the logistics deployed to connect with a mobile and scattered population and the categorisations and interpretations associated with the census questions, which are likely to have impacted on the successful outcome of census goals. At one level, this is surprising, since many of the contingencies faced were entirely predictable. At another level, it is not, because it reflects a continuing lack of meaningful engagement between citizens to be counted and the nation-state.

Despite the cultural importance in the Aboriginal world of the area between the Daly and Fitzmaurice Rivers, from a non-Aboriginal perspective this was one of the least-known parts of the continent until the mid 1930s and numbers resident there were simply guesstimated for prewar censuses and then incorporated into the general estimate for the full-blood Aboriginal population for the entire Daly River Census District. All this began to change with the establishment of the Catholic mission in 1935, first at Wentek Nganayi, then at Port Keats (now Wadeye) in 1939. From the very outset, a key task of mission administration in the region was regular census-taking. This was a requirement in the postwar years as part of annual reporting, initially to the Native Affairs Branch, then, from 1953, to the Welfare Branch of the Northern Territory Administration (Taylor 2005). Subsequently, the official count of the population has been sourced via the five-yearly ABS census. From 1976 to 1996, this provided a count of individuals present at Wadeye on census night, with those at outstations simply included as part of a much larger number representing the balance of the entire Daly Statistical Local Area. For the 2001 Census, however, outstations located in the Thamarrurr region were identified collectively for the first time as an Indigenous location. As we have seen, in the Realpolitik of community funding and representation, the TRC has also of late engaged in enumerating its population. Since census-taking is clearly not new to the region, why then—from observation—does it seem so difficult to accomplish?

One of the ABS responses to suggestions for improving the IES was to focus on form redesign. While the effect of changes made in this regard could be established at Wadeye only *a priori*, there was no doubt that the new census form proved to be a highly practical instrument to administer—leaving aside issues to do with the actual questions on the form and their interpretation. In all likelihood, it would not be wrong to suggest that the single-form approach was of greater assistance to interviewers and respondents than the multi-form approach in working through what was an increasingly crowded census schedule. This, as it turned out, was the least of the issues at stake (for further comments, see Appendix B).

The fact is, no matter how good the form structure, in small-scale communal settings such as those found typically in remote Australia, other more structural and systemic issues dominate. These relate to levels of community preparedness, participation and sense of ownership in what is a substantial and highly visible interaction with government. If these are not the primary focus and concern of the IES then the task of enumeration is reduced to a direct encounter between the ABS and individual householders—a much more difficult task than working in full partnership with their representative organisations. This is not least because the IES methodology insists on a dwelling-count approach to capturing a mobile population, which heightens the need for a sufficient, knowledgeable, authoritative and experienced local census workforce. The way to secure such expertise is to strengthen the existing relations between the ABS and communities and ensure the participation of representative organisations in statistical matters as a continuing priority throughout the entire inter-censual period.

The thwarted attempts to assemble an adequate census workforce at Wadeye provide a case in point. These attempts were not assisted by a growing feeling of detachment from the census process on the part of community representatives, by disruptive communal tensions leading up to the census, by competing local demands for skilled workers and by the fact that Wadeye was just one port of call on the CFO's vast administrative canvas. Before dismissing these as constraints that were unique to Wadeye, my point is that they were entirely to be expected and likely to be increasingly systemic in the absence of drastically improved resourcing for remote community services and governance. The consequence was an effective census team of just four people to cover the largest Aboriginal settlement cluster in the Northern Territory. This resulted in a much longer than planned for enumeration period, difficulty in establishing census coverage and a loss of capacity for data-quality checking in the field.

In the inter-cultural world of remote Aboriginal communities, the idea that a single CFO plus an Assistant can successfully negotiate, instigate and manage the census enumeration across a vast area in a compressed period without full local support is fanciful. Rather than suggesting a case for more CFOs, however, the more radical solution here is to build greater capacity for continuing ABS relations with community organisations so that by the time the census comes around every five years, both parties are better positioned to work together in the process. Part of the problem at Wadeye, it would seem, was that the census came to be viewed solely as an ABS activity—much more so than in the mainstream census, where the responsibility is on the individual householder to self-enumerate, and increasingly so given online census access. In the IES, errors can arise precisely because the householder has far less control over the process and is much more dependent on the logistical capabilities of ABS officers and procedures (this is not to deny that the IES, as conceived, is a device to enhance Indigenous participation in the census). To foster closer collaboration, or partnership, it might help to pursue notions of rights and responsibilities around census-taking in much the same way that Shared Responsibility Agreements (SRAs) work for other areas of government activity. For example, at Wadeye, ABS access to the TRC population database for guidance on DOB data and data-quality checking might have been more likely to have eventuated if ground rules and modus operandi regarding confidential data access were negotiated more fully in advance.

Ultimately, the census has two broad objectives. The first is to measure accurately the number and key characteristics of people in Australia on census night and the dwellings in which they live. The second is to provide timely, high-quality and relevant data for small geographic areas and small population groups, to complement the rich but broad-level data provided by ABS surveys (ABS 2006a). The IES, of necessity, contravenes the simultaneity condition of the first of these objectives, and by so doing compromises its capacity to deliver on the second. The dominant finding from observation of events at Wadeye is that this structural weakness of the IES could be greatly ameliorated if Indigenous people and their representative organisations were adequately positioned and resourced to engage more meaningfully in the census process and thereby assume more—not less—responsibility for 'self-enumeration' in line with the rest of the Australian community.

6. What sort of town is Fitzroy Crossing? Logistical and boundary problems of the 2006 enumeration in the southern Kimberley

Kathryn Thorburn

Fitzroy Crossing is a major service centre in the central western Kimberley. The nearest towns are Derby, 250 kilometres to the west, and Halls Creek, 290 kilometres to the east (see Figure 6.1). The majority of residents in Fitzroy Crossing are Indigenous, and there are a significant number of Indigenous-run non-governmental organisations (NGOs), including Marra Worra Worra (MWW) and Bunuba Inc., which, at the time of the census, were funded by the Western Australian and Commonwealth governments to service town-based Indigenous communities and outstations.

Fig. 6.1 Fitzroy Crossing and surrounding region

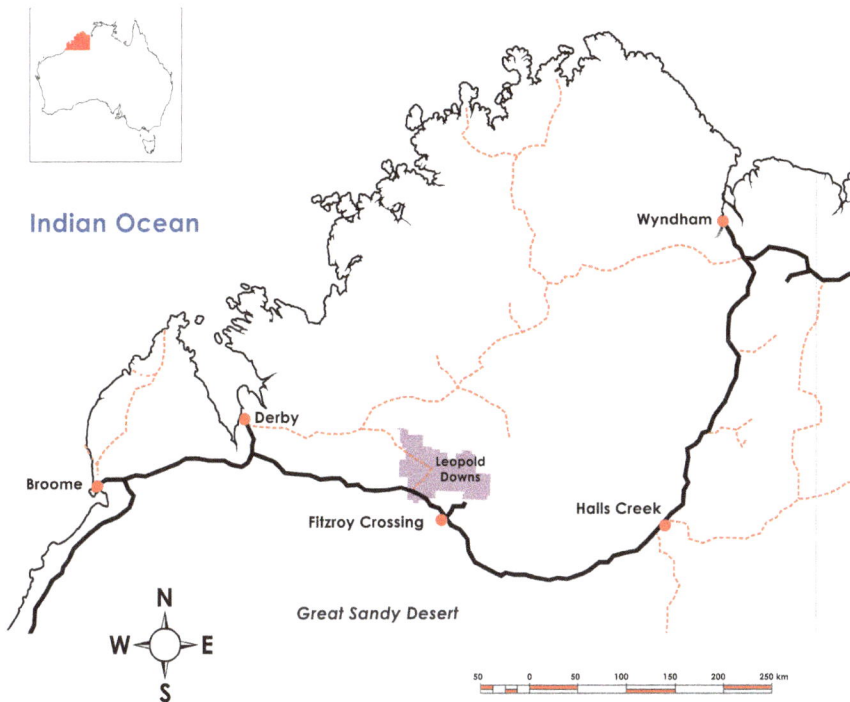

There are also a large number of non-Indigenous residents: about 45 per cent, according to the 2001 Census. Many of these non-Indigenous people work in service industries—health, education, administration and the like—as well as in various trades. Because Fitzroy Crossing is a town that services surrounding communities and pastoral stations in an area known as the Fitzroy Valley (estimated population 3500), there is much movement into and out of the town. In a sense, therefore, the 'population' of the town is rather unstable, and fluctuates seasonally and on the basis of various events such as festivals or funerals.

In addition, the Indigenous population of Fitzroy Crossing internally contains significant linguistic and cultural diversity. There are five major language groups resident in the town—Walmajarri, Wangkatjunga, Gooniyandi, Nyikina and Bunuba—as well as others, such as Djaru and Mangala. Bunuba are the traditional owners for the country on which Fitzroy Crossing sits. They have been associated with Bunuba Inc. since 1999, and before that with Junjuwa Community Inc. MWW has historically looked after the interests of non-Bunuba language groups in the town and on outstations and communities throughout the Fitzroy Valley.

While the brief of this research was to observe the effectiveness of the Indigenous Enumeration Strategy (IES) in capturing Indigenous residents in the town of Fitzroy Crossing, the 'mixed-up' nature of sections of the town meant I inevitably crossed paths with the mainstream, non-Indigenous count and collectors.

In its analysis of census data, the Australian Bureau of Statistics (ABS) separates out three 'discrete Indigenous communities' from the Fitzroy Crossing data: Junjuwa, Kurnangki and Mindi Rardi. In these areas of the town, the non-Indigenous population sits at less than 1 per cent of the total. For these areas, applying the IES would be predicted to be fairly unproblematic. Many other parts of the town—considered as distinct communities by their residents—are also enumerated under the IES. These are not separated out in the ABS's analysis but are incorporated into the 'discrete Indigenous communities' already mentioned, probably because their populations are too small. These include Burawa, Bungardi, Darlngunaya and Loanbung.

It is also noteworthy that the communities in which the IES is applied are characterised by their particular leases—mostly Aboriginal Lands Trust (ALT) reserves—which means that their municipal services, housing and so forth are managed by an Indigenous organisation, rather than by the local Derby/West Kimberley Shire. In Fitzroy Crossing, the two organisations in question are Bunuba Inc., which services Junjuwa, Burawa, Bungardi and Darlngunaya, as well as other outstations on the pastoral leases of Leopold Downs, and MWW, which services Kurnangki, Mindi Rardi and Loanbung in town, but also looks after 30 or so other communities throughout the Fitzroy Valley. These two organisations represent the primary point of articulation for outside interests wishing to engage with these Indigenous communities. As such, their role is vital in achieving community interest in the process and in providing resources including storage space, transport for census workers and other forms of support to ensure the census rolls out smoothly.

Those Indigenous people not living in the communities described above—that is, living in parts of town that were not on ALT leases or reserves—were enumerated along with the non-Indigenous population. These parts of the town included the town site itself, other peripheral areas around the town, such as blocks on either side of the river to the town's north, and an area adjacent to the school. Some of the houses in these areas are privately owned or rented; others are houses owned by local NGOs, which are leased to other such organisations for their staff. In the town itself, there are two streets in particular that are for public housing, and many local Aboriginal families live in this part of the town. According to the Western Australian Department of Housing and Works Derby office, there were at least 35 Aboriginal families living in this public housing at the time of the 2006 Census—that is, 35 separate households. This figure was the minimum number of Indigenous households that were enumerated with the mainstream, but the figure was likely to be higher, especially because of the number of houses that were owned by local Indigenous corporations, and that were likely to have had Indigenous families living in them.

This study differs, then, from the other three reported on in this monograph on two fronts. First, because of the nature of Fitzroy Crossing, the IES and the mainstream approach literally bumped against one another, sometimes overlapping and sometimes not meeting up and hence leaving gaps. Second, unlike in the Northern Territory, the approach throughout Western Australia was to *attempt* to complete the Indigenous count in the week of 7–11 August, with a three-week mop-up period. As will become apparent, by the end of the count, it was looking more like a time-extended, rolling count than a standard one. The Fitzroy Crossing study is nevertheless comparable with the others across the various aspects of the count, such as the workability of the household forms, the approach to staffing and training, the role of the Census Field Officer (CFO) and so forth.

Getting started

By the time I arrived in Fitzroy Crossing in mid July 2006, the CFO had already made progress in recruiting collector-interviewers (CIs) and Community Coordinators (CCs). The first training session took place on 18 July. Because of the particular character of the town, it was decided that there would be two training sessions: one for those CIs and the CC collecting Bunuba people's forms, the other for the remaining language groups whose data collection was being managed by MWW.

Two CCs were identified for the MWW communities, one of whom was also the Chief Executive Officer (CEO) of MWW; the other was a senior staff member of MWW. In other words, both already had full-time jobs in a very busy community organisation. Nevertheless, they were the two identified by MWW as most able to carry out the tasks. The brief of these two CCs did not include Bunuba people, who made up about 300 people in the town of Fitzroy, and who had been allocated their own CC to work out of the Junjuwa office.[1]

The MWW CC's catchment incorporated the constituents of MWW, which included the three non-Bunuba communities in 'town' and a number of surrounding communities and outstations. The structuring of the census very much reflected the authority of these two crucial NGOs—a division that also affected my observation to a degree, since there were two parallel management structures and hierarchies in action simultaneously in Fitzroy Crossing. My main focus was on those communities associated with Bunuba Inc., simply because of my historical familiarity with those people[2] and vice versa. I did, however, remain in contact with the CCs at MWW, and with the town-based Area Supervisor—who was concerned with the rest of the town—throughout the census period.[3]

Training, planning and preparation

The approach to Indigenous enumeration in Western Australia was 'standard'—that is, to attempt to count everybody, everywhere, in the same week. This was very different to the approach adopted in the Northern Territory, which was a 'rolling count'—that is, to train and then count, move to the next place, train and then count, and so on. I shall refer to the area covered by the CFO as the 'southern Kimberley'—an area stretching from Balgo and Mulan in the east to Jarlmadangah/Mt Anderson in the west, and incorporating the dozens of localities in between.[4] The first step was to coordinate across this vast area and to organise training sessions for community members at semi-centralised locations. These training dates did not always eventuate—people might have had more pressing matters to attend to or might simply have forgotten. Already we seem to be seeing how the 'standard' count might not work. The time lags between the first, introductory visit—in which the CFO might meet the chairperson and make an administrator aware of a return date for training—and the return to train was problematic. The CFO, from the outset, therefore had to backtrack, to attempt again to train in communities that might have missed out

---

[1] Junjuwa is the Fitzroy Crossing community with a majority Bunuba population and it is where the Bunuba Inc. office was located in 2006.

[2] I spent the first six months of 2005 working with Bunuba Inc. as part of my doctoral fieldwork.

[3] 'Area Supervisor' is the ABS term for the non-Indigenous coordinators.

[4] The distance between Mulan and Jarlmadangah is 780km, incorporating approximately 350km of dirt road.

on his first run. This pattern of backtracking—returning to places throughout his area to catch up—was to become quickly established. The size of the area, and the time required to drive between these communities—some of them, such as Balgo, are more than 300 kilometres of dirt road away from the main highway—clearly jeopardised the CFO's ability to coordinate the exercise.

It was not clear how much use had been made—or could have been made—of the report from the CFO of the 2001 Census. The 2006 CFO commented that this report was not of much use, since the 2001 Census depended on collaborating with a number of smaller Community Development Employment Project (CDEP) organisations that had ceased to exist, so there was a vacuum in many localities at the organisational level. It was also notable that this same CFO had been involved in conducting the Community Housing and Infrastructure Needs Survey (CHINS) only two months before, yet the CHINS data seemed to have no role in informing the planning process for the census—for example, planning the number of forms (on average, one for each house) for each community. That fundamental matters such as the number of forms required had not been estimated before the count—so that forms were still being ordered from Perth during the official census week (8–11 August)—set the whole process back further.

Training

On the first training day in Fitzroy Crossing for Bunuba CIs, only three people came out of six who had been identified by the CC from Junjuwa. The training for MWW was the next day and was attended by two different Bunuba people to replace those who had not shown up the day before, and one of the original team. Fortunately, on both training days, the Bunuba Inc. vehicle was available to 'round up' people who had agreed to attend, as the training was between 5 and 10 kilometres away from people's home communities. Had this vehicle not been available, there could have been much poorer attendance. The MWW training was well attended and included both of the CCs already mentioned. As people accustomed to managing the intrusion of bureaucrats and other outsiders, they encouraged all the CIs present to ask questions—there certainly were many more questions on this second day than on the first. These two CCs also stated in the MWW training session that *they* were to be the contact people if any CIs encountered difficulties—they were both infinitely more available, via phone or in the office, than the CFO, who returned to Fitzroy Crossing only periodically. In any event, I reluctantly took on a similar role for Bunuba people, mainly in contacting the Perth Census Management Unit (CMU) when necessary, or attempting to follow up CIs' and CCs' inquiries with the CFO after hours, via phone, or when he was camping at Fitzroy Crossing, generally on his way to somewhere else. I was able to do this because, unlike the CCs and the CIs, I had a mobile phone; this meant that I could call the CFO after hours, but it also meant that he could call me after hours and leave a message to pass on to the Bunuba census team. A more thorough planning process would have considered what avenues for communication were available.

Even at this early stage of the process, the CFO was under pressure and was rushed; the training suffered as a result. The CC of Bunuba, for example, who was to be managing five other people and attempting to coordinate the enumeration of more than 100 households, received barely more training than did the CIs. Nor did she receive a *Community Coordinator Manual*, which probably would have been very helpful, especially the 'frequently asked questions' section. That the CFO was already rushing at this stage seems to have compounded other difficulties that arose later.

For example, there was little opportunity for questions during the training, and indeed few arose in the first session I attended—perhaps no surprise given that none of the CIs tried out the form on each other (as was supposed to happen). The training essentially consisted of watching the training DVD, followed by the CFO reading through the Interviewer Household Form (IHF) and then people filling out the various forms to enable them to be paid. As I did not observe the CFO training, I cannot comment on the adequacy of the CFO's own training in informing his understanding of some of the issues that would arise with particular questions. Critically, Questions 11 and 12 (see Appendix A), which attempted to distinguish between people who were away and people living and/or staying at a dwelling, were not well explained. In particular, people did not understand that those written down as normally here but away and unlikely to be counted elsewhere were supposed to be moved 'inside the form' to Question 12. I doubt a single form in any of the Bunuba communities was completed in this way—resulting in very limited information being collected for these residents. In any case, CIs were repeatedly unsure how to handle the various states of 'being a resident' that they encountered, and were quite relieved to leave people off (to be caught up with 'later', which often did not happen) when, for example, they were down at the supermarket, or doing contract mustering.

Part of the reason why the training was not especially effective, it seems to me, is that it did not succeed in contextualising the whole census exercise. There could have been greater effort in the DVD to demonstrate what the census information was used for—or, if not in the DVD, the CFO himself could have gone through some of the previous census data for that region, and for particular communities that people came from. In other words, it might be useful for people to consider what the impacts are when the count is not accurate in terms of a concrete example from their own community, which they can relate to. For example, 'If we do not count all the kids under the age of five living in Fitzroy Crossing now, then the number of kids in each of the classrooms will just keep getting bigger because the government won't know to send more teachers for us.'

In addition, the training sessions took place on 18 and 19 July—that is, at least two weeks before any CIs started interviewing. Arguably, even if the training had been adequate, the CIs would still have forgotten some of the more subtle or tricky aspects of the form outlined in the training. Adopting the 'standard' approach—especially when it entails such a time lag between training and the real count—should require that there is an avenue for questions to be answered. Such an avenue might be provided by, for example, a toll-free phone number. The manual provided by the ABS was not referred to by any of the CIs I was observing, perhaps because very limited reference was made to it during the training.

Between the training and the beginning of the count in Junjuwa, the CFO and I went out with an older man and traditional owner for some of the station country to Leopold Downs Station to ascertain roughly how many people, and houses, might be on the pastoral excision communities. This seemed to be part of the brief of the CFO—that is, these particular outstations, but not the station itself. The station *workers*—that is, those living at the homestead rather than on pastoral excision communities—were not, however, considered part of the brief of the CFO, despite the fact that the station in question was owned by Aboriginal people. While there was a non-Indigenous manager there, he had five Indigenous people working alongside him and reckoned there were another five or so out on the stock camp. Enumerating these workers, as well as the non-Indigenous station staff, was, however, deemed to be the responsibility of the mainstream enumerator for the area. One can but wonder at the efficiency of having two different ABS staff visit the same station—which is some 60 kilometres from Fitzroy Crossing—the one to enumerate Indigenous communities there, the other to enumerate staff and workers, the majority of whom were in fact Indigenous.

Managing the paperwork

A crucial part of the planning was to establish the correct Master Dwelling Checklist (MDC) and draw from that the Interviewer Dwelling Checklists (IDCs) that were to guide the CIs.[5] In the case of Bunuba, the CC did not understand this process, although the MDC for the largest community, Junjuwa, was begun with the CFO's help, on the basis of a map of Junjuwa provided by the Bunuba Inc. housing officer. All except one of the MDCs and related IDCs were drawn up along the way, or even after the count had been done, on the basis of the number of IHFs filled in for a particular community or outstation. The validity of the MDCs and IDCs as checking mechanisms after the fact was completely undermined—although in my observation they were in fact largely accurate, apart from one house that was missed on the MDC and the IDC and was not enumerated at all. The main reason, it seemed, why CIs filled in IDCs was their

[5] For a full description of the 'ideal' procedure in the field, see Chapter 1.

understanding that it was on the basis of these forms that they were to be paid. Indeed, the CFO would never have realised that the IDCs and MDCs had been created after the count—rather than before it—if it had not been for the fact that the Collection District (CD) numbers to be filled in at the top right corner of each were missing. He had neglected to explain to the CC what these numbers were, or to provide her with the list for her area to ensure that none were missed.

The correct procedure was for the CFO to work with the CC in drawing up the MDCs, being sure to include the correct CD number and the correct regime of Census Record Numbers (CRNs). The CC was not, however, informed about CRNs until the data collection was complete, except for a handful of houses. The MDCs and IDCs were therefore drawn up *yet again*. Fixing the CRNs on the IHFs was a little trickier and required lots of scribbling out and, in some cases, necessitated filling out a whole new form.

The IDCs were very useful for identifying for the CC—who would follow up such things—if houses had been missed, for example, if there was no one at home at the time that the CI first called. It was, however, never clear to her, or to me, what the 'persons counted' boxes—for males and females—on the MDC and the IDC were for, when they were to be filled in, or by whom. Were they, for example, to be filled in by the ICs once they considered their interviewing work done, or by the CC once she and the CFO had checked the forms and made certain they were correct? It was also not clear whether they were to include visitors at the house in these totals, or people written down who were normally there, but who were away for the interview. This would, of course, have impacted on whether people were paid correctly.

The role of the Census Field Officer

The role of the CFO was absolutely pivotal in the success or otherwise of the 2006 Census. Indeed, it seems that the extent of responsibility placed on this individual in the whole process was a very risky strategy. There are a few elements to this burden that need to be unpacked. Firstly, the area to be covered by the CFO in question was significant. This vast area contains dozens of communities, some consisting only of a single family group, and some with highly variable occupancy. Obviously the CFO could not visit and coordinate all of these smaller places, so the approach was taken to engage with community-based organisations that provided services across the southern Kimberley. This engagement was, however, very informal and patchy. It involved the CFO having a chat with a councillor, chairman or administrator, identifying a CC, carrying out a morning's training, dropping off forms and then returning to pick up forms a few weeks later. The patchiness of these interactions was not always the CFO's fault: some of these organisation offices are not always staffed, so making contact by telephone to arrange a visit can be difficult. In addition, those community members trained to be CIs might not live in the community where the office is situated or might not have a telephone, and again, therefore, communication becomes problematic. In addition, the resources of these community-based organisations, and their staff, tend to be extremely overcommitted, and the lack of early engagement with these bodies meant that the census—and the requests to the CFO for assistance—was not always given priority.

In order to cover the ground he needed to cover, the CFO estimated that he was spending 50 per cent of his time driving.[6] In my observation, the time he spent in any given community was highly variable. While some communities received only a morning's training, in others the CFO was present for a week or two, because he had to help with the count itself. Therefore, he had no capacity to monitor what was happening anywhere except where he was on the day, or to provide CIs or CCs with any support, should they need it. That is, he had responsibility for everything, but no capacity to *be* responsible across the entire area. While he did have a satellite phone, he checked messages only in the evening. Very few members of his 'team' across the southern Kimberley, however, had a phone number to leave for him to get back to them.

That he had to return regularly to Broome to pick up supplies—extra IHFs, hats, satchels and so forth—added enormously to his time on the road. Having a base where materials could be stored, and perhaps an administrative assistant in Fitzroy Crossing, would have freed him up enormously. As it stood, once the training was completed, it was never quite clear when the CFO might be returning to Fitzroy Crossing. There were no other contacts given to the census workers for ABS staff in the Perth CMU, so if they had any questions, or needs such as more forms, there was no option but to attempt to contact the CFO. As noted above, this process was by no means straightforward.

The count

The CFO encouraged the Junjuwa CIs to start the count a week early—a suggestion that made a lot of sense given their enthusiasm and my availability as an observer and as a logistical resource with a car and a licence, and the fact that the week before census week was 'slack week'.[7] Since people's finances are getting low, there is generally much less drinking or mobility during slack week; people are easier to find and are less likely to be distracted by all of the activity that occurs during pay week; and there are less likely to be so many

---

[6] Between 12 March and 29 September—that is, 29 weeks (the period including the earlier CHINS data collection)—the CFO travelled a distance of 34 287 kilometres, an average of 1182 kilometres a week. Arguably, however, the fact that the CHINS stage was a lot more straightforward and required little or no backtracking suggests that most of this travel occurred during the census period—that is, in the final three months. The CFO also estimated that he was in Perth for at least two weeks of this time, for training.

[7] Slack week is the week between pay weeks, although some people—such as pensioners—are paid in this 'in between' week.

visitors in town for shopping. Of course, counting this community early raises questions about the potential for double-counting of people counted in Junjuwa and then counted again somewhere else in census week.

There were four CIs working in the community of Junjuwa and each was allocated 15 houses. In addition, there were a number of much smaller communities that this group of collectors was responsible for: Darlngunaya, Bungardi, Burawa, Biridu, Galamunda and Warangarri.

By and large, the CC took responsibility for these other communities, in part because I had a car and therefore she and I could go off and count those people. One young man was trained up to do the count in Darlngunaya, where he resided. This is the largest of the smaller communities, containing about 10 houses.

In the event, the real count began on 1 August. The CC and I drove around Junjuwa, finding the CIs, giving them their forms and the map on which the CC had allocated them particular areas. We then drove over to Burawa, a small community of about six houses, to begin the interview process. This was the first time the CC had attempted to fill in a form, since that process did not occur during the training. This first interview took 45 minutes, in part because the CC was trying to recall points made in the training video—two weeks earlier—about individual questions on the form.

In total, there were five CIs, one CC and myself engaged in the census for Bunuba Inc. Apart from the young man counting Darlngunaya, the four remaining CIs were in fact two couples, who worked together. This seemed a very effective arrangement for a range of reasons. One partner could act as a backup interviewer if there was a person in the house with whom the other partner had an avoidance relationship. One person might be far more confident in writing, so they could write the answers while the other asked the questions. Finally, it is more enjoyable and socially acceptable not to work alone.

One issue that arose was with people who worked full time. There were a number of houses that I visited with the CC where no one was home during the day. The CC herself was a mother of five children and, not owning a motor car, she was unable to chase up these people in the evening. The current approach seems to be based on the assumption that Indigenous people will be at home and available for interview during working hours, and does not seem to make provision for people in such communities who work full-time—apart from the CC or CI following them up after hours, which is not always possible if the census staff do not live in the same community. Such situations must surely arise regularly in Indigenous communities. In the end, the CC made the decision to leave a form at these households, to be collected later.

The effectiveness of having locals enumerating locals

The problem with observational reporting is that it is not necessarily so obvious to the observer what is working well, as opposed to what is not working well, in the current system. An opportunity did arise, however, to observe a context in which the census process worked less well. Mindi Rardi is a largely non-Bunuba community in Fitzroy Crossing, which was MWW's responsibility in this context. The CC, however, offered to help out the MWW staff, so the four CIs from Junjuwa and I spent two mornings enumerating the people there.

In general, the CIs were less comfortable working in this other community, even though they knew many people there. They were much keener to get forms over and done with quickly, and would not push people for answers. For example, the count of children in Mindi Rardi will be very much less than it should be, for the CIs would write down only the immediate response to the question 'Who stops here?', which often overlooked children. Others also would have been missed, since there was no follow-up or return visit to record people who happened to be at card games or at the supermarket on the day. While some of these people might have been noted when the forms were checked at MWW, those who were visitors would not have been recorded at all.

Marra Worra Worra

One of the CCs stated at the training that she hoped to have the parts of Fitzroy Crossing for which MWW was responsible completed by 3 August. After that date, she was going on leave for four weeks; however, the count for MWW's Fitzroy Crossing communities did not begin until well into the official census week, after 7 August. Part of the reason for the late start was that MWW still did not have enough forms (they were about 120 short) well into census week.

In any case, a single MWW staff member did most of the count of people in town at Kurnangki and Loanbung, as well as other communities such as Djimbalakudindj, about 100 kilometres to the west. By this time, this particular MWW staffer was acting CEO, so was having to carry out this work after hours.

The 'visitor' question

When people are really visitors—that is, when the are not just extended family members from outstations—for example, if they are in-laws from a different language group, the interviewers sometimes did not feel comfortable asking them the full range of questions. On one occasion, I was asked by the two CIs to enumerate a house of eight young people from as far south as Jigalong who were still in town after a funeral, and who were camping in one of the older houses at Mindi Rardi. In a sense, it was handy for the CIs to have someone like me around, a kind of neutral figure, to ask and explain these 'rude' questions to strangers in town.

The style of the count

According to the CFO *Field Manual*, there are three types of enumeration: standard (the approach taken in the Kimberley), rolling and assisted. Arguably, while the first kind of approach worked sufficiently well in certain areas, the problem was that because there was absolutely no oversight in many communities no one was aware if nothing had been done until it was almost too late. Taking the third approach[8] would have meant that the progress on the count could at least have been monitored. Taking the first approach and applying it across the board does not acknowledge the fact that there can be significant variations in human capacity across communities—a truism that might not be apparent to a CFO, especially one with a relatively short-term relationship with communities and community members. The approach, then, has potential to be very 'hit and miss'.

The intent with the census was that the majority of the southern Kimberley would be completed in some sense by the end of the week of 7 August. What ensued was that the CFO was still training in that week and that, for a significant number of communities, absolutely nothing happened once the training ended. Some very large communities were not enumerated until well into September when the CFO was joined by an ABS colleague from Perth and by two other CFOs who had finished their areas. The communities of Wankgatjungka, Yiyili, Looma and Jarlmadangah all required unplanned-for help from outside. My understanding was that the absolute deadline for forms to be 'in the mail' was 15 September, the date I was to leave Fitzroy Crossing. The count was, however, still under way when my observations ceased.

Issues specific to towns of the Fitzroy Crossing type

Although my brief was to observe the taking of the Indigenous part of the census, as already mentioned, I was aware that there were significant numbers of Indigenous people who lived in what is known as the 'town site'. The mixing up of people in certain areas should be relatively easy for the census to manage—it simply requires some form of continuing communication between the CFO and the non-Indigenous equivalent—the Area Supervisor—and some dedicated effort in the planning stage. As stated in the 2006 Census IES: 'For 2006, the role of the Census Field Officer in areas covered by Area Supervisors [mainstream managers] will be adjusted so that lines of responsibility and communication between these staff are clearer.' Regrettably, that did not occur, and not only did the CFO never even meet either of the Area Supervisors, the latter did not even meet each other! No 'Indigenous Assistants' were engaged

---

[8] The assisted approach is defined in the IES thus: '(W)here people from the community are recruited and trained and then the Census is conducted in the community. The census is completed before the CFO moves on to the next community.'

to help with either the enumeration of Fitzroy Crossing 'town site', or with the stations and tourists enumerator who was attempting to count people across a similarly huge area—one quite distinct from, yet overlapping in parts with, the CFO's area. The Area Supervisor in Fitzroy Crossing—a non-Indigenous woman but 'married-in' and resident for some 10 years—was aware that there were about 30 Indigenous households being enumerated in the mainstream collection. The Indigenous Assistant she thought she had recruited did not help out in the end, because she was already burnt out from working on the census at the nearby community of Bayulu. While the Perth ABS staff had encouraged the Area Supervisor to find an Indigenous Assistant to help out, in the end she was unable to.

Beyond the town of Fitzroy Crossing itself, there was much anecdotal evidence that similar issues were arising, such as that already mentioned relating to the pastoral stations. If census staff on the ground are not communicating with each other, and have been given the sense that they are not to collect from 'the other', significant gaps can easily emerge, as was the case. Overlaps can occur too, as when the CFO and the Area Supervisor on occasions visited the same stations, unaware of what the other was doing—this despite the fact that they were regularly camping at the same caravan park in Fitzroy Crossing. Arguably, the approach of enumerating Indigenous people separately has the potential to greatly improve the accuracy of the count, however, the process needs to be tempered with commonsense, so that, in some instances, the Indigenous CIs might also collect data from non-Indigenous people. The census will, of course, never be absolutely effective in these areas, but it seems that there are some quite simple matters to be remedied that would see it being a lot *more* effective next time around.

Conclusion

Undoubtedly, the 2006 Census count in Fitzroy Crossing took much longer and was more problematic than was planned for. Lack of planning and lack of resources—especially the very limited availability of the CFO—seriously undermined the efficiency of the exercise of census-taking across the entire area of this CFO's responsibility. There would clearly be a major benefit in terms of cost, efficiency and accuracy in devoting more time and resources to planning the census, with local NGOs, but also between ABS personnel (between the non-Indigenous and Indigenous census-takers), paying some considerable attention to the experience of previous census-takers.

The value of local knowledge cannot be overemphasised, and should be sought early in the planning process. Certain mobility trends, for example, are fairly predictable, such as the number of people—Indigenous and non-Indigenous—working in stock camps in August in the Kimberley. Others are less so, such as funerals, which might or might not be taking place locally but which will nevertheless impact enormously on mobility. What might be worth considering is more CCs to coordinate efforts on a smaller scale, and a long enough lead time for the ABS to recruit locals to fill these roles, including time for them to plan properly. Recruiting people who are not concurrently trying to do another full-time job might also increase the effectiveness of the count, although again such recruitment would probably require a longer lead time. An essential element of the planning is contingency planning—or planning for the unplanned. In other words, there needs to be more flexibility and scope built into the timetable to allow for unforeseen events. This CFO, for example, hit a bullock on the road to Billiluna in early September, which took him out of action for nearly a week at a very crucial time in the whole process.

The role played by local Indigenous organisations is also crucial. Sanders (Chapter 3) demonstrates clearly how a strategic engagement of the ABS with a local NGO can be extremely beneficial. Similarly, Taylor (Chapter 5) demonstrates how a lack of this engagement can undermine the effectiveness of the IES. These organisations are critical in two regards: as a source of day-to-day local knowledge and in terms of the support they can provide logistically—vehicles, office space, storage space and so forth. This recommendation, however, needs to be tempered by two issues. The first is that recent trends suggest the number of Indigenous community-based organisations—at least in remote Australia—are decreasing (see, for example, Taylor 2006b: 57); and changes to the CDEP program might see even fewer such organisations in the future. The ABS might want to consider how it could engage with remote communities that have no such administrative centre. The second issue is that not all of these organisations have the same resources and capacity—again, this is where contingency needs to be built into the planning, to account for those organisations whose capacity to provide support to the census process might be variable or limited.

7. After the count and after the fact: at the Darwin Census Management Unit

Frances Morphy

Before embarking on a description of processes at the Census Management Unit (CMU), I will present some interim comments about the organisational structure of the Indigenous Enumeration Strategy (IES). I will use the debriefing of the Census Field Officers (CFOs) in Darwin as a frame for doing so, for two reasons:

- in the course of the debriefing, the CFOs raised many of the issues that I would like to raise myself
- as the people who were responsible for the practical implementation of the IES strategy, their perspectives on what worked and what did not are significant.

That being said, I am presenting my comments from the point of view of an outside observer. I am interested here in what the CFOs perceived as the problems, as an element of my own analysis. They sometimes saw similar problems, but offered different solutions. In some cases, the recommendations that we make in Chapter 9 coincide with solutions offered by some or all of the CFOs. In other cases, they are different.

The CFO debriefing

The debriefing session took place on 15 September, when many of the CFOs were still attempting to complete the counts in their regions. In some respects, then, they had not had a chance to gain any distance from the process and some, like the CFO I had been shadowing, were feeling tired and discouraged.

The topic of time—or lack of it—featured prominently in the discussion. It was felt that their own training had been too compressed, that the time allowed for pre-census publicity in the communities was insufficient and that the Community Housing and Infrastructure Needs Survey (CHINS) work had interfered with their census publicity efforts. The time allowed for training the Community Coordinators (CCs) and collector-interviewers (CIs) was insufficient, given people's levels of skill and knowledge, but they saw problems in keeping people engaged in longer training sessions. Finally, given the size of their regions and the logistical difficulties involved in keeping track of what was happening at more than one place at a time, they felt under constant time pressure. There was no time and little opportunity to carry out the validation checks that they had been asked to do in the field. Most had been unable to complete the count in the six to seven-week window, and they were concerned about the implications of this for the accuracy of the count, given people's mobility.

All of these time pressures are symptomatic of one thing: the current remote IES arrangements are unviable. One could level criticisms of the individual sub-strategies employed by some of the CFOs, such as making too much use of vehicles and not enough use of planes. This does not, however, alter my view that, fundamentally, the CFO's job as currently constituted is inherently impossible. These CFOs were hard-working and conscientious people. They were putting in tremendously long hours under often physically demanding conditions—sometimes to the point of exhaustion—and they all felt that they were not able to do the job as well as they would have liked, or as was required.

In part, it is an issue of the resources that the Australian Bureau of Statistics (ABS) is willing to put into the IES. The CMU staff and the CFOs were unanimous in their opinion that the whole exercise was under-resourced. The more fundamental question is the uses to which the available resources are put. More resources might indeed be necessary, but they also need to be deployed differently. This issue is discussed in detail in Chapter 9.

Many of the CFOs were critical of the outdated technology that they had to operate with. Although they had been given laptop computers for the CHINS exercise, they were not allowed to keep them for the census enumeration. They were forced to carry around huge amounts of paperwork and, unless they took their own laptops with them, they were unable to keep up-to-date electronic reports as they went along. It would have been useful to have electronic access to databases such as the recently completed CHINS and the Discrete Indigenous Communities Database (DICD), and they would have been able to update the latter electronically as they went. They were happy with the level of support that the CMU had attempted to provide, but had to rely on fairly unreliable satellite phones as their main means of communication. Having spent some time at the Data Processing Centre (DPC) in Melbourne, I find the contrast between the high-tech environment there and the low-tech environment visited on the CFOs startling.

The CFOs were generally critical of the ABS publicity for the census; they felt there was not nearly enough targeting of the IES areas with IES-specific information. The mainstream information that was disseminated was more confusing than helpful. They also felt it was largely a waste of time to target publicity at the general population in Indigenous communities. The effort should be targeted more to local organisations, and more time should be spent training the CIs in an understanding of the purpose of the census, so that they in turn could explain it properly to the interviewees. Several were highly critical of the materials they had been given to use in training. The DVD was 'not relevant to the bush' and the storyboard was a 'shame job'.

I am sympathetic to the CFOs' criticisms. The census remains an alien project to most people in remote Indigenous communities, and publicity campaigns of short duration will not change that. It is no longer enough to simply tell people that the census is a good thing because it measures levels of need in housing and other basic services. This has been true for decades, and census results, in the eyes of many, have had no discernable effect on the government departments responsible for delivering these services.

The CFOs and the assistant CFOs all felt that the introduction of the Assistant role was a good thing. As one of the CFOs put it: 'The [region name], that's a lonely place down there. You need someone to offload with. There are lots of reasons to be working in pairs.'

Having two people also increased flexibility, with the CFO sometimes being able to leave the Assistant to supervise the count at one community, while moving on to start the training at another. They felt, however, that the respective roles and responsibilities of the CFO and Assistant CFO had not been mapped out clearly enough, and that this was a potential source of tension between them. They also thought that the Assistant CFOs had been brought on board too late in the exercise.

There was a discussion about the role of CCs, which it was felt was not differentiated sufficiently from that of the CIs. One suggestion was that CCs should be recruited and trained much earlier, and that they should be given responsibility for—and paid for—publicity activities and the recruitment of CIs. There was universal agreement that the training offered to CCs in 2006 was inadequate. In practice, because time was short, they were not given any more training than the CIs. One person suggested that the TAFE system could be used to deliver an accredited community-based training course on working for the census as a CC.

The CFOs were also very critical of the payment system for the CCs and CIs—it was complex, cumbersome and inefficient. Getting the pay details organised took up a substantial amount of time on the training day. They felt that people lost motivation because their pay was so delayed. Recruitment and retention of CCs and CIs in sufficient numbers had been an almost universal problem. The CFO for the Yolngu-speaking area brought up the example of a community of 1500 people in which he had been able to recruit only four people.

On the subject of their own training, the CFOs felt that their comments during the training had been vindicated. Not nearly enough time was spent on the content and implications of the questions on the form. They were particularly concerned about the 'persons temporarily absent' (PTA) question, feeling that they had been ill-prepared to assist the CCs and CIs in how to make decisions about moving people from the PTA table into the main body of the form. This comment can be linked to another, made by one of the CMU staff, that the longer the count went on the more complex this problem became. She felt that the count needed to be concentrated into three weeks at most, but acknowledged that this would require major changes to the organisation of the IES, and better resourcing. She suggested that one way of achieving the count in a shorter time might be to employ many more CFOs and give them responsibility for much smaller areas.

The CFOs also had some thoughts about the organisation of the CMU. There were three main issues. They thought that there should have been an IES-specific unit within the CMU—the managers to whom they were reporting had too many roles that involved them in the mainstream count, and this sometimes made it difficult to get the support that they needed in the field (at least one of the CMU managers concerned agreed strongly). They were critical of the lack of coordination and communication between themselves and the Area Supervisors of the mainstream count, and they questioned whether the State Indigenous Manager's role had been sufficiently well defined.

All in all, the outcome of this debriefing session was a fairly comprehensive critique of the IES in 2006, with a variety of solutions proposed to particular problems. In Chapter 9, we draw from this critique and from our own field observations to make our recommendations.

The post-count checking process at the Census Management Unit

In the second part of this chapter, I focus on the preliminary checking of the Interviewer Household Forms (IHFs) at the CMU, and on certain global problems with the data that emerged from the process. Checking was undertaken mainly at weekends by members of the CMU staff. From time to time, some of the CFOs were present, and the opportunity was taken to put outstanding queries to them about the regions in which they had worked. Several of the CFOs spent some time at the CMU helping to process the forms themselves.

There were two main tasks in the checking process. The first was undertaken in order to ensure that the forms were in maximally good order before being sent to the DPC in Melbourne. I learned later in Melbourne that not all CMUs had done this, and the DPC staff was very grateful to the Darwin CMU for its efforts. That Darwin focused on this exercise can be attributed to the fact that the person overseeing the IES had herself worked in the DPC in Sydney in 2001, and therefore had an understanding of the issues that would cause problems at the DPC if they were not addressed in Darwin. I draw attention to this as a classic example of the usefulness of 'local knowledge'. Because this person had an understanding of the context into which the forms were being sent, she was able to ensure that the forms were well prepared for that context.

The necessity for the second task emerged as a result of this 'grooming' process. It quickly became apparent that there were very large numbers of PTA, and that the CFOs, CCs and CIs had not been consistent across the board in the way that these people had been treated. Many who should have been moved 'into the form' (see Chapter 2) because they were unlikely to be counted elsewhere had not been moved, and the sheer number of PTAs raised concerns about whether even those who were said to be somewhere where they should, theoretically, have been counted, had in fact been counted at that place. The second task, then, was to deal with the problem of PTAs.

I will devote most of this chapter to that second problem. When it became obvious, I decided that among other things, I would focus on the forms from the area where I had observed the count, reasoning that by doing so I would be able to undertake a detailed quantitative analysis of the scale and nature of the PTA problem in that particular area.

Grooming the forms

When the boxes of IHFs from a particular Collection District (CD) arrived at the CMU, they should have had the following accompanying documentation:[1]

- Indigenous Community Information form from the DICD
- Interviewer Dwelling Checklists (IDCs) for Indigenous dwellings
- separate IDCs for non-Indigenous and non-private dwellings
- Master Dwelling Checklist (MDC)
- checklist for CFO.

On the last of these, which the CFO was expected to complete before sending the forms to the CMU, the CFO was required to crosscheck, among other things, that:

- the DICD form had been updated with available information
- an IHF had been completed for each unoccupied dwelling
- IHFs had been checked for Indigenous status non-response and followed up if necessary
- IHFs had been checked for duplications between the PTA list at Question 11 and the people listed as present at Question 12
- IHFs had been checked for usual address (Question 15)
- Question 10 ('Are there any persons who live here most of the time but are away?') had been marked appropriately 'no' or 'yes'

---

[1] Note that the checklists were said to be applicable to a 'community', whereas in fact the IHFs were grouped into CDs. This is a potential source of error. For example, some small outstations in the area where I made my observations were included in the wrong CD, and one was nearly missed altogether (see Chapter 4).

- each IHF had its correct CD number, Census Record Number and form numbers (where more than one form had been used for a dwelling), and that these corresponded with the numbering on the MDC and IDCs
- every dwelling on the MDC had been included on an IDC
- non-Indigenous dwellings and non-private dwellings had been listed on separate IDCs
- every dwelling listed on an IDC had been included on the MDC
- counts had been checked against available estimates (with a note that at minimum these were the 2001 Census and the 2006 CHINS figures).

In practice, many of these CFO checklists were not filled in, so the CMU could not know whether or not the CFO had carried out the checks asked for, and very little attempt had been made to update the DICD forms. In many cases, the IDCs were also missing.[2]

The community checklist for the CMU had two sections. One—theoretically to be completed while the CFO was still in the field—asked the CMU checker to make sure that the CFO had recorded and reported the counts for people, dwellings and unoccupied dwellings. At the CMU, these counts were then checked against available estimates and the CFO notified of discrepancies for follow-up. In practice, this happened after the forms had been returned to the CMU and the CFO was either no longer in the field or was in a different CD, necessitating in some cases a return to particular CDs, or a follow-up by phone or fax.

The second part of the CMU checklist involved inspecting the forms to ascertain whether the CFO had carried out all the checks that they had been asked to do on the CFO checklist. In addition, the checkers at the CMU were asked specifically to do the following:

- check the CD number on each form
- check that the number of male and female—and total—persons listed at Question 12 for each dwelling corresponded with the number listed on the MDC
- check that Question 18 on Indigenous status had been answered (and, if it had not been, to answer it in the positive if, on the evidence available on the form, the person was incontrovertibly Indigenous)
- check Question 15 (usual address)
- check that the details for PTA (Question 11) had been filled in

---

[2] In the case of the region in which I observed the count, this was because the contents of these lists had changed so often that they were almost useless as a record of what each CI had done. I suspect this could have been the case generally (see also Chapters 5 and 6).

- check that people who had been moved to Question 12 ('inside the form') had also been crossed off the PTA table, and that the details of their sex and date of birth had also been transferred inside the form
- where a dwelling had people listed as PTA, but no one listed at Question 12, the checkers were instructed to amend the status of the dwelling to 'unoccupied' on the MDC
- double-check that the grand totals on the MDC were correct.

All of these checks—and most of the checks that the CFOs were asked to undertake—were concerned ultimately with ensuring the *consistency* of the 'head count' aspect of the census and ensuring that as far as possible basic information about residence and Indigenous status had been recorded. All things being equal, they were designed to ensure that the forms sent to the DPC were internally consistent with respect to the number, sex ratio, usual residence and Indigenous status of the population. In terms of the *accuracy* of the count, the checks were initially more general in nature: the CMU was concerned if the population count for a particular CD or the number of dwellings for which forms existed was very different from the recently acquired CHINS data and/or the count at the 2001 Census. There were several cases in which CFOs were sent out again to investigate the reasons for discrepancies.

There were several issues where the checkers were told not to try to 'fix' discrepancies, for example, anomalies in ages and/or in the data on relationships between the members of the household. They were told that they had insufficient information to make changes and that the DPC had rules and procedures that applied in such cases. Again, this was an example of the application of prior knowledge about the context into which the forms were being sent.

The 'persons temporarily absent' problem

Another problem quickly emerged as a result of the detailed scrutiny of the PTA question. One of the first CDs to be scrutinised consisted of small communities that were close to a regional centre. Many of the PTAs on these forms were said to be 'shopping' or 'visiting family' in the regional centre. There was no way of knowing, a priori, whether these people had gone only for the day or whether they had gone to stay in the regional centre for a while, and might have been counted there. In this case, the CFO who had been in charge of this CD happened to be in the CMU for the day. His local knowledge of the communities was tapped. His judgment was that people from these communities normally just went into town for the day, and that, moreover, the enumeration in the regional centre happened at a different time from the enumeration in these communities, so on both counts it was unlikely that these PTAs would have been 'caught' in town. Accordingly, they were all moved to Question 12 on their forms. In this case, it was not thought necessary to go through all the forms for the regional centre to try to find people counted there.

It is notable that the CFO had not himself made these judgments about moving PTAs before the forms were sent back to Darwin. Had he done so—and had he asked the CIs to go back and collect full details for the PTAs who were moved inside the form—many more people in the population of this CD would have had their full details recorded. Unfortunately, I did not think to ask him why he had not taken this step. There are several possible reasons: he had not understood the circumstances under which PTAs should be moved; he had not checked the forms closely (as per the CFO checklist) before sending them to Darwin; he simply ran out of time and had to make a judgment that it was better to get the forms in by the deadline he had been set than to spend more time chasing the details of PTAs. Given that the original CIs who had completed the forms might no longer be available, this could have been a lengthy process.

Similar problems kept coming up. It became clear that many CIs had not followed the instruction—or had not been instructed clearly enough—to move people from the PTA table in clear cases where they would not have been counted elsewhere, such as being away at 'sorry business'. It was also clear that most CFOs had not questioned the CIs' original allocations of people to the PTA category. In most cases, the reasons for moving people—or not moving them—were undocumented.

It also became clear that the prolonged nature of the count, combined with the levels and range of mobility, posed real problems for judgments about whether PTAs were likely to have been counted elsewhere. Theoretically, it should have been possible to check the advance schedules that stipulated when each community in each CD was to be counted, so that, for example, a person listed as a PTA from a community counted in July, who was said to be at a community that was counted towards the end of August, stood a good chance of having returned home before the latter count took place. It would be reasonable then to move such a person back into the form. These judgments depended on schedules being adhered to and on the CFO (at the very least) being aware of the schedules for their own region and also for surrounding regions and major population centres such as Darwin and Alice Springs. The CIs who were assigning people to the PTA category certainly did not have this information and so were not in a position to make such judgments (see my comments in Chapter 4 on my own dilemma over this very point), and there is very little evidence that the CFOs attempted to make such judgments in the field. In any case, most of the advance schedules underwent substantial alterations in the field, so it was almost impossible, in practice, for any CFO to be aware precisely when communities outside their sphere of responsibility had been enumerated.

Some preliminary thoughts on tracking absent persons

In future censuses some of these problems could be ameliorated—but not eliminated—by better documentation, on several counts. Firstly, it should be documented whether people who are said to be 'visitors' at a dwelling have been asked how long they have been visiting for and whether or not they have been counted elsewhere.[3] Secondly, more details should be asked about where a PTA is, how long they have been away and when they are likely to return, and this should be documented. In particular, if a PTA is said to be in a large town—for example, Darwin or Alice Springs—it becomes well nigh impossible to crosscheck whether they have been counted unless some specific location within the town is recorded. Thirdly, the 'short form' used to enumerate the 'homeless' should allow for a person's usual place of residence to be recorded. Many people who go temporarily to Darwin and Alice Springs camp out. It is not possible to crosscheck whether such PTAs have been counted if their usual place of residence is not recorded (see Chapter 5).

The situation could also be ameliorated by better use of technology. If the schedule were in electronic form, and if it were kept updated by the CFOs, and if every CFO had access in the field to this database, it would be a straightforward matter to make judgments—in the field—about the likelihood of PTAs being counted elsewhere. The CFO would simply have to look at the database to see what progress had been made in the CD to which the PTA was said to have gone. If that CD was being counted at more or less the same time, the chances would be high that the PTA would be counted as a visitor there. In the case where a large number of PTAs were said to be in a particular community, it would be possible to check—in the field—whether they were being picked up there.

Thinking further along these lines, it might also be profitable to institute a 'funerals and festivals' database, which would also be updated constantly by the CFOs on the basis of local intelligence, detailing where and when ceremonies and festivals were taking place, and which communities were affected, in terms of being the site of such an event or the source of many attendees. Such a database would make planning around these events much more manageable.

Schedules set in stone at the beginning of the census exercise will never be an effective tool in the context of the remote Indigenous census. There are just too many contingent factors at play. I am suggesting here the use of modern technology as a tool to constantly update the schedule as contingencies come into play, and to keep all CFOs—and possibly the CCs as well, because they will be the source of much of the intelligence—updated on the situation, not only

---

[3] If people say they have been counted, they should of course not be counted again, but if they say they have not been counted it removes the necessity for checking to see if they have been counted at their usual place of residence.

in their own areas of responsibility but in neighbouring areas where 'their' PTAs are likely to be found.

Patterns of mobility and migration

In a snapshot such as the census, it is difficult to disentangle short-term mobility from longer-term migration. The feeling expressed by some at the CMU was that the count was down in remote areas, and that this most likely reflected migration since 2001 from remote settlements and homelands into regional centres and towns. There are, however, at least three other possibilities:

- that the 2001 count was inflated by double-counting and the 2006 count is a more accurate reflection of the real population in remote areas
- that the 2006 count in remote areas was an under-count in comparison with the 2001 count
- that short-term circular mobility between homelands, hub settlements and regional centres has increased in the intervening period, so that at any particular time fewer people are at their place of usual residence than was the case in 2001.

To these we can add the following possibility: that all these variables are at play to different degrees in different regions of the Northern Territory. Given this situation, it seems to me very unlikely that census data can be used to find definitive answers to questions about mobility or migration. There are, however, certainly indicative patterns that are worth noting for further investigation at a micro-demographic level.

In some areas, particularly in the arid and semi-arid zones, there were many small isolated homelands where all—or nearly all—the dwellings were empty. There are at least two possible reasons. One is migration into larger settlements and towns, which could well be a result of the closure of small Community Development Employment Projects (CDEP) programs and which is likely to increase if the Commonwealth government implements the policies it has foreshadowed for what it considers to be 'non-viable' small homelands, such as ceasing to provide funding for housing. If migration is involved, one would expect a corresponding swelling in the 'non-visitor' population of towns and regional centres—subject to the proviso that considerable numbers of people might nevertheless call themselves 'visitors' because they are not in their own 'country'. In some areas, however, it could simply reflect the seasonal occupation of homelands, with people moving regularly between their homelands and bigger hub settlements.

In particular instances (such as those described in Chapter 4), the emptiness of a settlement could reflect a very short-term movement, for example, to the site of a funeral ceremony or a festival. Such examples seem to occur commonly everywhere.

Another definite pattern emerged in the areas around service centres such as Tennant Creek or Mataranka. Here it was very common to find large numbers of PTA who were temporarily away in the service centre, shopping or accessing other services. This pattern was repeated on a smaller scale in all areas where a set of satellite communities looked to a particular hub community for basic amenities such as shopping, banking, health services and so on. In such cases, short-term mobility is a more likely explanation than migration, and in nearly all such cases the PTAs should have been put inside the form.

A pattern that was particularly discernable in the relatively densely populated Top End was intense levels of movement between adjacent settlements in culturally defined regions—such as, for example, the Yolngu-speaking region of Arnhem Land. In such regions, many PTA were said to be visiting relatives in nearby communities. Such patterns were also discernable in less densely populated regions, but more intermittently and over much larger areas (see Chapter 5). These patterns too are indicative of short-term mobility rather than migration.

In the next few years, government policy settings could well result in increased semi-permanent migration flows from remote settlements into towns. It will be a complex matter to disentangle the evidence for this migration from the 'noise' of mobility more generally, and given the complexity of the patterns described above it would be inadvisable to use census data as any kind of baseline measure. There is an urgent need for regional micro-demographic studies of the nature and causes of mobility and migration in remote Australia.

Documentation after the fact

When the extent of the PTA problem became apparent, the CMU manager attempted to introduce some consistency into the decision-making about who should be moved into the forms, and instructed the checkers to document their decisions on the CMU checklists. She also attempted to get a fix on the scale of the problem, while acknowledging that the CMU did not have the systems to do a proper evaluation. Since the IHFs were not as yet in electronic form on a database, it was extremely difficult and time-consuming to crosscheck for the presence of individuals on more than one form. For example, some large communities had 10 or more boxes of forms, so that if PTA from another community were said to be there, all 10 boxes had to be checked. The DPC manager nevertheless instituted a check on PTAs where this was practicable. In some areas it appeared, from my own observations of this process, that a majority of PTAs had not in fact been counted at the places where they were said to be visiting.

As long as people were listed as PTA at their usual residence, these discrepancies would not have serious consequences for the final estimated resident population

(ERP)—*if* PTAs were counted back into their communities for the purposes of the ERP. In such a case, however, the total Indigenous ERP of the Northern Territory would be significantly different from the total population counted in situ, since many of these PTAs did not appear inside *any* form unless they were moved back in at the CMU. Since PTAs are not counted back for the purposes of the ERP—and only those listed as visitors in other communities are counted back to their community—there will be a considerable under-count, because of the many PTAs unlikely to have been counted as visitors elsewhere.[4] There are also significant consequences for the quality of the data on all questions except the basic demographic variables of age and sex. There are no other data available for those originally listed as PTA on a form, and if they were not counted elsewhere as visitors then those data were not collected elsewhere either.

In a few cases, the manager of the CMU asked the CFO to go back and collect details of PTA who had been moved back inside the form, or to attempt to do so by phone, however, it was not possible to undertake this exercise across the board.

The Arnhem Land case-study area

I took the opportunity at the CMU to scrutinise thoroughly all the forms from the homelands where I had undertaken my observation of the enumeration, and also those from nearby hub communities, in order to get some idea of the scale of the PTA problem in that area, and to assist the CMU in making judgments about which PTAs to put back into the forms. I also attempted to ascertain how many people had been missed altogether and how many had been double-counted, based on my personal knowledge of the local population. The former was a harder task than the latter: noticing an absence is a very different task from finding two instances of a presence.

In Chapter 4, I detailed particular instances of double-counting that I picked up in the course of this exercise, and I will not repeat those here. There were several other instances, particularly of the kind where a person was listed as PTA in one community or homeland, and as a resident at another. I found that one small homeland (population 30) had been overlooked (it was then subsequently visited). I also found one 'vacant' dwelling at one homeland, where everyone had been absent at a funeral at the time of the count. It had been intended for a follow-up visit that never happened (the CFO phoned the household from Darwin and the IHF was duly filled in).

For the study-area homelands as a whole—after eliminating all known instances of double-counting—I found that the IHFs listed a total of 598 residents at their

---

[4] As noted in Chapter 1, this observation seems to be borne out by the published results of the post-enumeration survey (PES) exercise, conducted for the first time in 2006 in discrete Indigenous communities; see ABS (2007) and Taylor (2007b).

own dwellings, 105 PTAs and 51 visitors. On the raw figures therefore, 105 out of 703 usual residents (15 per cent) of the usual population were PTAs, and 51 out of 649 (8 per cent) of the people present at the count were visitors.[5] It must also be remembered that these counts were already something of a fiction (see Chapter 4)—for example, the inhabitants of A3 and A4 had been counted 'as if' they were at home, but the forms were filled in at community A, where they were attending a funeral.

I then went through the process of trying to crosscheck whether all PTAs had in fact been counted elsewhere. In some cases, PTAs were said to be at another of the homelands within the group, so crosschecking was relatively straightforward. In other cases, I had to trawl through all the boxes of IHFs from the hub communities in the region. In still other cases, people were said to be further afield and it was not possible to check most of these because the relevant boxes had already been sealed, awaiting transport to Melbourne.

As a result of this exercise, 70 of the 105 PTAs were put back into the forms, either because they were definitely not counted at the places where they were said to have been, or, in the cases where crosschecking was not possible, because they were unlikely to have been counted—for example, because they were at a funeral. That is, in the case of this set of communities, two-thirds of those who were originally listed as PTA—or 10 per cent of the usual resident population—would not have been counted *anywhere* unless this exercise had been undertaken. For this 10 per cent of the population, only very basic information is available: their sex, age, Indigenous status and usual place of residence.

Conclusion

Although I cannot extrapolate from my detailed findings about the PTA problem in the Arnhem Land homelands to the Northern Territory more generally, the overwhelming impression that I gained from being present at the CMU checking exercise when other areas were under scrutiny was that the problem would have been of the same order in many places. This is the key issue that emerges from this particular census exercise. It is a complex dilemma and the solution—which will never be perfect—is also complex, depending as it does on changes at many stages of the census exercise and at many sites within the ABS as an organisation. In the concluding chapter, we elaborate on these findings and make some recommendations for changes that will go some way to addressing them in the lead-up to the 2011 Census. In Appendix B, we discuss aspects of the IHF form design that probably contributed to the problem.

---

[5] These are not the real figures; I have, however, preserved the correct percentages.

8. The transformation of input into output: at the Melbourne Data Processing Centre

Frances Morphy

Introduction

I made several visits between November 2006 and March 2007 to the Data Processing Centre (DPC) in Melbourne, to observe the work of the Indigenous Processing Team (IPT). The creation of the IPT was an innovation for the 2006 Census, with a cohort of data-coders trained to deal specifically with the Interviewer Household Form (IHF). All Collection Districts (CDs) of Types 11, 12 and 13—all those consisting of or containing discrete Indigenous communities—went through the IPT. Since CDs of Types 11 and 13 also contained other kinds of communities that were enumerated via the mainstream form, the IPT coders had to deal with both kinds of forms.

I observed aspects of most stages of the data processing, from the grooming of the forms and the compilation of the Census Record Books (CRBs) before the electronic capturing of the data to coding of the first and second-release data.[1] I also attended the IPT coders' training sessions on the processing of household and family data, and of data relating to occupations and qualifications. I was given the opportunity to meet with individuals responsible for instituting and overseeing general systems and procedures within the DPC, and this helped me to gain an overview of the Indigenous Enumeration Strategy (IES) coding within the broader context of DPC activities.

As a field site, the DPC was very different from the remote area where I observed the enumeration and from the Darwin Census Management Unit (CMU). During the enumeration, I had been working in an environment that I knew well and where I had undertaken a similar exercise in 2001—and, as a result, I had an overview of the process that was informed by my prior local knowledge. Also, since the filling in of the IHF was a protracted exercise, it was possible to make very detailed observations of the initial data collection, in 'real time' as it were. At the CMU, although the institutional environment was initially unfamiliar, I was observing a relatively small-scale operation—in contrast with the DPC—and one in which, although use of information technology was a significant component, face-to-face interactions—for example, in the training sessions—and

---

[1] For the mainstream count, the CRBs were compiled in the field and the DPC had to reconcile discrepancies between the counts on the form and those in the CRBs. For the IHF forms, however, the compilation of the CRBs took place at the DPC.

manual processing of the IHFs (with people talking about what they were doing as they worked) were important elements of the process. The data were also arriving at a pace and in a form in which I could 'capture' it for the purposes of my own analysis.

In contrast, the DPC is a very large and complex—and highly technologised—environment. I had to rely largely on others for the information that would allow me to understand its workings, rather than observing for myself. Although I was able to observe the training of the data-coders in a manner similar to my observation of the training of the Census Field Officers (CFOs), once they started work the situation was very different. Whereas in the field and at the CMU the data were always in context—physically on a form that was in a box with other forms from the same place—once the data from the forms had been captured electronically at the DPC it was dissociated from those contexts. Although the coders could call up the electronic copy of the form if need be, for the most part they were working, at high speed, on snippets of information divorced from the wider context of the forms. In order to meet processing deadlines, they had to concentrate hard and work fast. There were fewer contexts for me to observe people's own commentary on what they were doing, and—with one exception, which I will note below—the data were not 'capturable' in the same way as in the earlier contexts.

In my work at the DPC, I was concerned less with analysing the organisational aspects of the exercise than was the case in the field, although I will make some brief general comments based on my rather superficial knowledge of what was a very complex and technologically sophisticated operation. My primary aim was to follow the progress of my own case-study IHFs, so I would have a complete picture of the journey of the data through various contextual frames, from its elicitation during the count to the coded end product.

There was not much more to observe as far as the basic 'head count' aspect of the census was concerned. The IES team did run another check on the internal consistency of the records while compiling the CRBs during 'pre-capture'. They also checked whether people who had been moved from 'persons temporarily absent' (PTA) status to 'inside the form' had then been eliminated from the PTA list at Question 11. By and large, this was not a problem with the Northern Territory forms—thanks to the work of the Darwin CMU—but quite a few 'duplicate' people were found in the IHFs from other States. In such cases, the person was usually retained inside the form at Question 12 and eliminated from the PTA list unless it was clear that they would have been counted elsewhere, for example, at boarding school. There were a few cases where the sex of individuals was missing, and these were imputed.[2]

---

[2] In some cases, ages were missing. These were imputed at a later stage during system edits.

I was most interested in the coding of the data that had as yet received little attention at any stage of the checking process in the field or at the CMU: this was the primarily socio-demographic information—household and family composition, language use, education, employment and so on. Many of the questions on the form relating to these issues required a written answer and, for the IHF, answers to such questions were coded manually. This was a major difference between the coding procedures for the standard form and the IHF.[3]

I was interested in the categorisations that underlie the coding process and how the data were fitted to those categories. As I have argued elsewhere (Morphy 2007), the categories in terms of which the national census is framed are derived from the culture of the mainstream and reflect the concerns of the nation-state. In Villaveces-Izquierdo's (2004: 178) words: '[T]he census is a tool through which the state envisions and acts upon the nation.' These categorisations, which also underlie the framing of the questions on the form, are opaque to those who fill in the forms—the collector-interviewers (CIs) and the interviewees.[4] In many cases therefore, the answers given to questions—particularly where written answers are required rather than simply the ticking of a box—are often difficult to interpret in terms of the preset coding categories. This was the main reason why such responses were coded manually.

In the field, I had been interested in the categories that Yolngu brought to bear in responding to the census questions, and what kinds of answers this produced. At the DPC, I was interested in how their answers were interpreted and slotted into the coding categories. I was interested in the demographic portrait of the Yolngu population that was produced as the end result of this process, and the degree to which it was commensurable with: a) the Yolngu view of themselves, and b) a depiction informed by anthropologically derived categories.

Some might argue that this is an unnecessary and even misconceived exercise, that the purpose of the census is, precisely, to gather demographic 'facts' that are comparable between different sectors of the population. My argument will be that, to the degree that these 'facts' are socio-demographic rather than socially neutral, they will be categorised differently depending on the cultural lens through which they are viewed. Census categories are not culturally neutral, and it cannot be assumed a priori that the categories of one socio-cultural system are translatable directly into those of another. To some extent, then, this chapter

---

[3] In mainstream processing and for some of the questions on the IHF, responses are coded automatically by the system. If a code cannot be determined automatically then manual intervention via an online coding system takes place. For the IHF forms, automatic coding (AC) is switched off for the majority of topics.

[4] This is true to some degree of all people who fill in a census form—with the exception of a small expert group of population specialists, including those employed by the ABS—but, in the case of people whose cultural categories diverge significantly from those of the mainstream, that opaqueness is compounded.

is less a commentary on my observations of the operation of the DPC and a more broad-ranging commentary on the nature of census data and its limitations.

The Indigenous Processing Team: a brief appraisal

Since I was not present at the DPC for the 2001 Census, I am not in a position to compare the functioning of that DPC with the 2006 DPC. It is possible, however, to assess whether the procedures put in place had strengths and weaknesses in their own right. My overwhelming impression—from my own observations and from conversations with IPT and other DPC staff—was that the IPT was a worthwhile innovation and that it should be retained for future censuses. It is needed for the same reason that the IES itself is needed—the 'difference' of Indigenous people in remote areas of Australia—and indeed it should be considered from now on as part and parcel of the IES.

It was found in 2001 that automatic coding (AC) was not successful in coding certain questions on the Indigenous forms, and for certain questions (as noted above) AC was switched off and the IPT coders were instructed to code manually. In this situation, there are advantages to the DPC in having to train only a small number of coders to work with the IHF, and having a small cohort allows for efficient quality assessment and feedback to the coders.

The IPT followed a policy of attempting to make minimal use of the option 'Not adequately described', and this meant the coders had sometimes to be quite lateral thinking in their coding solutions. In order to maintain consistency across coders, it was necessary to give feedback constantly to individuals and the group, and to monitor for patterns in the solutions adopted, particularly for less adequate solutions. When such patterns were noted, ad hoc tutorials were held to help the coders achieve better and more consistent solutions. All this would have been much more difficult to maintain rigorously with a larger number of coders.

The other major advantage of a specialist unit is that it can serve as a repository of specialist knowledge. A great deal of background research had been done to assist the coders in such matters as identifying the Indigenous languages that appeared on the forms and in compiling exhaustive lists of community names with their variants, and the family coding and the coding for occupation and qualifications required extra knowledge over and above what was required for the mainstream forms. Again, it is more efficient to train, monitor and assist a relatively small number of specialist coders rather than attempting a more general exercise involving all coders.

In assisting the coders to do their work, the DPC has to maintain a delicate balance. It must provide them with enough information to code accurately and quickly, while avoiding the pitfall of providing information that might bias them towards particular interpretations of the data. It is a cast-iron rule of coding that the coder must work with whatever information they have—and only that information—and this rule is in creative tension with the imperative to avoid coding a response as 'not adequately described' wherever possible.

The additional sources of information that were available to IPT coders included the community forms from the Discrete Indigenous Community Database (DICD) and the CFO and CMU checklists described in the previous chapter. They had access also—on request to the data-analyst on the floor—to extensive materials on Indigenous languages and on localities. These last two were invaluable and, for the Northern Territory at least, the CMU and CFO checklists often provided useful additional information, such as how the PTAs for a particular CD had been treated. The DICD forms were less useful, except as a check on the number of people and dwellings in a CD. As noted in earlier chapters, the CFOs had not, by and large, completed these in any great detail. Coders were encouraged to add to the forms, for example, by recording variant spellings of language names that appeared on the forms. If these forms are attended to and updated during the inter-censual period, they will potentially be an invaluable resource for the coders in 2011. This database is to be maintained by the National Centre for Aboriginal and Torres Strait Islander Statistics (NCATSIS), and we have suggested in Chapter 9 that the updating should be the responsibility of Indigenous Liaison Units—rather than a solitary State Indigenous Manager—located in the State and Territory offices.

Another procedure followed by the IPT that differed from the mainstream processing was to base processing on CDs. In the mainstream processing, coding was topic based, with different teams of coders working on different topics rather than on whole forms. The IPT procedures allowed the coders to become familiar with patterns of naming and other reoccurring information for particular communities, leading to more consistency in coding. From my observations, this generally worked very well. For example, once a coder became familiar with all the language names for a particular community, this speeded up the coding process considerably. It also helped the team managers in their quality-assessment work, since if a coder made a particular error it was likely to be repeated for the whole CD, showing up as a clear pattern.

In order to allow for flexibility in coding when faced with variety in the written responses to questions, the coders worked with colour-coded 'pick lists'. Some choices had to be exact matches, others allowed for close or approximate matches. As a last resort, the coder could choose to bypass the pick lists and go into a 'best-fit' process. In best fit, the coder was required to state their reason for choosing that path and this will presumably allow the ABS data-analysts to refine the pick lists for 2011. This seems to me to be a good idea, because it allows the coders some latitude with aberrant answers, and also allows them to signal 'gaps' in the options offered. It is unclear to me, however, how the subtleties of these procedures will be translated into the output data. I noted that coders differed in their propensity to opt for going into best fit. Some tried several pathways within the pick-list system and went to best fit only as a last resort, while others were quicker to opt for the best-fit solution.

Some global problems

The lists of localities for the coding of workplace addresses were provided by the State Transit Authorities (STAs), and were much less comprehensive than the ABS's own locality lists used in other questions. This was the case particularly for remote areas of the country—the majority of discrete Indigenous communities seemed to be missing.[5] This threatened to force the coders into a lengthy and tortuous coding process. They were essentially instructed to bypass the process and code the State, followed by 'Community further investigation'. It is hoped that these STA lists will be more comprehensive for 2011.

In family-coding mode, the coder had access to all the forms relating to a household—in instances where there was more than one form because there were more than 12 people in the household. This was not the case, however, when coding some other questions, such as the language question, and this caused problems if the answer was 'Same as Person 1'. If this answer appeared on the second or a subsequent form for the household, the coder no longer had easy access to the answer given for Person 1, on the first form. There seems no good reason why the system should not allow for the first form to be readily accessible for all coding.

In Chapter 7, I noted that at the Darwin CMU the answer to Question 15 ('Where does this person live most of the time?') was checked carefully for each individual. If this question had been left blank, and it was obvious from the answer to Question 12 that the individual was not a visitor, the 'This community' box was marked. It transpired that this was a very important exercise, since according to the coding conventions at the DPC the answer to Question 15 overrode the answer to Question 12. If the 'This community' box was left unchecked at Question 15, the individual could not be included in the family coding for the household even if they had replied, at Question 12, that they were not a visitor. This was one of several examples that I noted at various points in the process from data collection to data processing where a very small detail could have very large consequences. Thanks to the Darwin CMU, this will not have been a problem for the Northern Territory, but I do not know what happened in other CMUs.

---

[5] Given all the work that the IPT had put into compiling a comprehensive list of community names, this was irritating, to say the least.

There were other glitches in the system that required ad hoc coding solutions, but it seemed to me that these were dealt with efficiently through the impromptu tutorial sessions and the more formal training sessions.

Family coding: what is being coded, and why?

At the beginning of the training session on IHF family-coding procedures, the coders were reintroduced to the concept of the 'statistical family' that had been explained to them in the training for mainstream family coding. They were reminded: 'Statistical families are governed by a strict set of coding rules that conform to international standards. Often these statistical families do not reflect the true status of family members as seen by other family members and their community.'

They were told also that this 'applies even more' to some Indigenous households. The definition of the statistical family is: 'Two or more persons, one of whom is at least 15 years of age, who are related by blood, marriage (registered or de facto), adoption, step or fostering, and who are usually resident in the same household.'

Indigenous households pose particular problems for coding according to this definition, for several reasons. The ABS allows for only three statistical families in any household, and it allows for only three generations in a family. If there are more families, or more generations, additional families have to be merged with the 'primary' family in the household. In some cases, individuals who are closely related to someone in a household are classified simply as 'other relative' to the 'head' of the primary family once this process has dismantled their own family. It was interesting that the trainers anticipated that coders would find this unsettling—they were told to be 'unemotional' about following this procedure.

Other stray comments alerted me to the emotions that family-coding procedures could engender—in stark contrast with coding for occupation and qualifications, which were equally subject to a set of formal definitions and procedures. One visitor from the Darwin CMU advised a colleague, also visiting from Darwin, not to watch what was being done in family coding because of what it did to the data, and one of the coders who had lived in a discrete Aboriginal community also commented to me in passing how aware she was that family coding did not capture 'what is really out there'. It seems at first glance that matters to do with family strike an emotional chord that is at odds with a 'statistical' approach; it seems to make people uneasy to see relationships being objectified in this way. That is not the whole story. People would probably feel less ambivalent if they felt that what was being captured was somewhat closer to what is 'really out there'.

About halfway through the family-coding procedures, at a feedback session on the floor, the coders discussed difficulties they were having with family coding. They mentioned the three-generation and the three-family rules as problematic. One person also thought part of the problem was having to relate everyone to a single person, and suggested a matrix approach, in which everyone in the household was related to everyone else.

In my view, this last suggestion would be unworkable, given the size of many Indigenous households. For example, with a household of 20 people, according to my calculations, 190 different kinship dyads would have to be recorded. Even with a household of 10, 45 different kinship dyads would result. The chances of recording, in every case, the 'correct' Anglo-Celtic relationship would approach zero. The result would be more incoherent data, on a grander scale, and a coder's nightmare. There is little point in asking for further relationship details for other relatives, since the data that result have a good chance of being incoherent and misleading (see Morphy 2004, 2006). I have written in detail elsewhere (Morphy 2004, 2006, 2007) about the inherent difficulties of translating between incommensurable kinship systems and I will not repeat that discussion here. Nothing of what I observed in 2006 has, however, persuaded me against the recommendation that I made as a result of observing the count in 2001: that, for coding purposes, a new type of household should be added to the ABS list of definitions—the 'extended family household'. This type of household could potentially be useful for capturing information about more than just Indigenous households.

The default assumption, if evidence is missing or conflicting, would be that everyone in such a household is related to everyone else. Only where a person is stated explicitly to be something else—for example, a 'friend'—would they be classified as unrelated. In the 2006 Census, the large number of PTA who were moved back inside the form—at least in the Northern Territory—had to be classified as unrelated because there was no information on their relationships to other members of their households, whereas in fact it is much more probable that they *were* related to other members of the household (invariably so in the cases that I observed). In 2006, the large numbers of PTAs with no relationship data who were put back into the forms will generate a lot of spurious 'unrelatedness' in Indigenous households.

The sub-units within these households should not be called 'families'; they are, rather, sub-units of the extended family, and should be distinguished terminologically as conjugal *units*—with or without children—or single parent–child *units*. The terms 'couple family' and 'lone-parent family' should be reserved for households consisting of such unit types, and applied to them only.

I also see no useful purpose in maintaining the arbitrary cap on the number of such units that occur in a household. Nor do I see any useful purpose in assigning members of the grandparental generation arbitrarily to one unit or another, when they are equally closely related to members of several units. If this convention is abandoned, the necessity for the arbitrary cap on the number of generations within a 'family' also disappears.

Questions 31 and 32 (see Appendix A) should stay for 2011 as a means of identifying the sub-units within the extended family household. The collectors just need to be trained to implement them better. There is more chance of a 'match' between Anglo-Celtic and Indigenous systems when dealing with very close core kin. Indigenous CIs can in general cope with translation between Indigenous terms and the Anglo-Celtic terms 'father', 'mother', 'son' and 'daughter'.

During family coding, the coders were asked to document on paper the solutions they reached for the more complex households. This was invaluable for me in my analysis of what happens in the translation process. In my opinion, however, they would be of limited use as a basis for attempting a new classification of the internal structure of Indigenous households. They do not record what is really 'out there'. They are not neutral representations of Indigenous family structures, but artefacts of the current coding system (see Morphy 2007).[6]

In conclusion to this section, I pose the same question that I posed in 2001: what is family coding for? In their training, the coders were told that 'we do not try to capture relationships in terms of carers and finances'. Perhaps this is precisely what the census *should* be trying to capture and compare across different sections of the population. In socioeconomic terms, the family—however it is constituted—is the bedrock institution of any society, the site where children are raised, supported and socialised, and where those not in the workforce are supported by those who are. Family policy is almost invariably directed to these aspects of the family as a social institution. The question of precisely which categories of kin do or do not live in the same household is—or should be—a secondary consideration at most. The terms 'couple family' and 'lone-parent family' carry with them cultural assumptions about the nature of such families that cannot be projected simply from one cultural setting to another. For example, the child of a single mother who is living in an extended family household—where other adults besides the mother play a large part in their care—is in a very different situation to a child whose mother lives without such a supportive kin-based network.

---

[6] These family trees will be shredded when the DPC winds up, so cannot be used in this way in any case.

Occupation: CDEP and the invisible economy

Very wisely, the DPC had instituted a dedicated 'pick list' for Community Development Employment Project (CDEP) occupations.[7] The majority of 'employed' Indigenous people in remote Australia are CDEP participants (see, for example, Gray and Chapman 2006: 117). The instructions to the coders were to use this pick list as the first port of call whenever CDEP was mentioned, no matter which of the employment-related questions it appeared in. They were also warned that some people who worked for CDEP organisations were not CDEP participants, and to exit the CDEP pick list into the mainstream occupation coding options when a person's job description evidently did not fit within the CDEP listings. There was a concern that sometimes the level of CDEP-related jobs might be understated. For example, if someone said that they were a 'receptionist', this should not be automatically coded to 'administration or clerical work' on the CDEP pick list.

The CDEP pick list was compiled using responses from the 2001 Census, and this might have been an adequate strategy were it not for the case that CDEP was undergoing rapid and radical change at the time of the 2006 Census (DEWR 2005a, 2005b, 2006). The process of refocusing CDEP towards training people for 'real jobs' was encouraging the relabelling of 'traditional' CDEP jobs. Women who had previously been receiving their CDEP for 'home management' or 'home duties' were now working in 'environmental services' or 'community care', for example, as were many former 'rubbish collectors'. These changes to CDEP were very recent at the time of the census, and in Arnhem Land I had observed some people still using the older categories. By the time of the next census, if CDEP is still in existence, I would expect most CDEP participants to be more aware of their 'official' job descriptions, since each CDEP participant is now given a written formal job description and training plan. It would be advisable then to construct the CDEP pick list primarily from the Department of Employment and Workplace Relations' (DEWR) list of job descriptions in 2011, possibly supplemented by information from the 2006 responses.

The increasingly significant role of the Indigenous Protected Area (IPA) scheme and associated ranger programs was evident in the responses to CDEP questions. The closest equivalent in the CDEP pick list was 'park ranger'. It was decided to best fit 'community ranger'—the most common description of ranger jobs associated with IPAs—to 'park ranger' rather than simply picking it from the list, as a way of alerting the data-analysts to the gap in the pick list. By 2011, depending on the continuing success of the IPA program and the ability of these ranger programs to attract funding, many of these ranger positions could be non-CDEP jobs.

---

[7] The special CDEP coding was used only for IHF forms from remote communities, and not for coding the occupations of Indigenous people enumerated on mainstream forms.

The instruction to use CDEP as the entry to job classification wherever it appeared in the answers to work-related questions was a relaxation of normal coding procedures—but a sensible one. In general, respondents are not able to discriminate very clearly between questions that ask for a distinction between a job description and the list of tasks performed, nor are they able, in many cases, to provide a coherent or accurate description of what their 'employer' does. The questions on the census form are designed with mainstream employment situations in mind, and do not have salience for people who are not employed in the mainstream. Had the coders been faced with attempting to code CDEP responses as if they were mainstream responses, their task would have been much more arduous and frustrating.

As in 2001, I was struck forcibly by the silences—the gaps in information—that the form of the census questions on economic participation engendered. The overwhelming impression of remote Indigenous Australia is of economically marginalised people, in low-paid, part-time, low-skilled, 'dead-end' occupations. The biggest silences concern the subsistence economy and participation in the art industry. Some commentators (Hughes 2007; Johns 2006) dismiss subsistence hunting and gathering as merely recreational, whereas in many areas of remote Australia—particularly in outstation communities—there is evidence that these activities contribute significantly to the health and wellbeing of the population (see, for example, ABC News Online 2006; Barber 2005; McDermott et al. 1998; Morice 1976; Watson 2007). There is, however, nowhere on a census form where people are encouraged to record these activities—not even in the question on unpaid domestic work. Perhaps for the next census that question could be reworded to make it less 'feminine' and 'hunting, fishing or gathering bush food' could be included among the suggested options.

The Indigenous arts industry is a major component of the remote economy (see, for example, Altman 2003). The study area where I observed the enumeration in 2006 contained one extremely successful art centre, many successful and well-known artists and many others who were learning from the more established artists. Despite the inclusion of 'artist' in the list of suggestions for occupations, however, only one or two people put this down as their occupation. It is clear that the majority of people do not really think of art production as a job, and the emphasis in the census questions on sources of regular income—as opposed to intermittent and somewhat unpredictable income—conspires with this attitude to render an important source of income and economic engagement essentially invisible.

From the Yolngu point of view therefore, art production is not a 'job', even if it is a source of income. There are, however, some things considered by Yolngu to be 'jobs' that the mainstream categories ignore. Several senior Yolngu who were CDEP participants described their occupation as 'leader' or 'community leader'. Needless to say, there was no match for these in the CDEP pick list, and it is very unlikely that such are their 'official' CDEP job descriptions. It proved very difficult to deal with such cases even in 'best fit' or by exiting the CDEP module, since equivalent jobs in the mainstream generally imply high levels of formal (Western) education and qualifications, and incomes to match. From the point of view of these senior Yolngu, however, this is indeed their most important job, and it can be demanding and time-consuming.

It is extremely interesting to see these cultural differences in the idea of what is and is not 'work' being played out through the census process. What is frustrating is that none of this complexity is evident in the official output of the census—the tables representing the 'facts and figures' of Indigenous employment. Arguably, however, if effective measures are to be put in place to improve the economic circumstances of Indigenous people, it is as necessary to understand differences in perceptions and values as it is to understand the 'facts' as they appear through the lens of the mainstream.

Conclusion: the representation of Indigenous Australians in the census

In considering this question in the context of the DPC, the most obvious point to be made is: coders can code only what is there in the forms. No matter how advanced and sophisticated the technology, no matter how expert, well-trained and dedicated the staff, no matter how effective the systems for checking internal consistency, the fact remains that one gets out what one puts in. And what is put in is a very partial representation of the Indigenous 'facts', couched in the categories of the mainstream. It was somewhat disconcerting to see such care, thought, expertise and expense being devoted to the processing of this data—in particular, the household data.

The data are partial in at least two senses. Firstly, because of the intercultural difficulties of the enumeration exercise, many data are missed, or presented incoherently. The forms are filled in incompletely or the answers are hard to interpret. Secondly, the data are partial in the sense that it captures only a partial representation of Indigenous lives and circumstances. Some would argue that this is necessary and desirable—the state needs to know only so much about its citizens in order to plan and deliver policy and services. What is more, the census is a broad-brush instrument. It is not designed to capture the subtleties of social life. There are, however, unhelpful cultural biases in this partiality that could be addressed, so that a more *accurate* partial picture emerges—one that would make Indigenous people more recognisable to themselves in the output of the census. To that end, I have gone into some detail on the subject of the representation of the family structures of Indigenous households.

9. Accommodating agency and contingency: towards an extended strategy for engagement

Frances Morphy, Will Sanders and John Taylor

The National Census is a broad-brush instrument with two major objectives: to provide an accurate count of the national population and to collect data on demographic and socioeconomic characteristics that are comparable across different sectors of the population, variously defined. The Indigenous Enumeration Strategy (IES) has evolved through the years in response to the perceived 'difference' of the Aboriginal and Torres Strait Islander populations of Australia. In the 2006 Census, we were in a unique position to observe the workings of the IES, from the design of the collection instrument through to the processing of the data collected in the field. Our findings suggest that the IES has probably reached a point in its development where the injection of ever-increasing resources into essentially the same generic set and structure of activities could begin to produce diminishing returns to output (data quality) unless there is some fundamental reworking of the way in which the strategy is delivered. In particular, we suggest that the manner in which the Australian Bureau of Statistics (ABS) engages with local communities and their organisations needs to change.

We begin with a short discussion of the Interviewer Household Form (IHF) before turning to what emerged as the major theme of our 2006 research: the difficulties of using a dwelling-based count that assumes a sedentary lifestyle to capture a highly mobile population—a population that manifests little consciousness of or interest in the purposes of the census. We will frame this discussion in terms of agency—the agency of Indigenous people and the organisations that sit on the interface between local Indigenous populations and the state—and contingency—the need to accept the contingent factors that influence Indigenous mobility and to build a response to contingency more explicitly into the collection strategy. We argue that to contain the effects of contingency it is necessary for the ABS to make much more productive use of local knowledge at the regional and the local level. In part, this entails building the agency of local institutions into the process much more effectively.

The Interviewer Household Form: from data collection to data coding

As indicated in Chapter 1, evaluation of the IHF was initially a primary objective of the research since the IHF—as a single matrix form—was considerably different from the two-form collection instrument of 2001. In all four case-study accounts (Chapters 3–6), there is a sense that the new IHF (see Appendix A) worked quite well. The most obvious of the remaining structural problems is the ordering of the questions on persons temporarily absent (PTA) before the questions about who was at the dwelling—residents and visitors—at the time of the count. We discuss this issue—which could have had a substantial effect on the adequacy of the count—in Appendix B. All four case studies also contain comments about questions that did not work very well for various reasons. These too are discussed in detail in Appendix B.

After the census count, the observation of the final checking of census forms at the Darwin Census Management Unit (CMU) and the conversion of paper-based returns to computer-read unit record data at the Data Processing Centre (DPC) in Melbourne allowed us to follow raw data all the way from collection to processing. This has provided a unique basis for evaluating census output. Questions such as how household structures are compiled, how occupations are determined and what contributes to final head counts have never before been analysed in this way. While we note the intense, often highly technical, scrutiny of census returns that uses a mix of formulaic criteria and almost forensic guile, at the end of the day there remains an inevitable sense of human agency in decision-making about certain data categorisations, not least because the overarching framework for this in terms of the ultimate purpose of data collection remains, inevitably, a function of state administration.

Observation of the family-coding procedures (Chapter 8) confirmed our findings in 2001 (Morphy 2002, 2004, 2006; see also Morphy 2007) that the census cannot capture fully the complex family structures of Indigenous households and in many ways it is better if it does not try to do so. We conclude that the 2006 questions about relationships within households (Questions 13, 30 and 31) worked better than the 2001 questions, but they could still be improved somewhat (see Appendix B). We argue again also for the recognition of a new coding category of 'extended-family household'.

In the case of occupation coding, the current checklist for the majority of employed Indigenous people in remote Australia working on a Community Development Employment Projects (CDEP) does not adequately identify all economic activity. A significant proportion of the remote-area Indigenous economy therefore remains invisible in the 2006 Census.

These observations on coding point to the very partial way in which the census captures Indigenous social and economic life in remote Australia. We return to this question in a postscript to this chapter.

Common themes

In this section, we focus on common themes that emerged from the four case studies in the field. These observations of the process in 2006 lead to a critique of the structure and processes of the IES and to suggestions for its improvement in 2011. One general initial point to be made—which arises out of the multi-sited nature of the census—is the need for constant monitoring of the flow of information to and from the central administration of the ABS, the regional offices, the Census Field Officers (CFOs) and the field staff, and the need for knowledge and local insights to be kept available locally for the next census exercise and not just fed back to the centre. Where vital links in the information chain failed—as occurred in some instances in regard to the proper placing of PTA on census forms, or in non-response to the Indigenous status question—this had major repercussions down the line, with complications emerging in the determination of final classifications at the DPC. One suggestion for resolving some of the translation issues involved in moving from field encounters to the production of statistical information would be to swap the roles of former DPC and CMU staff—at least in the training of each—so as to bring the different skills, experiences and insights to bear at each end of the process.

The role of the Census Field Officer

In all the case-study areas, with the possible exception of the Alice Springs town camps, the case studies show that the role of the CFO, as presently conceived, is inherently impossible. Various factors contribute to this situation. The size of the areas for which the CFOs are responsible and the logistical difficulties arising from the remoteness of many discrete Indigenous communities from the main concentrations of population—and hence from administrative centres—is an intractable problem. The difficulties the CFOs experienced in three of the case-study areas in recruiting and retaining sufficient numbers of Community Coordinators (CCs) and collector-interviewers (CIs) threatened at times to undermine the whole exercise. In the way that the count is currently organised, the CFO cannot maintain control of the process across the entire region.

The training of the CFOs did not prepare them adequately for the realities of their task. Observation of this training (reported in Chapter 2) revealed two standout issues.

The combination of conducting the Community Housing and Infrastructure Needs Survey (CHINS), compiling the Discrete Indigenous Communities Database (DICD) and promoting upcoming census activities as a preliminary to census training proved a useful device for acquainting newly recruited CFOs with their field areas of responsibility, but the compression of these multiple tasks—especially the CHINS and the compilation of the DICD—into a single short field exercise also served to dilute the efficacy of efforts spent on census preparation and promotion.

Not only were CFOs new to the field operations they were about to encounter, so were those training them. The result was an inability to inject much corporate memory into the training process and this resulted in limited preparation for the many practical issues that individuals would face. To be fair, not all contingencies of this sort could be anticipated, but the truth is that many of the nuances involved in conducting the census were perforce learnt on the job. Essentially, CFO training requires more focus on practicalities and less on process. Greater attention should be given to the content of census forms and this could be aided by more explanation of the concepts, ideas and intentions that underpin form design. For example, the question of PTAs was rightly worrying the CFOs during their training, but they received only limited conceptual or substantive guidance on how to deal with them.

The support offered to the CFOs in the field was limited by structural and technological factors. Lack of access to computerised records that would have informed them of the progress of the count in nearby regions made it impossible for them to check, in the field, whether people 'temporarily absent' from where they were said to be residents were likely to have been counted in the places to which they were said to have gone. Lack of computers in the field also made keeping and updating their own records of progress much more arduous than necessary. They had no email access to the CMU, and were forced to use often-unreliable satellite phone links to maintain contact with the CMU. In the Northern Territory the managers at the CMU were responsible for many other tasks besides overseeing the IES, and often could not respond as quickly as was desirable to queries from the field.

It is significant that the most successful count observed in 2006 was in the Alice Springs town camps, where there was a vast improvement between 2001 and 2006. This can be attributed to two factors: the redesigned IHF and better engagement between the ABS and Tangentyere Council, the organisation that services and represents the town camps. Even in Alice Springs, however, there were factors that prevented the CFO and Tangentyere from cooperating fully with each other. For example, Tangentyere had developed a list of town camp residents through its own research work in 2005, but despite some early ideas about how it might be used, it was not in the end used to assist the census collection process.

At Wadeye and its outstations, there were signs of cooperation early in 2006 between the ABS and the Thamarrurr Regional Council (TRC), but when a suggested workshop at Wadeye failed to eventuate, the TRC began to feel little ownership of the coming census. Thereafter, the 2006 Census at Wadeye was destined to become an encounter between the ABS and individual households, with only limited involvement from the TRC. In the Arnhem Land case study, the local organisations felt no ownership of the census. They were not involved proactively in assisting the CFO, and little attempt was made to encourage proactive involvement. They were nevertheless willing to offer assistance of a limited kind when asked.

In Fitzroy Crossing, there were some boundary problems between the IES and the general census enumeration, which reflected Fitzroy Crossing's status as an open, roadside town in a pastoral area of the Kimberley with a complex mix of Indigenous and settler populations. It appears that there were no formal procedures in place to ensure that the CFO and the Area Supervisor were aware of each other's activities.

The role of the Community Coordinators and collector-interviewers

The recruitment and training processes for CCs and CIs were confounded by the contingencies of life in remote Indigenous communities. Acting as a CC or CI is a complex task. The individual, whose first language is not English in many cases, and who might not have highly developed literacy in English, must master the content of a long and complex form and the elaborate and unfamiliar administrative procedures (outlined in Chapter 1) involved in ensuring the consistency, accuracy and completeness of the count. The training was compressed because of the realistic perception that there was likely to be attrition in attendance if the training went for more than one day, but this compression, and the fact that the CFOs were not themselves trained as trainers, meant that the training delivered to the CCs and CIs was not very effective in many cases. We observed time pressures on the CFOs—the time it took to recruit people and ensure their attendance at training sessions, and the necessity because of this to deliver training to the CCs and CIs in a joint session rather than giving the CCs additional support and training. Time pressures too meant that very often the CFO could not provide sufficient backup and feedback to the CCs and CIs during the early days of the collection process because of the necessity to move on to another community to begin the process again.

As a result, administrative procedures often broke down in the face of the contingencies of everyday life. At Fitzroy Crossing, Master Dwelling Checklists (MDCs) and Interviewer Dwelling Checklists (IDCs) were used in an inverse administrative process for bringing together the paperwork after the enumeration, rather than as a planning tool before the enumeration. At Wadeye and in Arnhem Land, CCs and CIs did not follow the IDCs that they had been given, and arguably this was inevitable when the presence or absence of so many people was contingent on so many factors external to the census enumeration.

Logistics, mobility and the time-extended rolling count

The census as it is currently constructed is essentially a dwelling-based count, which assumes some degree of sedentariness among the population being counted. Remote Indigenous populations, however, behave in 'radically uncontained' ways (Morphy 2007). In Chapter 3, it is shown how this led to major problems for census administration in Arnhem Land, as dwellings—and even whole settlements—were often found empty and people were to be found in all sorts of different places during the extended period of the count. Sometimes people were found away from their usual dwelling, but wanted to be counted and were in fact counted 'as if' they were back there. There was an interesting political aspect to this 'as if' counting, as well as some practical administrative issues. At other times, where someone at least was present at a dwelling, many people were counted as PTAs; however, the ability to judge whether these people would also be enumerated elsewhere was limited.

The account of the Wadeye and outstations enumeration also addresses the theme of the high mobility of the population being counted. In this case, the issue is not just constant mobility between Wadeye, the outstations and nearby Indigenous communities, but a high level of dry-season mobility into Darwin. Although many of the people who were in Darwin were enumerated in the town camps as visitors from Wadeye, many others were camping out. There was concern that these last people were not being counted in Wadeye as PTAs, and also might not be counted in Darwin; or that if they were counted in Darwin on the 'Special Short Form' used for people not associated with a dwelling that this did not identify their community of usual residence, and so they were lost to Wadeye's final de jure count of usual residents.

The account of the 2006 IES in Fitzroy Crossing provides a useful widening of focus across a State/Territory border into Western Australia. The ABS administration in Western Australia clearly envisaged itself as doing a more 'standard' Indigenous enumeration than in the Northern Territory. The intention was that training of CCs and CIs would be done some considerable time before enumeration and that the time extension of enumeration would be kept to a minimum. At least in Fitzroy Crossing, however, and the southern Kimberley, there was not really that much difference from the time-extended rolling count that had been planned for the Northern Territory. Once training was done, there was encouragement to get on with the count straight away in case it took a while. Indeed, the enumeration dragged out in the southern Kimberley in just the same way as in the Northern Territory case studies.

Residents, visitors and 'persons temporarily absent'

There are definitional factors at play in the difficulties encountered by the ABS in enumerating the highly mobile remote Indigenous population. There is the question of how people define 'resident' and 'visitor'; this binary categorisation relies on a settler Australian view of relationship to place that, as the case studies and the observations at the CMU show, is in tension with an Indigenous view that rests on a sense of 'belonging' to a particular place. Then there is the question of what to do about 'residents' who are absent at the time of the count, and how to decide whether or not they are likely to be counted elsewhere.

In the Alice Springs town camps, there was a big improvement on the situation in 2001. Then, many visitors who were present at census time were nonetheless not counted due to the attempt to apply a 'usual residents' or de jure basis for enumeration. In 2006, a de facto approach was adhered to, with the result that all of those present were counted, at least as far as could be ascertained. While the same conceptual approach was adopted at all other sites, some confusion was observed about whether to count certain individuals as 'present' and precisely who qualified as a PTA. The observations at the CMU after the count revealed that this confusion was widespread in the Northern Territory. This was partly a consequence of the instruction to interviewers to be flexible and include people who were away but might not be counted elsewhere—a judgment call that was difficult to make at times for interviewers and interviewees. A fundamental difficulty also arose due to the rolling nature of the enumeration over several weeks, as this lent itself to the possibility of individuals—even households—being overlooked altogether or being double (or even triple) counted.

The reasons for and the regional patterning of PTA phenomena in 2006 need to be analysed in detail—centrally and at the CMU level—so that adequate training on how to treat different kinds of cases can be delivered, to the CFOs initially and then on down the line. Training on this issue should have a scenario component, in which people are presented with a range of 'real-life' examples to decide on. This should happen at all levels of training. It is hoped that the detailed information contained in our observations will allow the ABS to devise a better articulated strategy for dealing with PTAs in 2011. Our research shows that while mobility is pervasive, it is not random, and it also points to other factors that might reduce the scale of the problem: shortening the time frame of the rolling count and making better use of local knowledge.

Suggestions for a new manner of engagement

There will always be problems in enumerating a mobile population in terms of a dwelling-based count. The situation can, however, be ameliorated in three ways: by making better use of local knowledge, by having more and better-trained temporary staff on the ground and by reducing the time during which the enumeration takes place. All of these suggestions point in one direction: to a better form of engagement between the ABS and local institutions and agencies that are repositories of local knowledge and employers of local people.

The involvement of local organisations

Among the CFOs, opinion was divided on the question of how to involve local organisations in the census process. Some felt that they should be involved much more directly in the organisation of the count, so that best use could be made of their local knowledge and of their resources. They saw a need to develop a skill set out in the communities that could be tapped into at census time. Others thought that organisations should be kept at arm's length because they had a conflict of interest: it was felt to be in their interests to maximise the census count in their area because this had resource implications.[1] Given this division of opinion, it is helpful that the evidence from our observations is unequivocal: the single most important factor that can enhance the quality of delivery and outcome from the IES is greater and more sustained engagement with local organisations and their personnel. In the Northern Territory in the future, this sector will include the new regional authorities as well as local community organisations.

The IES is designed in part to take advantage of the local knowledge of CCs and CIs, but it is clear that in the current social dynamic that operates in most communities it is unrealistic to expect the CFOs to be able to find and recruit sufficient numbers of adequately qualified and strongly motivated local Indigenous field staff. A variety of factors are involved, including low levels of literacy and numeracy in remote communities, which reduces the size of the potential pool of workers. Nearly all other major problems with the count follow from this. With inadequate numbers of collectors, the process becomes unduly prolonged and the problem of ensuring an accurate count is compounded by the mobility of the population. Moreover, those collectors who are recruited are faced with very burdensome workloads and, not surprisingly, many of them lose motivation, particularly when the payment system is slow and unsatisfactory. Most recruits are people with many other social obligations and it is easy for those obligations to take precedence over working for the ABS, particularly if people have to work long hours for a prolonged period to complete their workload.

In 2006, it was also possible that the general political climate had alienated many of those people who might have acted as CCs and CIs—that is, those who were more literate and more aware of events in the world beyond the local. Such people are no longer persuaded that taking part in the census delivers benefits

---

[1] The question of the count in CHINS is a different issue: here organisations might legitimately include a 'service' population rather than simply a resident population, since they need the resources to service all of their clients in a mobile population.

to them and their communities. Moreover, there is no sense among the general remote Indigenous population—at least in the communities where we observed the count—that the census enumeration is anything other than yet another 'government' intervention in their lives, which serves no direct purpose as far as they can see. It is viewed as irrelevant to their concerns, so more immediate local events always take precedence over taking part in the census. The inability to recruit sufficient numbers of field staff was a widespread phenomenon, and blame cannot be laid at the door of individual CFOs. The problem lies with the general nature of the engagement between the ABS and local populations.

In 2006, the lack of CCs and CIs, combined with the size of the regions they had to cover, made the job of the CFOs and their assistants well nigh impossible. One of the solutions advocated at the CMU debriefing was, in effect, to throw more bodies into the fray by increasing the number of CFOs next time, and maybe even the number of non-Indigenous CCs and CIs. It was suggested that greater use might also be made in 2011 of the team of Indigenous Assistants from Darwin. Such a solution begins to negate the rationale behind the use of local Indigenous people in the IES, and denies the value of their local knowledge.

There is another way to approach the problem, and that is to increase the sense of ownership of the census process at the local level, not so much by attempting a mass education campaign, but by strategic long-term engagement with local Indigenous organisations and their Indigenous and non-Indigenous staff, and with the staff of the regional authorities in the Northern Territory—once established. Such a relationship could be of mutual benefit.

At the moment, there is not enough capacity to deal with the inevitable contingencies that arise from the unpredictability and the scale of short-term mobility of remote Indigenous populations. It cannot be otherwise when the ABS's primary engagement with remote Indigenous populations is on a short-term basis once every five years.

Harnessing local knowledge more effectively

The detailed description of the course of the census count in part of the Yolngu area of Arnhem Land (Chapter 4) highlighted the major causes of mobility in that particular region: funerals, first and foremost, and other contributory factors such as the need to visit service centres and visit kin in other communities. Although contingent and therefore unpredictable events such as the death of a particular person initiate episodes of mobility, once that mobility is in train its patterns are to some extent predictable to people with detailed knowledge of the networks of kinship and ceremonial connections in a particular region—in other words, to locals with local knowledge. The IES could make much better use of this store of knowledge than it does at the moment, by giving greater responsibility for the planning of the count to locals. It could not do this at the moment, because locals are not qualified to take on such a responsibility.

The CC position therefore needs substantial rethinking, in the context of continuing engagement with local organisations and regional authorities. The emphasis should be on training selected employees—Indigenous and non-Indigenous—in basic demographic methodology, and on their employment on micro-demographic projects and other surveys between censuses, as has happened at Wadeye and Tangentyere, so that, come census time, there is for each Collection District (CD) a set of people already trained for the enhanced CC role. This will decrease the burden on the CFO, who will be able to take a genuinely regional approach to their task and make better and more systematic use of the local knowledge of the CCs. For example, CCs could be alerted to watch out for patterns in the PTA data as they emerge in the field, so that crosschecking with other communities can take place at that point, rather than after the fact. They could also be instrumental in preparing access to local administrative data sets that could assist in providing vital demographic data such as dates of birth.

The enhanced CC role should be extended to responsibility for recruitment and training of the CI workforce. This should enable the training of CIs to take place in a less hurried manner—because it will not be dependent on the presence of the CFO—and will most likely improve recruitment and retention rates because the CCs will be local, will not have to leave the area during the count and will have received some basic training in the management of their CI workforce.

These individuals would be a permanent resource that the ABS could call on. They could be involved actively in promoting the census to their own communities, in engaging and training the CI workforce for the census and in planning the count itself. The role of the CFO would be transformed, and the current regional structure could probably be maintained. In effect, what we suggest is an enhancement of the role of the CC, who would now be a trained person with experience in other survey work for the community, and a corresponding change in the CFO role to that of a regional coordinator and facilitator, with specialist knowledge of census procedures. The CFOs would still provide the CCs with training to carry out the particular census tasks, but they would be training people who already had the skill set required for the job.

These recommendations, if implemented, should also result in less drawn-out counts. It seems incontrovertible that the more the period of the count is extended, the more complex the PTA problem becomes, and the more scope there is for double-counting and for missing people altogether.

All of these recommendations would also improve other aspects of the count. They would result in substantially more complete sets of data for the questions on the form that relate to factors other than just basic age, sex and usual residence. More highly trained CCs would also be able to deliver better training to the CIs on the purposes and meaning of the questions, resulting in improvements in the quality of the data collected.

Underpinning all these changes there should be a much better use of information technology. Databases that are updated in the field for their areas of responsibility by the CFOs and/or the CCs to show the current progress of the count—and that are accessible to all CFOs—would make the task of assessing PTA data much easier in the field, particularly where mobility is occurring across regional boundaries.

It is likely that the institutional landscape of remote Australia, particularly in the Northern Territory, will look very different in 2011. The Northern Territory government's plans for the development of regional authorities and shires is proceeding apace, and many local community organisations will cease to exist, or will be amalgamated into larger organisations with altered functions. The need for good local population data will, however, still be there. Many of the well-established organisations will survive. They will continue to deliver services and infrastructure under contract to their local shires, and increasingly they will become agencies that support and deliver economic development to their members. Unless the ABS keeps abreast of these changes it will experience considerable logistical difficulties in the field in 2011.

At one level, this reorganisation of service delivery in remote parts of the Territory will simplify the task of the ABS: there will be fewer organisations on the ground. At another level, it could increase the difficulty of compiling and updating information at the level of the community or the CD, unless the new regional authorities have the capacity to assist the ABS in this task.

The mutual benefits of continual engagement

For their part, many community organisations—and regional authorities once they are established—would probably welcome a continuing engagement with the ABS. Good-quality demographic data at the local level would help them in their planning at many levels, yet they do not currently have the expertise, time or resources to gather these data effectively for themselves. As a result, local administrative data sets are often very inadequate, and although there is much informal knowledge about patterns of mobility and their effects, formal analyses of mobility are almost non-existent. The ABS—by involving itself creatively in training staff of regional authorities and local organisations to carry out such work—would be helping them help themselves, while simultaneously building capacity in individuals that could be utilised at census time, and also in the context of other ABS surveys.

The symbiotic relationship between the ABS and regional authorities and community organisations would have benefits for all. It would lead to a vast improvement in local administrative data sets and to a more cooperative attitude on the part of organisations in allowing these to be used to validate the census count. Locally based research on patterns of mobility could also contribute significantly to our understanding of population mobility in remote Australia.

Keeping abreast of socio-demographic change

Between now and 2011, there will be considerable changes in the Indigenous landscape in remote Australia, particularly in the Northern Territory, as a result of Commonwealth government policy settings. It is possible that many small outstation or homeland communities will cease to exist, owing to the withdrawal of funding for community housing and infrastructure. It has been proposed that the Community Housing and Infrastructure Program be abolished and that new initiatives to address the need for housing should '[c]ontinue the shift away from building housing on "on country" outstations and homelands and focus on building new housing where there is access to education, health, law and order and other basic services' (PricewaterhouseCooper 2007: 23). Recent changes to—and indeed the abolition of—the CDEP program, and the projected removal of the remote-area exemption for Newstart participants could also have the effect of turning many outstation dwellers into 'economic migrants', compelled to move to larger population centres in pursuit of 'real' jobs. Once again, the ABS needs to monitor these processes in the period leading up to the 2011 census, and the most efficient way to do so is to enlist the local knowledge of the staff of regional authorities and local community organisations.

A new way of thinking

These suggestions involve a new way of thinking about the engagement between the ABS and the Indigenous public, as mediated by the census. They would involve a radical change in the IES. Instead of being an intermittent strategy that manifests itself temporarily every five years, it would become a continual process of engagement. This would obviously have implications for the internal structure of the ABS, at least in the Northern Territory. It would involve the development of an Indigenous engagement unit to replace the single State Indigenous Manager. The unit's initial role would be to make an audit of regional authorities and community organisations to assess their potential as, and interest in being, sites for the training of local people as, in effect, population specialists. The unit could also be responsible for keeping the DICD for its State or Territory up to date. As noted above, given the likelihood of sweeping changes in the institutional landscape of remote Australia in the next few years—and the possibility of substantial changes in settlement patterns—this will be an important task if the ABS is to have good local knowledge in 2011. The development of training materials and local projects would necessitate creative engagement with the TAFE system and/or Charles Darwin University and other tertiary institutions around the country. Certain projects could be university-based research projects with the local organisations as contributing partners.

What is being advocated here is not just incremental improvements to the IES and therefore to the quality of census data on Indigenous Australians. It is a proposal for a new kind of engagement with Indigenous organisations and local government agencies that will ultimately yield high-quality micro-demographic data that will be of substantial benefit to local communities, while simultaneously contributing to the success of future censuses. It is a proposal to harness the agency of local Indigenous people more effectively, in an organisational setting, in pursuit of a strategy that better addresses the complex contingencies that the census process confronts in the field in remote Indigenous Australia.

Postscript: the census and the construction of Indigenous identity

In this book, we have largely taken the existence and the nature of the census as 'given', as a necessary part of the armoury of the modern nation-state. We have focused on ways to make the census in remote Indigenous Australia more effective, in its own terms. We have also pointed to the limitations of the census as a means of capturing and elucidating the social processes and cultural values that pattern the 'facts' of Indigenous demography. We have drawn attention to the culturally constructed nature of Indigenous responses to such questions as those on language and religion, and to the distortion of Indigenous family and household structures that occurs when Western categorisations are imposed on them (see also Morphy 2007). We have also drawn attention to the 'silences' in the data. In particular, the census is silent on significant aspects of remote Indigenous economic activity, such as income derived from art production and the contribution of subsistence activities such as hunting and gathering. This wider question of how Indigenous populations are represented in the census is discussed in most detail in Chapter 8. It has also been addressed previously to some extent in the literature (Ellanna et al. 1988; Jonas 1992; Martin et al. 2002; Martin and Taylor 1996; Morphy 2004, 2006, 2007; Smith 1992).

In making such observations, however, we are also alluding to a literature that we have not addressed explicitly in this monograph: the work of anthropological demographers who critique the cultural assumptions underlying the construction of demographic categories (for example, Bledsoe 2002; Kertzer and Fricke 1997; Szreter et al. 2004), and who examine the role of state instruments such as the census in the construction of sub-national identities (for example, Kertzer and Arel 2002). Taken together, critiques such as these point to the essentially political nature of the census as a tool by which the state makes its citizens 'legible' and thus able to be acted on (Scott 1998). Benedict Anderson (2006: 163) calls the census—specifically in the context of colonial states—an 'institution of power'. As colonised subjects, the Indigenous people of Australia find themselves being categorised and made legible in terms of the assumptions of the settler state that now encapsulates them. The view of them that is constructed in this way feeds in turn into government policy settings and programs. Currently the state—through measures such as the 'National Emergency' intervention in the Northern Territory—is inserting itself ever deeper into the lives of Indigenous people in remote areas. As bodies such as the United Nations recognise (Taylor 2007a), there is an urgent need for a critique of the categories that underlie the census and also other survey tools that the state deploys to capture the demographic and socioeconomic characteristics of Indigenous Australians.

Appendix A. The 2006 Interviewer Household Form

Australian Bureau of Statistics

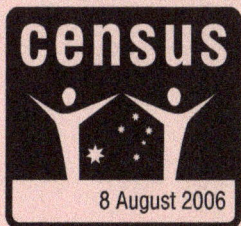

census

8 August 2006

Interviewer Household Form

CD Number | Check Letter | Record Number

□□□□□□□ – □ – □□□□

Form [ ] of [ ]

WHAT YOU NEED TO DO

- Use this form to record details of **all persons** (including visitors) who are staying at this dwelling.
- You can record the details of **twelve** persons on this form. If more than twelve persons are staying at this dwelling, continue on another form.
- Ask **all** questions for **every** person, unless the form asks you not to.
- If a person **does not know** an answer, ask them to give the best answer they can.
- For persons who live at this dwelling most of the time but are **away**, record their details in the table on page 3 (see Questions 10 and 1...

HOW TO ANSWER

- Please use a **black or blue pen.**
- Mark boxes like th : ▬
- Start numbers in the first box. `3 2 1`
- Write in **CAPIT**A. l tters and keep each letter within on : `A R T I S T`
- Use every bo... turn and only miss a box to leave a space between words. `M O T O R   M E C` `H A N I C`
- If you mak .. mistake in a mark box, draw a line through the box like this, or ✦
- dra ... .e through the box and re-w... .e the letters like this: `P A I N T N̶G̶ I N` `G`

Address of dwelling:

P ase use **CAPITAL** letters only.

House number, if any | Street name, if any

[ ][ ][ ][ ][ ] | [ ]

Community name

[ ]

Suburb, rural locality or town

[ ]

State/Territory | Postcode

[ ][ ][ ][ ] | [ ][ ][ ][ ]

These questions ask about this dwelling.

2 **Is this dwelling occupied? (Interviewer to answer)**
- Mark the appropriate box.

☐ Yes
☐ No ▶ **Answer Question 3 only**

3 **Is this dwelling a house? (Interviewer to answer)**
- Mark the appropriate box.

If the dwelling is *unoccupied*, do not answer any more questions.

☐ Yes
☐ No - caravan, tin shed or cabin
☐ No - humpy, tent or sleepout ▶ **Go to 8**

4 **How many bedrooms are there in this dwelling?**
- If the dwelling has no bedrooms, mark the 'None' box like this: ▬

☐☐ Number of bedrooms
☐ None

5 **What is the total amount being paid for this dwelling *each fortnight*?**
- A fortnight means two weeks.
- Include rent and mortgage repayments.
- Exclude electricity, repairs, council rates etc.
- If no payments, please mark the 'Nil payments' box.

$ ☐☐☐ . 0 0 per fortnight
☐ Nil payments

6 **Is this dwelling being rented?**
- Mark the appropriate box.

☐ Yes, rented
☐ No, being bought ▶ **Go to 8**
☐ No, owned ▶ **Go to 8**
☐ No, being occupied rent-free
☐ No, other ▶ **Go to 8**

7 **Who is this dwelling rented from?**

☐ Community or co-operative housing group
☐ Government Housing Authority
☐ Employer - Government
☐ Employer - Private
☐ Other person not in this dwelling

8 **How many registered motor vehicles were parked at this dwelling *last night*?**
- Include vans and work vehicles kept at home.
- Exclude motorbikes and motor scooters.

☐☐ Number of motor vehicles
☐ None

9 **Can the Internet be accessed at this dwelling?**
- Include any Internet service regardless of whether or not paid for by the household.
- If more than one type of connection in dwelling, mark the higher type.

☐ No Internet connection
☐ Yes, broadband connection (including ADSL, Cable, Wireless and Satellite connections)
☐ Yes, dial-up connection (including analog modem and ISDN connections)
☐ Other (include Internet access through mobile phones, etc)

These questions ask about people who live here most of the time but who are away.

10 Are there any persons who live here most of the time but are away?

- ☐ No, no-one away ▶ Go to Question 12 (on page 4)
- ☐ Yes, someone away ▶ Go to Question 11 below

11 For each person who is *away*, fill in the table below:

- For persons who are ***unlikely to be counted elsewhere*** (e.g. away hunting or fishing, away on sorry business, etc) record details at Question 12 on the next page and answer remaining questions on the form as though they are here.

Person away	Name	Sex	Date of Birth OR Age	Where are they? • If another community, write that community name. • If in a town or city, write street number, street name and suburb if known.	Why are they away?
A	First or given name Surname or family name	☐ Male ☐ Female	Day Month Year OR Age Years	Community name/Suburb, locality or town	Reason for being away
B	First or given name Surname or family name	☐ Male ☐ Female	Day Month Year OR Age Years	Community name/Suburb, locality or town	Reason for being away
C	First or given name Surname or family name	☐ Male ☐ Female	Day Month Year OR Age Years	Community name/Suburb, locality or town	Reason for being away
D	First or given name Surname or family name	☐ Male ☐ Female	Day Month Year OR Age Years	Community name/Suburb, locality or town	Reason for being away
E	First or given name Surname or family name	☐ Male ☐ Female	Day Month Year OR Age Years	Community name/Suburb, locality or town	Reason for being away
F	First or given name Surname or family name	☐ Male ☐ Female	Day Month Year OR Age Years	Community name/Suburb, locality or town	Reason for being away
G	First or given name Surname or family name	☐ Male ☐ Female	Day Month Year OR Age Years	Community name/Suburb, locality or town	Reason for being away
H	First or given name Surname or family name	☐ Male ☐ Female	Day Month Year OR Age Years	Community name/Suburb, locality or town	Reason for being away

These questions ask about people who are living or staying here now.

Person Number

12 For the persons *present in this dwelling*, complete the following questions:
- Record the head of house as **Person 1** and, if present, their spouse or partner as **Person 2**.
- Record details for all adults, children, babies and visitors.
- Record details for persons who are away but who are unlikely to be counted elsewhere (e.g. away hunting or fishing, away on sorry business, etc.)

	Name	Is the person a visitor?	Sex	Date of Birth OR Age
Person 1	First or given name / Surname or family name	No / Yes	Male / Female	Day Month Year OR Age Years
Person 2	First or given name / Surname or family name	No / Yes	Male / Female	Day Month Year OR Age Years
Person 3	First or given name / Surname or family name	No / Yes	Male / Female	Day Month Year OR Age Years
Person 4	First or given name / Surname or family name	No / Yes	Male / Female	Day Month Year OR Age Years
Person 5	First or given name / Surname or family name	No / Yes	Male / Female	Day Month Year OR Age Years
Person 6	First or given name / Surname or family name	No / Yes	Male / Female	Day Month Year OR Age Years
Person 7	First or given name / Surname or family name	No / Yes	Male / Female	Day Month Year OR Age Years
Person 8	First or given name / Surname or family name	No / Yes	Male / Female	Day Month Year OR Age Years
Person 9	First or given name / Surname or family name	No / Yes	Male / Female	Day Month Year OR Age Years
Person 10	First or given name / Surname or family name	No / Yes	Male / Female	Day Month Year OR Age Years
Person 11	First or given name / Surname or family name	No / Yes	Male / Female	Day Month Year OR Age Years
Person 12	First or given name / Surname or family name	No / Yes	Male / Female	Day Month Year OR Age Years

If there are more than 12 persons in this dwelling, continue on to a second form.

13 How is the person related to Person 1/Person 2?
- Some examples of other relationships are: BROTHER, SISTER, UNCLE, AUNT, SON-IN-LAW, DAUGHTER-IN-LAW, FRIEND, UNRELATED.

14 Is the person married?
- 'Married' refers to registered marriage.
- If the person is in a traditional Aboriginal or Torres Strait Islander marriage, mark the 'Married' box.

Person No.

Person 1

No answer to this question required for Person 1

- Never married
- Widowed
- Divorced
- Separated but not divorced
- Married

Person 2

- Husband or wife of Person 1
- De facto partner of Person 1
- Child of Person 1
- Grandchild of Person 1

Other relationship to Person 1 - please specify

- Never married
- Widowed
- Divorced
- Separated but not divorced
- Married

Person 3

- Child of both Person 1 and Person 2
- Child of Person 1 only
- Child of Person 2 only
- Grandchild of Person 1

Other relationship to Person 1 - please specify

- Never married
- Widowed
- Divorced
- Separated but not divorced
- Married

Person 4

- Child of both Person 1 and Person 2
- Child of Person 1 only
- Child of Person 2 only
- Grandchild of Person 1

Other relationship to Person 1 - please specify

- Never married
- Widowed
- Divorced
- Separated but not divorced
- Married

Person 5

- Child of both Person 1 and Person 2
- Child of Person 1 only
- Child of Person 2 only
- Grandchild of Person 1

Other relationship to Person 1 - please specify

- Never married
- Widowed
- Divorced
- Separated but not divorced
- Married

Person 6

- Child of both Person 1 and Person 2
- Child of Person 1 only
- Child of Person 2 only
- Grandchild of Person 1

Other relationship to Person 1 - please specify

- Never married
- Widowed
- Divorced
- Separated but not divorced
- Married

Person 7

- Child of both Person 1 and Person 2
- Child of Person 1 only
- Child of Person 2 only
- Grandchild of Person 1

Other relationship to Person 1 - please specify

- Never married
- Widowed
- Divorced
- Separated but not divorced
- Married

Person 8

- Child of both Person 1 and Person 2
- Child of Person 1 only
- Child of Person 2 only
- Grandchild of Person 1

Other relationship to Person 1 - please specify

- Never married
- Widowed
- Divorced
- Separated but not divorced
- Married

Person 9

- Child of both Person 1 and Person 2
- Child of Person 1 only
- Child of Person 2 only
- Grandchild of Person 1

Other relationship to Person 1 - please specify

- Never married
- Widowed
- Divorced
- Separated but not divorced
- Married

Person 10

- Child of both Person 1 and Person 2
- Child of Person 1 only
- Child of Person 2 only
- Grandchild of Person 1

Other relationship to Person 1 - please specify

- Never married
- Widowed
- Divorced
- Separated but not divorced
- Married

Person 11

- Child of both Person 1 and Person 2
- Child of Person 1 only
- Child of Person 2 only
- Grandchild of Person 1

Other relationship to Person 1 - please specify

- Never married
- Widowed
- Divorced
- Separated but not divorced
- Married

Person 12

- Child of both Person 1 and Person 2
- Child of Person 1 only
- Child of Person 2 only
- Grandchild of Person 1

Other relationship to Person 1 - please specify

- Never married
- Widowed
- Divorced
- Separated but not divorced
- Married

15 Where does the person live most of the time?

- If another community, write that community name in the 'Elsewhere - please specify' boxes.
- If another town or city, write street number and street name (if known), suburb, rural locality or town in the 'Elsewhere - please specify' boxes.
- If another country, write name of that country in the 'Elsewhere - please specify' boxes.

Person No.

1
- ☐ This community
- ☐ Elsewhere - please specify

State/Territory

2
- ☐ This community
- ☐ Elsewhere - please specify

State/Territory

3
- ☐ This community
- ☐ Elsewhere - please specify

State/Territory

4
- ☐ This community
- ☐ Elsewhere - please specify

State/Territory

5
- ☐ This community
- ☐ Elsewhere - please specify

State/Territory

6
- ☐ This community
- ☐ Elsewhere - please specify

State/Territory

7
- ☐ This community
- ☐ Elsewhere - please specify

State/Territory

8
- ☐ This community
- ☐ Elsewhere - please specify

State/Territory

9
- ☐ This community
- ☐ Elsewhere - please specify

State/Territory

10
- ☐ This community
- ☐ Elsewhere - please specify

State/Territory

11
- ☐ This community
- ☐ Elsewhere - please specify

State/Territory

12
- ☐ This community
- ☐ Elsewhere - please specify

State/Territory

16 Where did the person live most of the time one year ago?

- If the person is a **baby** less than one year old, leave the question blank.
- If another community, write that community name in the 'Elsewhere - please specify' boxes.
- If another town or city, write street number and street name (if known), suburb, rural locality or town in the 'Elsewhere - please specify' boxes.
- If another country, write name of that country in the 'Elsewhere - please specify' boxes.

Person No.

1
- ☐ This community
- ☐ Elsewhere - please specify   State/Territory

2
- ☐ This community
- ☐ Elsewhere - please specify   State/Territory

3
- ☐ This community
- ☐ Elsewhere - please specify   State/Territory

4
- ☐ This community
- ☐ Elsewhere - please specify   State/Territory

5
- ☐ This community
- ☐ Elsewhere - please specify   State/Territory

6
- ☐ This community
- ☐ Elsewhere - please specify   State/Territory

7
- ☐ This community
- ☐ Elsewhere - please specify   State/Territory

8
- ☐ This community
- ☐ Elsewhere - please specify   State/Territory

9
- ☐ This community
- ☐ Elsewhere - please specify   State/Territory

10
- ☐ This community
- ☐ Elsewhere - please specify   State/Territory

11
- ☐ This community
- ☐ Elsewhere - please specify   State/Territory

12
- ☐ This community
- ☐ Elsewhere - please specify   State/Territory

17 Where did the person live most of the time five years ago?

- If the person is a **child** less than five years old, leave the question blank.
- If another community, write that community name in the 'Elsewhere - please specify' boxes.
- If another town or city, write street number and street name (if known), suburb, rural locality or town in the 'Elsewhere - please specify' boxes.
- If another country, write name of that country in the 'Elsewhere - please specify' boxes.

Person No.

1
- ☐ This community
- ☐ Elsewhere - please specify

State/Territory

2
- ☐ This community
- ☐ Elsewhere - please specify

State/Territory

3
- ☐ This community
- ☐ Elsewhere - please specify

State/Territory

4
- ☐ This community
- ☐ Elsewhere - please specify

State/Territory

5
- ☐ This community
- ☐ Elsewhere - please specify

State/Territory

6
- ☐ This community
- ☐ Elsewhere - please specify

State/Territory

7
- ☐ This community
- ☐ Elsewhere - please specify

State/Territory

8
- ☐ This community
- ☐ Elsewhere - please specify

State/Territory

9
- ☐ This community
- ☐ Elsewhere - please specify

State/Territory

10
- ☐ This community
- ☐ Elsewhere - please specify

State/Territory

11
- ☐ This community
- ☐ Elsewhere - please specify

State/Territory

12
- ☐ This community
- ☐ Elsewhere - please specify

State/Territory

Person No.	18 Is the person of Aboriginal or Torres Strait Islander origin? • If the person is of both Aboriginal and Torres Strait Islander origin, mark the 'Yes, both Aboriginal and Torres Strait Islander' box.		19 Was the person's father born in Australia?	20 Was the person's mother born in Australia?
1	☐ Yes, Aboriginal ☐ Yes, Torres Strait Islander	☐ Yes, both Aboriginal and Torres Strait Islander ☐ No	☐ Yes, Australia ☐ No, other country	☐ Yes, Australia ☐ No, other country
2	☐ Yes, Aboriginal ☐ Yes, Torres Strait Islander	☐ Yes, both Aboriginal and Torres Strait Islander ☐ No	☐ Yes, Australia ☐ No, other country	☐ Yes, Australia ☐ No, other country
3	☐ Yes, Aboriginal ☐ Yes, Torres Strait Islander	☐ Yes, both Aboriginal and Torres Strait Islander ☐ No	☐ Yes, Australia ☐ No, other country	☐ Yes, Australia ☐ No, other country
4	☐ Yes, Aboriginal ☐ Yes, Torres Strait Islander	☐ Yes, both Aboriginal and Torres Strait Islander ☐ No	☐ Yes, Australia ☐ No, other country	☐ Yes, Australia ☐ No, other country
5	☐ Yes, Aboriginal ☐ Yes, Torres Strait Islander	☐ Yes, both Aboriginal and Torres Strait Islander ☐ No	☐ Yes, Australia ☐ No, other country	☐ Yes, Australia ☐ No, other country
6	☐ Yes, Aboriginal ☐ Yes, Torres Strait Islander	☐ Yes, both Aboriginal and Torres Strait Islander ☐ No	☐ Yes, Australia ☐ No, other country	☐ Yes, Australia ☐ No, other country
7	☐ Yes, Aboriginal ☐ Yes, Torres Strait Islander	☐ Yes, both Aboriginal and Torres Strait Islander ☐ No	☐ Yes, Australia ☐ No, other country	☐ Yes, Australia ☐ No, other country
8	☐ Yes, Aboriginal ☐ Yes, Torres Strait Islander	☐ Yes, both Aboriginal and Torres Strait Islander ☐ No	☐ Yes, Australia ☐ No, other country	☐ Yes, Australia ☐ No, other country
9	☐ Yes, Aboriginal ☐ Yes, Torres Strait Islander	☐ Yes, both Aboriginal and Torres Strait Islander ☐ No	☐ Yes, Australia ☐ No, other country	☐ Yes, Australia ☐ No, other country
10	☐ Yes, Aboriginal ☐ Yes, Torres Strait Islander	☐ Yes, both Aboriginal and Torres Strait Islander ☐ No	☐ Yes, Australia ☐ No, other country	☐ Yes, Australia ☐ No, other country
11	☐ Yes, Aboriginal ☐ Yes, Torres Strait Islander	☐ Yes, both Aboriginal and Torres Strait Islander ☐ No	☐ Yes, Australia ☐ No, other country	☐ Yes, Australia ☐ No, other country
12	☐ Yes, Aboriginal ☐ Yes, Torres Strait Islander	☐ Yes, both Aboriginal and Torres Strait Islander ☐ No	☐ Yes, Australia ☐ No, other country	☐ Yes, Australia ☐ No, other country

21 Does the person speak an Aboriginal or Torres Strait Islander language at _home_?
- If Aboriginal or Torres Strait Islander language, please write the name of the language.
- If more than one language, indicate the language that is spoken most.

22 How well does the person speak _English_?

Person No.

1
- Yes - write name of language
- No, speaks only English

☐ Very well ☐ Not well
☐ Well ☐ Not at all

2
- Yes, same as Person 1
- Yes, other - please specify language
- No, speaks only English

☐ Very well ☐ Not well
☐ Well ☐ Not at all

3
- Yes, same as Person 1
- Yes, other - please specify language
- No, speaks only English

☐ Very well ☐ Not well
☐ Well ☐ Not at all

4
- Yes, same as Person 1
- Yes, other - please specify language
- No, speaks only English

☐ Very well ☐ Not well
☐ Well ☐ Not at all

5
- Yes, same as Person 1
- Yes, other - please specify language
- No, speaks only English

☐ Very well ☐ Not well
☐ Well ☐ Not at all

6
- Yes, same as Person 1
- Yes, other - please specify language
- No, speaks only English

☐ Very well ☐ Not well
☐ Well ☐ Not at all

7
- Yes, same as Person 1
- Yes, other - please specify language
- No, speaks only English

☐ Very well ☐ Not well
☐ Well ☐ Not at all

8
- Yes, same as Person 1
- Yes, other - please specify language
- No, speaks only English

☐ Very well ☐ Not well
☐ Well ☐ Not at all

9
- Yes, same as Person 1
- Yes, other - please specify language
- No, speaks only English

☐ Very well ☐ Not well
☐ Well ☐ Not at all

10
- Yes, same as Person 1
- Yes, other - please specify language
- No, speaks only English

☐ Very well ☐ Not well
☐ Well ☐ Not at all

11
- Yes, same as Person 1
- Yes, other - please specify language
- No, speaks only English

☐ Very well ☐ Not well
☐ Well ☐ Not at all

12
- Yes, same as Person 1
- Yes, other - please specify language
- No, speaks only English

☐ Very well ☐ Not well
☐ Well ☐ Not at all

23 What is the person's ancestry?
- Record up to two ancestries.
- Some examples of 'Other-please specify' are:
  SCOTTISH, MALAY, NEW GUINEAN, ENGLISH,
  MAORI, CHINESE, SAMOAN, IRISH,
  AUSTRALIAN SOUTH SEA ISLANDER.

24 What is the person's religion?
- Answering this question is OPTIONAL.
- Some examples are: TRADITIONAL BELIEFS,
  ANGLICAN (CHURCH OF ENGLAND), CATHOLIC,
  UNITING CHURCH, LUTHERAN, BAPTIST,
  ABORIGINAL EVANGELICAL MISSIONS.
- If no religion, mark the 'No religion' box.

25 For each female, how many babies has she ever given birth to?
- Include live births only.
- Exclude adopted, foster and step children.

Person No.

1
Aboriginal / Torres Strait Islander / Other - please specify
Write religion here / No religion
Number of babies / None

2–12
Aboriginal / Torres Strait Islander / Other - please specify
Same as Person 1 / Other - please specify / No religion
Number of babies / None

Person No.	26 Does the person ever need someone to help them do everyday things such as eating, washing themselves, dressing or using the toilet?	27 Does the person ever need someone to help them move around? For example, getting out of bed, walking, climbing stairs, getting out of a chair.	28 Does the person ever need someone to help with understanding other people or being understood by other people?	29 Why does the person need help in the areas shown in questions 26, 27 and 28? • Mark all reasons for needing help or assistance.
1	Yes, always / Yes, sometimes / No	Yes, always / Yes, sometimes / No	Yes, always / Yes, sometimes / No	No need for help / Short-term health condition (lasting less than 6 months) / Long-term health condition (lasting 6 months or more) / Disability (lasting 6 months or more) / Old or young age / Difficulty with English language / Other cause
2	Yes, always / Yes, sometimes / No	Yes, always / Yes, sometimes / No	Yes, always / Yes, sometimes / No	No need for help / Short-term health condition (lasting less than 6 months) / Long-term health condition (lasting 6 months or more) / Disability (lasting 6 months or more) / Old or young age / Difficulty with English language / Other cause
3	Yes, always / Yes, sometimes / No	Yes, always / Yes, sometimes / No	Yes, always / Yes, sometimes / No	No need for help / Short-term health condition (lasting less than 6 months) / Long-term health condition (lasting 6 months or more) / Disability (lasting 6 months or more) / Old or young age / Difficulty with English language / Other cause
4	Yes, always / Yes, sometimes / No	Yes, always / Yes, sometimes / No	Yes, always / Yes, sometimes / No	No need for help / Short-term health condition (lasting less than 6 months) / Long-term health condition (lasting 6 months or more) / Disability (lasting 6 months or more) / Old or young age / Difficulty with English language / Other cause
5	Yes, always / Yes, sometimes / No	Yes, always / Yes, sometimes / No	Yes, always / Yes, sometimes / No	No need for help / Short-term health condition (lasting less than 6 months) / Long-term health condition (lasting 6 months or more) / Disability (lasting 6 months or more) / Old or young age / Difficulty with English language / Other cause
6	Yes, always / Yes, sometimes / No	Yes, always / Yes, sometimes / No	Yes, always / Yes, sometimes / No	No need for help / Short-term health condition (lasting less than 6 months) / Long-term health condition (lasting 6 months or more) / Disability (lasting 6 months or more) / Old or young age / Difficulty with English language / Other cause
7	Yes, always / Yes, sometimes / No	Yes, always / Yes, sometimes / No	Yes, always / Yes, sometimes / No	No need for help / Short-term health condition (lasting less than 6 months) / Long-term health condition (lasting 6 months or more) / Disability (lasting 6 months or more) / Old or young age / Difficulty with English language / Other cause
8	Yes, always / Yes, sometimes / No	Yes, always / Yes, sometimes / No	Yes, always / Yes, sometimes / No	No need for help / Short-term health condition (lasting less than 6 months) / Long-term health condition (lasting 6 months or more) / Disability (lasting 6 months or more) / Old or young age / Difficulty with English language / Other cause
9	Yes, always / Yes, sometimes / No	Yes, always / Yes, sometimes / No	Yes, always / Yes, sometimes / No	No need for help / Short-term health condition (lasting less than 6 months) / Long-term health condition (lasting 6 months or more) / Disability (lasting 6 months or more) / Old or young age / Difficulty with English language / Other cause
10	Yes, always / Yes, sometimes / No	Yes, always / Yes, sometimes / No	Yes, always / Yes, sometimes / No	No need for help / Short-term health condition (lasting less than 6 months) / Long-term health condition (lasting 6 months or more) / Disability (lasting 6 months or more) / Old or young age / Difficulty with English language / Other cause
11	Yes, always / Yes, sometimes / No	Yes, always / Yes, sometimes / No	Yes, always / Yes, sometimes / No	No need for help / Short-term health condition (lasting less than 6 months) / Long-term health condition (lasting 6 months or more) / Disability (lasting 6 months or more) / Old or young age / Difficulty with English language / Other cause
12	Yes, always / Yes, sometimes / No	Yes, always / Yes, sometimes / No	Yes, always / Yes, sometimes / No	No need for help / Short-term health condition (lasting less than 6 months) / Long-term health condition (lasting 6 months or more) / Disability (lasting 6 months or more) / Old or young age / Difficulty with English language / Other cause

	30 Is the person's mother staying in the dwelling?	31 Is the person's father staying in the dwelling?	32 Is the person attending a school or any other educational institution?
Person No.	• Include birth, adoptive, step or foster mother. • The Person number is listed at Question 12 on page 4.	• Include birth, adoptive, step or foster father. • The Person number is listed at Question 12 on page 4.	• Include school of the air, external or correspondence students. • Include pre-school students. • Include students of other education or training providers.
1	Yes - please specify **mother's** Person number (see Question 12 on page 4) ☐☐ ☐ No	Yes - please specify **father's** Person number (see Question 12 on page 4) ☐☐ ☐ No	☐ No ☐ Yes, full-time student ☐ Yes, part-time student
2	Yes - please specify **mother's** Person number (see Question 12 on page 4) ☐☐ ☐ No	Yes - please specify **father's** Person number (see Question 12 on page 4) ☐☐ ☐ No	☐ No ☐ Yes, full-time student ☐ Yes, part-time student
3	Yes - please specify **mother's** Person number (see Question 12 on page 4) ☐☐ ☐ No	Yes - please specify **father's** Person number (see Question 12 on page 4) ☐☐ ☐ No	☐ No ☐ Yes, full-time student ☐ Yes, part-time student
4	Yes - please specify **mother's** Person number (see Question 12 on page 4) ☐☐ ☐ No	Yes - please specify **father's** Person number (see Question 12 on page 4) ☐☐ ☐ No	☐ No ☐ Yes, full-time student ☐ Yes, part-time student
5	Yes - please specify **mother's** Person number (see Question 12 on page 4) ☐☐ ☐ No	Yes - please specify **father's** Person number (see Question 12 on page 4) ☐☐ ☐ No	☐ No ☐ Yes, full-time student ☐ Yes, part-time student
6	Yes - please specify **mother's** Person number (see Question 12 on page 4) ☐☐ ☐ No	Yes - please specify **father's** Person number (see Question 12 on page 4) ☐☐ ☐ No	☐ No ☐ Yes, full-time student ☐ Yes, part-time student
7	Yes - please specify **mother's** Person number (see Question 12 on page 4) ☐☐ ☐ No	Yes - please specify **father's** Person number (see Question 12 on page 4) ☐☐ ☐ No	☐ No ☐ Yes, full-time student ☐ Yes, part-time student
8	Yes - please specify **mother's** Person number (see Question 12 on page 4) ☐☐ ☐ No	Yes - please specify **father's** Person number (see Question 12 on page 4) ☐☐ ☐ No	☐ No ☐ Yes, full-time student ☐ Yes, part-time student
9	Yes - please specify **mother's** Person number (see Question 12 on page 4) ☐☐ ☐ No	Yes - please specify **father's** Person number (see Question 12 on page 4) ☐☐ ☐ No	☐ No ☐ Yes, full-time student ☐ Yes, part-time student
10	Yes - please specify **mother's** Person number (see Question 12 on page 4) ☐☐ ☐ No	Yes - please specify **father's** Person number (see Question 12 on page 4) ☐☐ ☐ No	☐ No ☐ Yes, full-time student ☐ Yes, part-time student
11	Yes - please specify **mother's** Person number (see Question 12 on page 4) ☐☐ ☐ No	Yes - please specify **father's** Person number (see Question 12 on page 4) ☐☐ ☐ No	☐ No ☐ Yes, full-time student ☐ Yes, part-time student
12	Yes - please specify **mother's** Person number (see Question 12 on page 4) ☐☐ ☐ No	Yes - please specify **father's** Person number (see Question 12 on page 4) ☐☐ ☐ No	☐ No ☐ Yes, full-time student ☐ Yes, part-time student

33 What type of educational institution is the person attending?

- Mark one box only.
- Include school of the air, external or correspondence students.
- Include secondary colleges and senior high schools under the 'Secondary school' category.

Person No.

For each person (1–12), the following options are provided:

	None	Infants/Primary school	Secondary school	Tertiary Institution	Other education or training provider
	Pre-school	Government Catholic Other non-government	Government Catholic Other non-government	TAFE Institution/College University or other higher educational institution	

Person 1 through **Person 12** each repeat the above set of options.

34 What is the highest year of primary or secondary school the person has *completed*?

- Mark one box only.
- For persons who have gone back to school, mark the highest year they have completed.
- For persons who did schooling in the mission days, mark the 'Year 8 or below' box.

35 Has the person *completed* a trade certificate/apprenticeship, TAFE course, university course or other course?

- Mark one box only.

Person No.

For each person (1–12), the following options are provided:

Question 34:
- Person aged under 15 years
- Did not go to school
- Went to primary school
- Finished primary school
- Year 8 or below
- Year 9 or equivalent
- Year 10 or equivalent
- Year 11 or equivalent
- Year 12 or equivalent

Question 35:
- No
- No, still studying for first qualification
- Yes, trade certificate/apprenticeship
- Yes, other qualification

36 What is the level of the *highest* qualification that the person has *completed*?

- For example: TRADE CERTIFICATE, BACHELOR DEGREE, ASSOCIATE DIPLOMA, CERTIFICATE I, CERTIFICATE II, ADVANCED DIPLOMA.

37 What is the main field of study for the *highest* qualification that the person has *completed*?

- For example: PLUMBING, HISTORY, ABORIGINAL HEALTH, PARK MANAGEMENT.

Person No.

1
Level of qualification
☐ No qualification, or still studying for first qualification
Field of study
☐ No qualification, or still studying for first qualification

2
Level of qualification
☐ No qualification, or still studying for first qualification
Field of study
☐ No qualification, or still studying for first qualification

3
Level of qualification
☐ No qualification, or still studying for first qualification
Field of study
☐ No qualification, or still studying for first qualification

4
Level of qualification
☐ No qualification, or still studying for first qualification
Field of study
☐ No qualification, or still studying for first qualification

5
Level of qualification
☐ No qualification, or still studying for first qualification
Field of study
☐ No qualification, or still studying for first qualification

6
Level of qualification
☐ No qualification, or still studying for first qualification
Field of study
☐ No qualification, or still studying for first qualification

7
Level of qualification
☐ No qualification, or still studying for first qualification
Field of study
☐ No qualification, or still studying for first qualification

8
Level of qualification
☐ No qualification, or still studying for first qualification
Field of study
☐ No qualification, or still studying for first qualification

9
Level of qualification
☐ No qualification, or still studying for first qualification
Field of study
☐ No qualification, or still studying for first qualification

10
Level of qualification
☐ No qualification, or still studying for first qualification
Field of study
☐ No qualification, or still studying for first qualification

11
Level of qualification
☐ No qualification, or still studying for first qualification
Field of study
☐ No qualification, or still studying for first qualification

12
Level of qualification
☐ No qualification, or still studying for first qualification
Field of study
☐ No qualification, or still studying for first qualification

38 What was the name of the educational institution where the person *completed* their *highest* qualification?
- Include institutions where the person has completed external or correspondence studies.
- Include other training providers.

39 Did the person *complete* this qualification before 1998?

Person No.

Person 1
Name of educational institution

☐ No qualification, or still studying for first qualification

☐ Yes, before 1998
☐ No, 1998 or later
☐ No qualification, or still studying for first qualification

Person 2
Name of educational institution

☐ No qualification, or still studying for first qualification

☐ Yes, before 1998
☐ No, 1998 or later
☐ No qualification, or still studying for first qualification

Person 3
Name of educational institution

☐ No qualification, or still studying for first qualification

☐ Yes, before 1998
☐ No, 1998 or later
☐ No qualification, or still studying for first qualification

Person 4
Name of educational institution

☐ No qualification, or still studying for first qualification

☐ Yes, before 1998
☐ No, 1998 or later
☐ No qualification, or still studying for first qualification

Person 5
Name of educational institution

☐ No qualification, or still studying for first qualification

☐ Yes, before 1998
☐ No, 1998 or later
☐ No qualification, or still studying for first qualification

Person 6
Name of educational institution

☐ No qualification, or still studying for first qualification

☐ Yes, before 1998
☐ No, 1998 or later
☐ No qualification, or still studying for first qualification

Person 7
Name of educational institution

☐ No qualification, or still studying for first qualification

☐ Yes, before 1998
☐ No, 1998 or later
☐ No qualification, or still studying for first qualification

Person 8
Name of educational institution

☐ No qualification, or still studying for first qualification

☐ Yes, before 1998
☐ No, 1998 or later
☐ No qualification, or still studying for first qualification

Person 9
Name of educational institution

☐ No qualification, or still studying for first qualification

☐ Yes, before 1998
☐ No, 1998 or later
☐ No qualification, or still studying for first qualification

Person 10
Name of educational institution

☐ No qualification, or still studying for first qualification

☐ Yes, before 1998
☐ No, 1998 or later
☐ No qualification, or still studying for first qualification

Person 11
Name of educational institution

☐ No qualification, or still studying for first qualification

☐ Yes, before 1998
☐ No, 1998 or later
☐ No qualification, or still studying for first qualification

Person 12
Name of educational institution

☐ No qualification, or still studying for first qualification

☐ Yes, before 1998
☐ No, 1998 or later
☐ No qualification, or still studying for first qualification

40 How much money does the person get each *fortnight* before tax or anything else is taken out?
- Mark one box only.
- A fortnight means two weeks.
- Include wages, Centrelink, government payments, CDEP money, pensions, art sales, and any other money, before tax or anything else is taken out.
- Do not take out automatic deductions such as rent and housing costs.

41 *Last week* did the person have a paid job of any kind?
- Answer for the **main job** only. The **main job** is the job in which the person works the most hours.
- A job means any type of paid work including casual or temporary work or part-time work if it was for one hour or more.
- If the person was off work because of holidays, sick leave, ceremony or cultural activities, then mark the appropriate "Yes" box for their main job.

Person No.

For each Person (1–12):

Question 40 options:
- Nil income
- $1-$299
- $300-$499
- $500-$799
- $800-$1,199
- $1,200-$1,599
- $1,600-$1,999
- $2,000-$2,599
- $2,600-$3,199
- $3,200-$3,999
- $4,000 or more

Question 41 options:
- Yes, CDEP job
- Yes, job not CDEP
- Yes, worked in own business
- No, did not have a job

	42 In the main job held *last week*, what was the person's occupation?	**43** What are the main tasks that the person usually performs in that occupation?

42: • For example: CLEANER, COUNCIL LABOURER, STATION HAND, REGISTERED NURSE, SHOP ASSISTANT, MOTOR MECHANIC, ARTIST.

43: • For example: CLEANS SCHOOL, COLLECTS RUBBISH, MUSTERS CATTLE, LOOKS AFTER OLD PEOPLE, SELLS FOOD AND SUPPLIES, FIXES CARS AND TRUCKS, DOES PAINTINGS TO SELL.

Person No.

1 Occupation — Did not have a job | Tasks or duties — Did not have a job
2 Occupation — Did not have a job | Tasks or duties — Did not have a job
3 Occupation — Did not have a job | Tasks or duties — Did not have a job
4 Occupation — Did not have a job | Tasks or duties — Did not have a job
5 Occupation — Did not have a job | Tasks or duties — Did not have a job
6 Occupation — Did not have a job | Tasks or duties — Did not have a job
7 Occupation — Did not have a job | Tasks or duties — Did not have a job
8 Occupation — Did not have a job | Tasks or duties — Did not have a job
9 Occupation — Did not have a job | Tasks or duties — Did not have a job
10 Occupation — Did not have a job | Tasks or duties — Did not have a job
11 Occupation — Did not have a job | Tasks or duties — Did not have a job
12 Occupation — Did not have a job | Tasks or duties — Did not have a job

44 For the *main job* held *last week*, who did the person work for?
- If it is the community council, write the community's name.
- For self-employed persons, write the name of the business.

45 For the *main job* held last week, where was the person's workplace?
- If it is not this community, write the name of the community, suburb, rural locality or town in the 'Elsewhere' box.

Person No.

No.	Name of employer/business	This community / Elsewhere
1	☐ Did not have a job	☐ This community / Elsewhere ☐ Did not have a job
2	☐ Did not have a job	☐ This community / Elsewhere ☐ Did not have a job
3	☐ Did not have a job	☐ This community / Elsewhere ☐ Did not have a job
4	☐ Did not have a job	☐ This community / Elsewhere ☐ Did not have a job
5	☐ Did not have a job	☐ This community / Elsewhere ☐ Did not have a job
6	☐ Did not have a job	☐ This community / Elsewhere ☐ Did not have a job
7	☐ Did not have a job	☐ This community / Elsewhere ☐ Did not have a job
8	☐ Did not have a job	☐ This community / Elsewhere ☐ Did not have a job
9	☐ Did not have a job	☐ This community / Elsewhere ☐ Did not have a job
10	☐ Did not have a job	☐ This community / Elsewhere ☐ Did not have a job
11	☐ Did not have a job	☐ This community / Elsewhere ☐ Did not have a job
12	☐ Did not have a job	☐ This community / Elsewhere ☐ Did not have a job

Sample only

46 For the *main job* held *last week*, what did the person's employer do?
- Describe using two words or more, for example: PROVIDES PRIMARY SCHOOL EDUCATION, BEEF CATTLE FARMING, COMMUNITY HEALTH SERVICE, COMMUNITY CARE SERVICE, MAKES ARTWORK OR CRAFTS.
- For self employed persons describe the type of industry, business or service provided by their business.

47 *Last week*, how many hours did the person work in all jobs?
- Add any overtime or extra time worked.
- Subtract any time off.

Person No.

No.	Industry, business or service of employer	Hours worked last week
1	Did not have a job	None / Did not have a job
2	Did not have a job	None / Did not have a job
3	Did not have a job	None / Did not have a job
4	Did not have a job	None / Did not have a job
5	Did not have a job	None / Did not have a job
6	Did not have a job	None / Did not have a job
7	Did not have a job	None / Did not have a job
8	Did not have a job	None / Did not have a job
9	Did not have a job	None / Did not have a job
10	Did not have a job	None / Did not have a job
11	Did not have a job	None / Did not have a job
12	Did not have a job	None / Did not have a job

48 How did the person get to work *last week*?

• If the person used more than one method of travel to work, **record all methods** used.

Person No.

1
- Walked only
- Car - as driver
- Car - as passenger
- Bus
- Truck
- Motorbike or motor scooter
- Bicycle
- Other
- Did not go to work
- Worked at home
- Did not have a job

2
- Walked only
- Car - as driver
- Car - as passenger
- Bus
- Truck
- Motorbike or motor scooter
- Bicycle
- Other
- Did not go to work
- Worked at home
- Did not have a job

3
- Walked only
- Car - as driver
- Car - as passenger
- Bus
- Truck
- Motorbike or motor scooter
- Bicycle
- Other
- Did not go to work
- Worked at home
- Did not have a job

4
- Walked only
- Car - as driver
- Car - as passenger
- Bus
- Truck
- Motorbike or motor scooter
- Bicycle
- Other
- Did not go to work
- Worked at home
- Did not have a job

5
- Walked only
- Car - as driver
- Car - as passenger
- Bus
- Truck
- Motorbike or motor scooter
- Bicycle
- Other
- Did not go to work
- Worked at home
- Did not have a job

6
- Walked only
- Car - as driver
- Car - as passenger
- Bus
- Truck
- Motorbike or motor scooter
- Bicycle
- Other
- Did not go to work
- Worked at home
- Did not have a job

7
- Walked only
- Car - as driver
- Car - as passenger
- Bus
- Truck
- Motorbike or motor scooter
- Bicycle
- Other
- Did not go to work
- Worked at home
- Did not have a job

8
- Walked only
- Car - as driver
- Car - as passenger
- Bus
- Truck
- Motorbike or motor scooter
- Bicycle
- Other
- Did not go to work
- Worked at home
- Did not have a job

9
- Walked only
- Car - as driver
- Car - as passenger
- Bus
- Truck
- Motorbike or motor scooter
- Bicycle
- Other
- Did not go to work
- Worked at home
- Did not have a job

10
- Walked only
- Car - as driver
- Car - as passenger
- Bus
- Truck
- Motorbike or motor scooter
- Bicycle
- Other
- Did not go to work
- Worked at home
- Did not have a job

11
- Walked only
- Car - as driver
- Car - as passenger
- Bus
- Truck
- Motorbike or motor scooter
- Bicycle
- Other
- Did not go to work
- Worked at home
- Did not have a job

12
- Walked only
- Car - as driver
- Car - as passenger
- Bus
- Truck
- Motorbike or motor scooter
- Bicycle
- Other
- Did not go to work
- Worked at home
- Did not have a job

Person No.	49 Did the person look for work at any time in the *last four weeks*? • Examples of looking for work include: being registered with Centrelink as a job seeker; checking or registering with any other employment agency; writing, telephoning or applying in person to an employer for work; advertising for work.	50 If the person had found a job, could the person have started work *last week*?
1	No, did not look for work Yes, looked for full-time work Yes, looked for part-time work	Yes, could have started work last week No, other reason No, already had a job to go to No, temporarily ill or injured Did not look for work
2	No, did not look for work Yes, looked for full-time work Yes, looked for part-time work	Yes, could have started work last week No, other reason No, already had a job to go to No, temporarily ill or injured Did not look for work
3	No, did not look for work Yes, looked for full-time work Yes, looked for part-time work	Yes, could have started work last week No, other reason No, already had a job to go to No, temporarily ill or injured Did not look for work
4	No, did not look for work Yes, looked for full-time work Yes, looked for part-time work	Yes, could have started work last week No, other reason No, already had a job to go to No, temporarily ill or injured Did not look for work
5	No, did not look for work Yes, looked for full-time work Yes, looked for part-time work	Yes, could have started work last week No, other reason No, already had a job to go to No, temporarily ill or injured Did not look for work
6	No, did not look for work Yes, looked for full-time work Yes, looked for part-time work	Yes, could have started work last week No, other reason No, already had a job to go to No, temporarily ill or injured Did not look for work
7	No, did not look for work Yes, looked for full-time work Yes, looked for part-time work	Yes, could have started work last week No, other reason No, already had a job to go to No, temporarily ill or injured Did not look for work
8	No, did not look for work Yes, looked for full-time work Yes, looked for part-time work	Yes, could have started work last week No, other reason No, already had a job to go to No, temporarily ill or injured Did not look for work
9	No, did not look for work Yes, looked for full-time work Yes, looked for part-time work	Yes, could have started work last week No, other reason No, already had a job to go to No, temporarily ill or injured Did not look for work
10	No, did not look for work Yes, looked for full-time work Yes, looked for part-time work	Yes, could have started work last week No, other reason No, already had a job to go to No, temporarily ill or injured Did not look for work
11	No, did not look for work Yes, looked for full-time work Yes, looked for part-time work	Yes, could have started work last week No, other reason No, already had a job to go to No, temporarily ill or injured Did not look for work
12	No, did not look for work Yes, looked for full-time work Yes, looked for part-time work	Yes, could have started work last week No, other reason No, already had a job to go to No, temporarily ill or injured Did not look for work

51 In the *last week* did the person spend time doing unpaid domestic work for their household?	**52** In the *last two weeks* did the person spend time providing unpaid care, help or assistance to anyone because they had a disability, a long term illness or problems related to old age?
• Include all housework, food/drink preparation and cleanup, laundry, gardening, home maintenance and repairs, and household shopping and finance management.	• Record persons who receive a carers benefit in the 'Yes, provided unpaid care, help or assistance' box. • Ad hoc help or assistance, such as shopping, should only be included if the person needs this sort of assistance because of his/her condition. • Do not include work done through a voluntary organisation or group.

Person No.

1
- No, did not do any unpaid domestic work in the last week
- Yes, less than 5 hours
- Yes, 5 to 14 hours
- Yes, 15 to 29 hours
- Yes, 30 hours or more

- No, did not provide unpaid care, help or assistance
- Yes, provided unpaid care, help or assistance

2
- No, did not do any unpaid domestic work in the last week
- Yes, less than 5 hours
- Yes, 5 to 14 hours
- Yes, 15 to 29 hours
- Yes, 30 hours or more

- No, did not provide unpaid care, help or assistance
- Yes, provided unpaid care, help or assistance

3
- No, did not do any unpaid domestic work in the last week
- Yes, less than 5 hours
- Yes, 5 to 14 hours
- Yes, 15 to 29 hours
- Yes, 30 hours or more

- No, did not provide unpaid care, help or assistance
- Yes, provided unpaid care, help or assistance

4
- No, did not do any unpaid domestic work in the last week
- Yes, less than 5 hours
- Yes, 5 to 14 hours
- Yes, 15 to 29 hours
- Yes, 30 hours or more

- No, did not provide unpaid care, help or assistance
- Yes, provided unpaid care, help or assistance

5
- No, did not do any unpaid domestic work in the last week
- Yes, less than 5 hours
- Yes, 5 to 14 hours
- Yes, 15 to 29 hours
- Yes, 30 hours or more

- No, did not provide unpaid care, help or assistance
- Yes, provided unpaid care, help or assistance

6
- No, did not do any unpaid domestic work in the last week
- Yes, less than 5 hours
- Yes, 5 to 14 hours
- Yes, 15 to 29 hours
- Yes, 30 hours or more

- No, did not provide unpaid care, help or assistance
- Yes, provided unpaid care, help or assistance

7
- No, did not do any unpaid domestic work in the last week
- Yes, less than 5 hours
- Yes, 5 to 14 hours
- Yes, 15 to 29 hours
- Yes, 30 hours or more

- No, did not provide unpaid care, help or assistance
- Yes, provided unpaid care, help or assistance

8
- No, did not do any unpaid domestic work in the last week
- Yes, less than 5 hours
- Yes, 5 to 14 hours
- Yes, 15 to 29 hours
- Yes, 30 hours or more

- No, did not provide unpaid care, help or assistance
- Yes, provided unpaid care, help or assistance

9
- No, did not do any unpaid domestic work in the last week
- Yes, less than 5 hours
- Yes, 5 to 14 hours
- Yes, 15 to 29 hours
- Yes, 30 hours or more

- No, did not provide unpaid care, help or assistance
- Yes, provided unpaid care, help or assistance

10
- No, did not do any unpaid domestic work in the last week
- Yes, less than 5 hours
- Yes, 5 to 14 hours
- Yes, 15 to 29 hours
- Yes, 30 hours or more

- No, did not provide unpaid care, help or assistance
- Yes, provided unpaid care, help or assistance

11
- No, did not do any unpaid domestic work in the last week
- Yes, less than 5 hours
- Yes, 5 to 14 hours
- Yes, 15 to 29 hours
- Yes, 30 hours or more

- No, did not provide unpaid care, help or assistance
- Yes, provided unpaid care, help or assistance

12
- No, did not do any unpaid domestic work in the last week
- Yes, less than 5 hours
- Yes, 5 to 14 hours
- Yes, 15 to 29 hours
- Yes, 30 hours or more

- No, did not provide unpaid care, help or assistance
- Yes, provided unpaid care, help or assistance

	53 In the *last two weeks* did the person spend time looking after a child (kid), *without pay*? • Only include children (kids) who were less than 15 years of age. • Mark all applicable responses.	**54** In the *last twelve months* did the person spend any time doing voluntary work through an organisation or group? • Exclude anything the person does as part of their paid employment or to qualify for a Government benefit. • Exclude working in a family business.
Person No.		
1	☐ No ☐ Yes, looked after my own child (kid) ☐ Yes, looked after a child (kid) other than my own	☐ No, did not do voluntary work ☐ Yes, did voluntary work
2	☐ No ☐ Yes, looked after my own child (kid) ☐ Yes, looked after a child (kid) other than my own	☐ No, did not do voluntary work ☐ Yes, did voluntary work
3	☐ No ☐ Yes, looked after my own child (kid) ☐ Yes, looked after a child (kid) other than my own	☐ No, did not do voluntary work ☐ Yes, did voluntary work
4	☐ No ☐ Yes, looked after my own child (kid) ☐ Yes, looked after a child (kid) other than my own	☐ No, did not do voluntary work ☐ Yes, did voluntary work
5	☐ No ☐ Yes, looked after my own child (kid) ☐ Yes, looked after a child (kid) other than my own	☐ No, did not do voluntary work ☐ Yes, did voluntary work
6	☐ No ☐ Yes, looked after my own child (kid) ☐ Yes, looked after a child (kid) other than my own	☐ No, did not do voluntary work ☐ Yes, did voluntary work
7	☐ No ☐ Yes, looked after my own child (kid) ☐ Yes, looked after a child (kid) other than my own	☐ No, did not do voluntary work ☐ Yes, did voluntary work
8	☐ No ☐ Yes, looked after my own child (kid) ☐ Yes, looked after a child (kid) other than my own	☐ No, did not do voluntary work ☐ Yes, did voluntary work
9	☐ No ☐ Yes, looked after my own child (kid) ☐ Yes, looked after a child (kid) other than my own	☐ No, did not do voluntary work ☐ Yes, did voluntary work
10	☐ No ☐ Yes, looked after my own child (kid) ☐ Yes, looked after a child (kid) other than my own	☐ No, did not do voluntary work ☐ Yes, did voluntary work
11	☐ No ☐ Yes, looked after my own child (kid) ☐ Yes, looked after a child (kid) other than my own	☐ No, did not do voluntary work ☐ Yes, did voluntary work
12	☐ No ☐ Yes, looked after my own child (kid) ☐ Yes, looked after a child (kid) other than my own	☐ No, did not do voluntary work ☐ Yes, did voluntary work

Person No.	55 Does the person agree to his/her name and address and other information on this form being kept by the National Archives of Australia and then made publicly available after 99 years?

55 Does the person agree to his/her name and address and other information on this form being kept by the National Archives of Australia and then made publicly available after 99 years?

- Answering this question is **OPTIONAL**.
- A person's name-identified information will not be kept where a person does not agree or the answer is left blank.

1
- [ ] Yes, agrees
- [ ] No, does not agree

2
- [ ] Yes, agrees
- [ ] No, does not agree

3
- [ ] Yes, agrees
- [ ] No, does not agree

4
- [ ] Yes, agrees
- [ ] No, does not agree

5
- [ ] Yes, agrees
- [ ] No, does not agree

6
- [ ] Yes, agrees
- [ ] No, does not agree

7
- [ ] Yes, agrees
- [ ] No, does not agree

8
- [ ] Yes, agrees
- [ ] No, does not agree

9
- [ ] Yes, agrees
- [ ] No, does not agree

10
- [ ] Yes, agrees
- [ ] No, does not agree

11
- [ ] Yes, agrees
- [ ] No, does not agree

12
- [ ] Yes, agrees
- [ ] No, does not agree

56 Declaration

I have explained the requirements of question 55 to the household. I believe the household understood my explanation of question 55 and that I have correctly recorded the views of each person in the household at question 55.

Signature

Date

Thank you for completing this form.

Australian Statistician

Appendix B. Commentary on the 2006 Interviewer Household Form

A particular task of the 2006 Census observation was to consider the efficacy of changes made since the 2001 Census to the collection instrument—in particular, the streamlining of the interview process brought about by the change from a two-form to a single-form schedule. In this Appendix, we draw together our comments on the 2006 Interviewer Household Form in two main sections. The first considers the structure of the single matrix form that was used for the first time in 2006 (see Appendix A) and some of the consequences of that structure for the way in which the form was used in the field. We make suggestions for minor changes to the form's design. The second section looks at the content of the questions and their wording—in some cases drawing comparisons between the different field sites—to assess the likely effects on the quality of the data that were gathered.

Structure

The matrix form is considered to be a definite improvement on the previous arrangement of Household Forms and Personal Forms used in 2001. This was not just the view of the present researchers, but also that of others who had experience of both censuses. One of these was one of the Community Coordinators (CCs) at C3 in Arnhem Land, who had been a collector-interviewer (CI) in 2001. At the Census Field Officer (CFO) debriefing (see Chapter 7), a CFO from another area commented that several people who had worked on both censuses had said to him that the form was 'heaps better than last time'.

The single form was far less demanding of interviewers in a practical sense. Taylor comments that what appeared initially to CIs to be a daunting document was mastered in terms of its mode of application by most—though not all—of the team by day two of interviewing at Wadeye. The idea that dwelling information was sought in Questions 2–9, and that the people listed in Question 12 were then carried through sequentially by working down each subsequent page of questions through to the end of the schedule, was soon grasped. In practice, this was the way in which the form was filled in at all the field sites.

After observations at the Data Processing Centre (DPC) (see Chapter 8), Morphy thinks that too much emphasis was placed during the training of the CFOs and therefore of the CCs and CIs on the importance of using horizontal marks as opposed to ticks in the 'tick boxes' on the form. It is also questionable whether it is really necessary to require that written responses be in capital letters, and that each letter be written in a box. In Morphy's experience (personal as well as observational, see Chapter 4), writing in capital letters in boxes is laborious, time-consuming and highly conducive to spelling mistakes. The CIs that she observed in Arnhem Land frequently began with capital letters, but almost invariably switched to the easier and more natural upper and lower case printing at some stage on the form. Horizontal lines and capital letters are necessary for successful automatic coding. However, where data is being coded manually the images on the screen that are available to coders are of sufficient quality to distinguish ticks from crosses and to identify lower case letters.

Thorburn notes that as a general point, the interviewers tended not to read the fine print on the Interviewer Household Form (IHF), which explains each question. This fine print needs to be highlighted very strongly in the training.

As will be argued at length below, the form needs to be designed so that the 'persons temporarily absent' (PTA) table appears after, not before, the list of persons present. Therefore, when people are away, the reasons for their absence can be ascertained and those unlikely to be counted elsewhere can be added to the main form before the PTA table is drawn up. This procedure should be reinforced in training at every level: of the CFOs, the CCs and the CIs.

Length

The form contains too many questions for comfort. The sheer length of interviews in often large, multi-family households was tiring for the CIs and the interviewees. In Arnhem Land, Morphy observed consistently that people tended to start flagging once they hit the education questions (beginning at 32) and were worn out by the time they reached the employment questions (beginning at 40). Often, the CIs were lucky to have even one interviewee left at that point. The questions on education and employment are also those that people find most difficult to answer (see below), and for which the CIs are unlikely to know the answers themselves. It might be advisable to promote these questions higher up the form, so that the CI and interviewees are tackling them when they are feeling relatively fresh. The length of the form and other aspects of its design—notably the lack of sequencing discussed below—encouraged formulaic responses (also discussed below). We suggest that the Australian Bureau of Statistics (ABS) needs to look again at reducing the number of questions and better specifying questions and categorical answers in this form designed for discrete Indigenous communities in remote Australia.

Sequencing

All the observers noted that lack of sequencing in the IHF meant that in the latter part of the questioning—about people's educational and employment characteristics—there was a fairly heavy demand on CIs repeatedly marking redundant boxes such as 'No qualification' or 'Did not have a job'. Under the sequencing directions used in the 'mainstream' Household Form, these questions would have been skipped. With the IHF, however, interviewers had to rely on either minimal questioning or humour to get them through as they filled in boxes that indicated such obvious things as young children not having jobs, incomes or post-school qualifications. Often—particularly later in the interview—the CI would cease to fill in the redundant boxes.

We would argue that leaving out sequencing from the IHF was, however, still the correct decision. Sequencing works only if all questions for one person are asked before moving onto the next person. As anticipated in the design of the IHF, and as noted above in practice, this was not the predominant way in which the IHF was used. 'Working vertically'—or answering each question for all people listed before moving on to the next question—is the most attractive and efficient way of working with the IHF. Sequencing instructions could lead to questions being skipped for those to whom they apply as well as for those to whom they do not apply.

Sanders notes, however, that there could be some use made of instructions such as 'Only continue for persons aged 15 years or more', as in the general Household Form. This instruction could probably have been inserted at the top of Page 15 of the IHF before Question 34 about the highest year of primary or secondary school the person had completed. Such a system would also be easier to implement if the interviewers were encouraged to list adults first, then children, rather than grouping individuals into 'family groups'. One other way to reinforce this instruction would be to make the question pages after that instruction a different colour.

Another consequence of the lack of sequencing, noted by Morphy, is that the necessity to mark a lot of redundant boxes focused the attention of the CI on the form rather than on keeping the interviewees engaged in the interview process. In 2001, in Arnhem Land, the interview session tended to be a bit of a social event, and individuals were engaged because each had their own form. In 2006, the interview tended to be with one or two people, and everyone else was unengaged or even absent. At times, it was hard to keep even one or two engaged—Morphy observed several cases where the CI was left to fill in the form by themselves. Taylor notes that at Wadeye this repetition tended to cause CIs and respondents a good deal of irritation and consequent loss of flow in rapport during which time some respondents became diverted by events around them and it took considerable effort to regain momentum.

Given the design of the form, this is an intractable problem, but shortening the form and moving the education and employment questions nearer to the front (as suggested above) might improve matters.

Formulaic and standardised responses

Thorburn observes that the people working for the census team at Junjuwa in the Fitzroy Crossing area have a long association with the place and the people there. She estimates that on average they probably knew about 80 per cent of the answers to the questions they were asking people; there were very few exceptions or surprises. The only time she saw someone's presumption proven wrong was with a woman in her late 40s, known as having 'grown up' many children. The interviewer had not realised that this woman had never actually given birth to any of these children. Arguably, biological motherhood is less salient than social motherhood for these women, for whom 'growing up' children is to 'have them'—but it is of some significance to the census.

A similar observation could be made about the local knowledge of the CIs in the Arnhem Land case study. By and large in these small kin-based communities everyone knows exactly how people are related to one another, how many children people have and so on. For these kinds of questions, it was common for the CI to fill in the form without much reference to the interviewee. The only questions, apart from date of birth, for which the CIs regularly had to ask for details were those relating to post-school qualifications.

As was observed to occur in 2001 (Martin et al. 2002), the CCs and the CIs very quickly developed standardised answers to many of the questions. This was a rational response to questions that had little meaning or relevance for people being asked (see below), and had the effect of speeding up the interviews. CIs would often ask the questions, just for the theatrical and humour value, but more often they would quietly fill in the answer for the respondent, while the latter waited for the next one that the interviewer might need confirmation for. People would regularly answer questions for others in the house who were away, or who had lost interest in the process and wandered off.

If anything, the 2006 form structure proved to be so convenient that at times it encouraged—even more than was the case in 2001—a formulaic filling in or ticking of boxes down the page. As a consequence, there was a tendency for CIs to give more similar responses to the same question for different individuals than would otherwise be the case. This is a likely effect of the interview method in general, as opposed to self-enumeration, and is particularly likely when the question asked does not relate well to the social context of the people being interviewed.

One instance of this, which Sanders has noted in the past, is asking people in Indigenous communities where most people do not have a job whether they looked for work in the past four weeks. If people without a job answer 'yes' to this question they will show up in subsequent analysis as unemployed, while if they answer 'no' they will show up in analysis as not in the labour force. How interviewers and interviewees together decide to answer that question for the people associated with a dwelling in such a community is pretty arbitrary and depends on many things. One is their understanding of the eligibility rules for Newstart or unemployment payment entitlements. If people are being told that they must look for work as a condition of that entitlement, they are probably more likely to answer 'yes' to the question about whether they have looked for a job, and hence turn up in subsequent analysis as unemployed. In 2001, only 11 per cent of people aged 15 years and over in the Alice Springs town camps answered this way, while 76 per cent showed up as not in the labour force having answered 'no' to this question (Sanders 2004: 6). Sanders predicts that in 2006, with a recent policy emphasis pushing people to do more to get off unemployment payments, the proportion answering 'yes' and hence being categorised as unemployed in the Alice Springs town camps will probably go up and the proportion answering 'no' and being categorised as not in the labour force will go down from 2001. This is largely 'policy noise' in the statistical system produced by a patterning of answers that arises from interviewer and interviewee knowledge of other policy systems, which have little to do with the ABS, but which affect the way in which these particular census questions are answered. Patterning of such answers under an interviewer process of enumeration is probably stronger than under a self-enumeration process, however, it can occur under both types of enumeration processes and is largely unavoidable.

In the Fitzroy Crossing area, the questions that were most commonly approached in a standardised way by the CIs were: Question 5 (amount of rent), Question 7 (who is this dwelling being rented from?), Question 9 (can the Internet be accessed?), Question 40 (income) and Questions 42–6 relating to a person's occupation (particularly where the respondent was on Community Development Employment Projects [CDEP]).

Thorburn notes that such standardisations are not necessarily the same across interviewers, for example, some put down every CDEP person they counted as working 32 hours, when it is very likely that what they meant was 16 hours—the standard for a week. A very valuable part of the training then would be to discuss some of these possible standards—rent paid for different kinds of housing, for example—so that answers are thought about and answered in the same way across interviewers.

This issue could also be addressed in the training if the CFO were aware of the questions to which people would be likely to develop standardised answers. It seems important for the ABS to acknowledge that such standardised answering procedures will develop spontaneously in any case; recognising this in the training would go some way to ensure consistency within communities, and across regions.

Content

Almost inevitably, given the processes of cultural translation that were necessary, issues surrounding the interpretation, understanding and relevance of certain questions arose. Just comparing the various site-based observations and the findings from 2001 (Martin et al. 2002), there seem to be perennial conceptual confusions in regard to such matters as usual place of residence, family composition, income and industry. Some of the new questions on the census form relating to unpaid and voluntary work also presented difficulties.

The 'resident' versus 'visitor' problem

After the count, when the Northern Territory forms were back at the Darwin Census Management Unit (CMU), the detailed checking of the whereabouts of PTA and people's place of residence threw up some interesting examples of definitional problems surrounding the concepts 'resident' and 'visitor' (see also Chapters 3 and 4). In mainstream terms, being a 'visitor' tends to denote a short-term stay in a place other than one's own residence. In the Indigenous world, the concept could be interpreted very differently. In desert areas, particularly, a person who has lived in a community for half a lifetime could still be considered a 'visitor' and be entered on the form as such at Question 12, but nevertheless respond to Question 15 that they live in 'this community' most of the time—and also did so one and five years ago. This is most likely because they are not living on their own country. There were even cases where the 'Person 1' on a household form was designated as a 'visitor'. Conversely, people might be listed in Question 12 as residents—because the settlement is on their country—but specify that they live 'elsewhere' at Question 15. In other cases—and this seemed more common in Arnhem Land than elsewhere—certain people did not have a clear idea of themselves as 'residents' in a single place. Typically, these were people who divided their time, for various reasons (seasonal, family or work-related) between a homeland and a hub settlement. Such people ran the risk of being designated as a PTA in one place and a resident elsewhere.

'Persons temporarily absent'

This question is treated in detail in all the case-study chapters (see Chapters 3–6) and also in Chapters 7 and 9. The way in which PTA were treated was a major problem at all the study sites, and possibly was one of the most significant factors contributing to the under-count of Indigenous people in Western Australia and the Northern Territory in 2006 (ABS 2007; Taylor 2007b).

In the Indigenous Enumeration Strategy (IES) documentation, it states that:

> [The] counting methodology will be 'as enumerated' but will have the flexibility to include people who may not be counted anywhere. People not present…will be listed on the Interviewer Household Form. If they are away hunting or fishing…and it is thought they will not be counted where they are, then they will be included as present and personal details should be completed for them. If they are in a town or city etc, where they should be counted, then they will be listed as being away and only summary details will be completed for them.

As noted above, we conclude that it was a mistake to have the PTA table before the 'people there now' question (12). Although most CIs grew used to this order of questions over time, it was not the most logical and often confused interviewees. The more logical order would be to ask first for people living or staying at the dwelling and then for usual residents who are currently away. As it was, the conceptual problems over 'resident' status compounded the problem and, all in all, it was much too easy to 'forget' to move people onto the main form, especially if there were a lot of people to be counted and if it was difficult to make judgments about whether they would be counted elsewhere.

The problem was compounded further by the lack of guidance in the training of the Northern Territory CFOs and therefore of the CCs and CIs about how to make judgments on the question of whether PTA would be counted elsewhere. There was also a lack of clarity—there was nothing explicit in the documentation and it was not covered in anyone's training—about whether the CIs were to be paid for everyone listed on the form, including PTA, or just for those listed at Question 12.

Thorburn notes that in Fitzroy Crossing the distinction was not understood by the CC or the CIs and perhaps not even by the CFO. Certainly in the day of crosschecking that she observed, with the CFO and the Bunuba CC, no questions were asked about whether or not people who were marked down as being away should have been included as present. In her observation, no forms for any of the Bunuba communities were reviewed in this way. Fieldwork at the DPC in Darwin (see Chapter 7) suggests that a large proportion of PTA would not have been counted on a form anywhere else, and so would have been missed in the population count.

Taylor observes that the phrasing of Questions 12 ('People who are living or staying here now') and 10 and 11 ('People who live here most of the time but are away') sometimes led to people who were just away at the shops or out bush being treated as PTA. He also noted that people he knew to be associated with dwellings who were away were simply not listed, either at 12 or 11. There was therefore not a clear sense among CIs and interviewees that this twofold categorisation was supposed to be exhaustive of people associated with the dwelling.

The issue could also be discussed in terms of demands and interest. Because the demands of the census are high and interest is low, any opportunity to minimise the amount of work to be done by *not* identifying more people to go on a form is quite likely to be taken by interviewees and CIs.

It was suggested to Sanders by a number of users of the form that the switch in order could be accommodated by having the questions about people who live at the dwelling but are currently away on the first spiral-bound right-hand page. That way all the people associated with a dwelling would be able to be seen in one opening, with those currently there on the left page and usual residents who are currently away on the right page. With this form design, people currently away would be effectively folded out of the way as the more detailed questioning began about those currently there.

In the event, in the Northern Territory, many people were not moved back inside the form to Question 12 until the forms reached the CMU (see Chapter 7). This means that for many people there is only very basic information recorded: age, sex, place where they are thought to be and reason for being away. It is regrettable that there is no information on their relationship to Person 1. At the family-coding stage (see Chapter 8), such people have to be coded as 'unrelated', and this will give a misleading picture of the structure of remote Indigenous households in 2006. Comparison with 2001 could yield a false impression that there are now significantly more households containing people who are not relatives.

'Household' and 'family' structure

The questions on relationships within the household (13–14 and 31–2) yielded more coherent and interpretable data than their equivalents in the 2001 Census (see Martin et al. 2002), although intractable problems of interpretation remained (see Chapter 8 and Morphy 2007). In Question 13 ('How is the person related to Person 1/Person 2?'), it was much clearer what to do with Person 1, but the specified relationships to Person 1 and 2 were structured on the assumption that 1 and 2 were a couple, and it sometimes caused difficulties if they were not. There also seems no good reason to have excluded some of the options that were allowed for on the mainstream form, particularly 'brother or sister of Person 1'. We are in favour of retaining a modified version of Question 13 for 2011, removing the assumption that Person 1 and Person 2 are a married couple and restricting the options to the following relationships to Person 1: father, mother, husband, wife, brother, sister, child, other relative, unrelated.

There were some instances in which Question 13 on family relationships was answered upside down (or back-to-front), with the relationship of Person 1 to Person x sought instead of the other way round. The research at the DPC revealed that this was an uncommon problem, but one that occurred sporadically everywhere. It is extremely difficult to think of a wording for the question that makes the direction of the relationship totally unambiguous.

Question 13 contains the category 'de facto', but this is not given as an option in Question 14 ('Is the person married?'). This was sometimes confusing to the CIs and the interviewees.

The addition of Questions 31 ('Is the person's mother staying in the dwelling?') and 32 ('Is the person's father staying in the dwelling?') was invaluable—particularly at the data processing stage in the DPC—although people were not always successful at filling them in consistently. These were a great improvement on the essentially unanswerable 2001 question about being 'more closely related to' someone other than Person 1.

Two researchers (Morphy and Thorburn) noted that these questions sometimes caused problems when a household was big enough to require more than one form, if the CIs had not been told to leave 'Person 1' and Person 2' blank on the second and subsequent forms. At Wadeye, these questions presented issues in the case of deceased parents and others who were in respite care or currently located with another relative. Interestingly, some respondents wanted to know how to respond if their parent was temporarily away, and yet this fact had not been recorded in answer to Question 11 relating to PTA.

Thorburn notes that in Fitzroy Crossing most interviewers presumed that these questions related to biological mothers and fathers. Given the earlier question (25) about babies that the mother had given birth to, rather than 'grown up', it is not surprising, and Thorburn suggests that Question 25 primes people to answer the later questions in a non-Indigenous way, which is precisely what they did—that is, defining mothers and fathers biologically, rather than as 'adoptive, step or foster', which are the descriptors given in the fine print.

Date of birth

In Wadeye and Arnhem Land, major difficulties arose in trying to establish age or date of birth (DOB) in Question 12. In numerous cases this item was left blank, and on the occasions where DOB was unknown and an attempt was made to establish age instead, this invariably became a more or less well-educated guess. So prominent was this omission in Wadeye that an attempt was made by one of the CCs to extract DOB information from the TRC population database, although this was unsuccessful owing to difficulties in establishing a procedure that preserved confidentiality. In Arnhem Land, the CFO tried to use the local health database to check, but was stymied by the multiple names problem (see Chapters 4 and 7).

Usual residence

In Arnhem Land and Wadeye, Questions 15, 16 and 17—regarding usual residence now, one, and five years ago—were treated essentially as the same and the tendency was for interviewers to rush through these with a standard response and little discussion. Given the different values surrounding the terms 'resident' and 'visitor' in mainstream and remote Aboriginal cultures this is not surprising, and these data cannot be interpreted as a reliable reflection of mobility patterns, either in the shorter or longer term.

Language

As in 2001, Question 21 ('Does the person speak an Aboriginal or Torres Strait Islander language *at home*?') and Question 22 ('How well does the person speak *English*?') revealed interesting regional differences in attitudes to language. The data gathered in these questions cannot be taken to be an objective measure of language use (cf. Kral and Morphy 2006).

People in Fitzroy Crossing did not answer Question 21 consistently. In Thorburn's view, this is because belonging to a 'language group' has become a marker of political identity, to an extent, particularly in terms of traditional ownership of country. That there is an organisation in Fitzroy Crossing called Bunuba Inc.—that is, called by a language group name—probably further confused matters. So stating that one is Walmajarri or Bunuba does not necessarily mean that one speaks that language the majority of the time; rather, it distinguishes one's identity in contrast with other language groups in town, and marks one as a member of a group. Some CIs also interpreted the question as meaning 'Can you speak language, and if so, which one?' This issue is probably something specific to those settlements and towns where a number of language groups coalesce. In any case, answers to this question were not consistent across interviewers and some tended to write down 'Kriol', the most accurate answer for the majority there.

In north-east Arnhem Land, where the majority of people speak a Yolngu-matha dialect as their first language, the data on real usage are more reliable. It is likely that a generational effect is beginning to be evident, with the language form '*dhuwaya*'—the term for the lingua franca that has developed in the eastern part of the Yolngu-speaking area—being recorded for the majority of people of about 40 years of age and below. This variety is replacing clan dialects spoken by the older generations, and whereas in 2001 interviewees were still volunteering their clan dialect as their 'language' (even if they were most of the time speaking *dhuwaya*), there seems to have been a shift in the intervening years to reporting real (rather than clan-identificational) usage.

Question 22 on English usage was for the most part considered patronising and/or confusing by people in Fitzroy Crossing. This question was interpreted as being similar to Question 28 ('Does the person ever need someone to help with understanding other people or being understood by other people?'), where it is not clear who the person is not being understood by. The implication seems to be it is non-Indigenous people who are not understanding, and that is certainly how the question was interpreted.

In Arnhem Land, in contrast, as in 2001, most people found this question unexceptionable. Answers tended to be formulaic, with infants classified as non-English speakers, children of primary-school age being classified as speaking 'not well' and nearly everyone else as speaking English 'well'. There was an occasional politically motivated response to the question (see Chapter 4). At Question 28, people felt it odd, even insulting, that language comprehension was put in the same category as disabilities such as deafness. None of the few people who responded 'yes' to this then ticked the 'difficulty with English' box at Question 29.

Religion

As with the language question, Question 24 ('What is the person's religion?') elicited culturally mediated responses. Thorburn comments that it is not clear whether the ABS really is seeking to ascertain how many Indigenous people maintain traditional beliefs and cultural practice. If it is seeking to capture that, more discussion needs to take place in the training, and perhaps other words suggested on the form. She is not sure that people in Fitzroy Crossing like to describe themselves as 'traditional' with its undertone of 'backward' (see Martin 2002 for similar comments with respect to Aurukun in 2001).

In the Yolngu area, as in 2001, some people wanted to put 'traditional beliefs' and a Christian option, while others disputed that traditional beliefs were the same thing as a religion. In this very 'traditional' region, where funerals made the count almost impossible (see Chapter 4), most people chose to put their Christian affiliation. Traditional beliefs were highly under-reported in the Yolngu region in 2001 and 2006.

We strongly recommend—as Morphy did in 2002—that if some attempt to get at traditional orientations is to stay, it should be separated from the religion question. At the very least, it should be possible to choose the 'traditional' and another option.

Number of babies ever born

Question 25 ('For each female, how many babies has she given birth to?'), which had been a worry to the ABS—and a focus of training—was relatively unproblematic, although Taylor comments that in Wadeye the question often generated discussion, perhaps not surprisingly given possible sensitivities.

In the Yolngu area, in general, female CIs asked this question. If there was no female CI the form was handed over to a female member of the household for the question to be completed. In some cases, the female CIs were able to add deceased children from their personal knowledge, but often only currently living children were counted. In Fitzroy Crossing, the question was understood well enough, but was certainly not one that was asked of older women by younger male interviewers.

Need for assistance

The four questions (26–8) about people needing help—which were designed to probe disability issues—were wordy and could be interpreted in very different ways. The Yolngu CIs had difficulty reading them out, and the interviewees in interpreting them. People understated their disabilities. They thought it odd that children had to be included—their reasons for needing help are different than for adults—and the 'old or young age' box did not come until Question 29.

In Fitzroy Crossing, these questions caused irritation at times and the tendency was for interviewers to focus more on Question 28 (whether the person needed help being understood) and then to interpret this primarily as a test of English-language ability in Question 29—in contrast with the Yolngu-speaking interviewees and CIs (see above).

Education and training

In the Yolngu area, as in Wadeye, Question 33 on attendance at an educational institution elicited fairly stock responses. At Wadeye, there was discussion at times as to whether the Thamarrurr Regional School was a primary or secondary institution given that it was, strictly speaking at the time, a primary school but with secondary-enrolled students—a common occurrence in remote Aboriginal settlements.

Question 34 on the highest year of schooling completed also presented subtleties at Wadeye and often two categories were ticked ('Went to primary school' and 'Finished primary school'). In the Yolngu area, the prompt on Question 34 to put 'Year 8 or below' for 'mission days' schooling was a good idea—it saved a lot of time and discussion.

There followed a series of questions containing default categories that, as previously noted, tended to disrupt the interview and cause it to lose momentum. Almost invariably at Wadeye and in the Yolngu-speaking area the answer to Question 35 on post-school qualifications was answered in the negative, so the answers to Questions 36–9 were also negative, yet each question had a box that required ticking. For Question 38 ('What was the name of the educational institution where the person completed their highest qualification?'), the CFO at Wadeye instructed CIs in training to write down for this question the name of the high school if that was the highest level of qualification, but no one did. For whatever reason, it was interpreted by CIs—correctly, although the form of the question was not unambiguous—as a question about education after school.

Income and employment

At Question 40 ('How much money does the person get each fortnight…') many incomes were understated in the Arnhem Land case study area; pensions were not included, by and large, nor were child allowance or intermittent income from artwork. In Fitzroy Crossing, this question was also problematic, and Thorburn suggested that a cheat sheet on people's pays depending on what government payment they received would have been very useful. Largely, people are not aware of the total amount of money they receive, as rent and often 'chuck-in' (communal savings) are removed immediately the pay goes into their account. Many people also are unaware of whether or not they are taxed. The question also presumes that a person's pay has not changed—that is, for people who are contract workers, or who change jobs often, the question could be hard to answer. More attention needs to be given in the training to some of the difficulties with calculating people's income.

All of the questions from 42 to 50, relating to work, also would have benefited from more discussion during the training sessions—in particular, how to answer the questions for those people on CDEP, who are the majority of employed people in these communities.

In Fitzroy Crossing, in answer to Question 42 ('In the main job held last week, what was the person's occupation?'), people wrote 'CDEP' where appropriate. For Question 44 ('For the main job held last week, who did the person work for?'), however, some CIs wrote the name of the community where the person worked, rather than the CDEP grantee organisation for whom they were working—indeed, the fine print encouraged them to do so. In the Fitzroy Valley, however, almost all of the smaller CDEPs have been transferred to Marra Worra Worra (MWW) in the past five years, so the smaller communities no longer run their own CDEP programs.

Question 46 ('…what did the person's employer do?') was most problematic in the Arnhem Land area: people do not know how to describe what their CDEP organisation does. Here, the CIs gradually worked out a formulaic response: 'Provides community services'. Thorburn comments that in the Fitzroy area MWW is a multi-million-dollar organisation that receives funding from various government agencies to provide all kinds of services to communities around Fitzroy Crossing. A descriptive tag such as 'community organisation' could have been decided on and adhered to by all CIs. Again, discussion in the training and the drawing up of a cheat sheet would have been very helpful in both locations.

As with Question 46, Question 47 ('Last week, how many hours did the person work in all jobs?') had very stable answers for most people in Fitzroy Crossing: either 'Did not have a job' or '16 hours'—the hours required under CDEP rules. As previously noted, however, one of the CIs wrote 32 hours for all CDEP respondents, thinking that, like the pay question, it was referring to a fortnight.

In Arnhem Land, the question was often filled in with daily rather than weekly hours. Morphy comments that it would make things much easier for the CIs if the same time frame applied to all income and job questions.

In Question 50 ('If the person had found a job, could the person have started work last week?'), two of the options given were 'No, other reason' and 'Did not look for work'. The latter was a 'default' category—as in the previous question—but this was very unclear in the context because it was not a coherent response to the real question asked.

Taylor comments that, at Wadeye, because many people do not have a job, Questions 42–8 were effectively redundant but nonetheless required filling out. By this stage—as in the other field sites—there was generally a sense that all participants wanted to move quickly to finish the proceedings. Consequently, Question 49 on looking for work was answered universally in the negative—whether people were registered with Centrelink was not asked. Question 50 on availability for work was then seen as another default situation.

Unpaid work, unpaid care and voluntary work

In the Yolngu-speaking area and at Wadeye, the final four questions tended to be answered speedily and without too much thought, with the CIs quickly establishing stock responses to what seemed rather irrelevant questions. In Arnhem Land, Question 51 (on unpaid domestic work) was a bit perplexing to some, as they were putting 'home duties' down as their CDEP employment in answer to an earlier question. The need to choose between several alternatives in terms of hours spent caused difficulties, until the CIs worked out some formulaic responses: boys, less than five hours; young men, none; girls, 5–14 hours; women, 15–29 hours. In Wadeye, this question was overwhelmingly answered 'yes', but the quality of the answers on hours spent appeared questionable as people had little measurable sense of this.

Interestingly, in the Yolngu-speaking area, nearly everyone from about the age of 10 up—boys as well as girls—was said to have looked after children in response to Question 53. In contrast, the concept of 'voluntary work' (Question 54) is foreign to people, and no one responded 'yes' to this question.

The keeping of information

Question 55, on the archiving of personal information, was treated differently by different CIs, and there could also have been an effect caused by the nature of the form. In the Yolngu-speaking area in 2001, when everyone had a personal form, they answered this question for themselves. The use of a matrix form in 2006, as noted above, led to less engagement with the process among members of the household and often only the CI and one interviewee were left by the end. The CIs had been told that people had to answer this question for themselves, so most of the boxes were left blank. Those people who did respond invariably responded in the affirmative, as in 2001.

In Fitzroy Crossing, the question was asked of Person 1 only (who invariably assented to archiving), and each of the boxes for other household members were then ticked in the same way. This was contrary to the instructions the CIs had received in training.

References

ABC News Online 2006, 'Researchers find Indigenous health Utopia', available at http://www.abc.net.au/news/newsitems/200610/s1760241.htm, accessed 14 June 2007.

Ah Kit, J. 2002, 'Ministerial Statement—Indigenous Affairs', *Debates—Ninth Assembly First Session, Parliamentary Record No. 3*, Northern Territory Hansard, Legislative Assembly of the Northern Territory, Darwin.

Altman, J.C. 2003, 'Developing an Indigenous Arts Strategy for the Northern Territory: Issues paper for consultations', *CAEPR Working Paper No. 23*, CAEPR, ANU, Canberra.

Anderson, B. 2006, *Imagined Communities* (revised edition), Verso, London.

Australian Bureau of Statistics (ABS) 2006a, *How Australia Takes a Census, 2006*, cat. no. 2903.0, ABS, Canberra.

Australian Bureau of Statistics (ABS) 2006b, *Census Field Officer's Manual: 8 August 2006 Census*, ABS, Canberra.

Australian Bureau of Statistics (ABS) 2007, *Census of Population and Housing: Undercount*, cat no. 2940.0, ABS, Canberra.

Barber, M. 2005, Where the Clouds Stand: Australian Aboriginal Relationships to Water, Place, and the Marine Environment in Blue Mud Bay, Northern Territory, PhD thesis, ANU.

Bledsoe, C.H. 2002, *Contingent Lives: Fertility, Time and Aging in West Africa*, The University of Chicago Press, Chicago.

Centralian Advocate 2006, Friday, 4 August 2006.

Commonwealth of Australia 2006, *Official Committee Hansard Senate Standing Committee on Community Affairs Estimates*, Thursday, 2 November 2006, Parliament House, Canberra.

Department of Employment and Workplace Relations (DEWR) 2005a, 'Building on success', *CDEP Discussion Paper 2005*, DEWR, Canberra.

Department of Employment and Workplace Relations (DEWR) 2005b, *Building on success: CDEP—Future Directions*, DEWR, Canberra.

Department of Employment and Workplace Relations (DEWR) 2006, 'Indigenous potential meets economic opportunity', *Discussion Paper*, November 2006, DEWR, Canberra.

Dillon, M.C. 2007, 'National security and the failed state in remote Australia', *Austral Policy Forum*, no. 0701A, 25 January, Nautilus Institute, RMIT University, Melbourne.

Ellanna, L., Loveday, P., Stanley, O. and Young, E.A. 1988, *Economic Enterprises in Aboriginal Communities in the Northern Territory*, North Australian Research Unit, ANU, Darwin.

Foster, D., Mitchell, J., Ulrik, J. and Williams, R. 2005, *Population and Mobility in the Town Camps of Alice Springs: A Report Prepared by the Tangentyere Council Research Unit,* Report 9, Desert Knowledge Cooperative Research Centre, Alice Springs.

Gray, M. and Chapman, B. 2006, 'Labour market issues', in B.H. Hunter (ed.), *Assessing the Evidence on Indigenous Socioeconomic Outcomes: A Focus on the 2002 NATSISS*, CAEPR Research Monograph No. 26, ANU E Press, Canberra.

Hughes, H. 2007, *Lands of Shame: Aboriginal and Torres Strait Islander 'Homelands' in Transition*, Centre for Independent Studies, Sydney.

Johns, G. 2006, 'Social stability and structural adjustment', Address to the Bennelong Society Sixth Annual Conference, *Leaving Remote Communities*, 2 September 2006, Melbourne, available at http://www.bennelong.com.au/conferences/pdf/Johns2006.pdf, accessed 14 June 2007.

Joint Standing Committee on Electoral Matters 2003, *Territory Representation: Report of the Inquiry into Increasing the Minimum Representation for the Australian Capital Territory and the Northern Territory in the House of Representatives*, The Parliament of the Commonwealth of Australia, Canberra.

Jonas, W. 1992, 'Aboriginal community and agency perceptions about the collection of social statistics', in J.C. Altman (ed.), *A National Survey of Indigenous Australians: Options and Implications*, CAEPR Research Monograph No. 3, CAEPR, ANU, Canberra.

Kertzer, D.I. and Arel, D. (eds) 2002, *Census and Identity: The Politics of Race, Ethnicity and Language in National Censuses*, Cambridge University Press, Cambridge.

Kertzer, D.I. and Fricke, T. (eds) 1997, *Anthropological Demography: Toward a New Synthesis*, The University of Chicago Press, Chicago.

Kral, I. and Morphy, F. 2006, 'Language', in B.H. Hunter (ed.), *Assessing the Evidence on Indigenous Socioeconomic Outcomes: A Focus on the 2002 NATSISS*, CAEPR Research Monograph No. 26, ANU E Press, Canberra.

McDermott, R., O'Dea, K., Rowley, K. et al. 1998, 'Beneficial impact of Homelands Movement on health outcomes in Central Australian Aborigines', *Australian and New Zealand Journal of Public Health*, vol. 22, pp. 653–8.

Martin, D. 2002, 'Counting the Wik: the 2001 Census in Aurukun, western Cape York Peninsula', in D.F. Martin, F. Morphy, W.G. Sanders and J. Taylor,

Making Sense of the Census: Observations of the 2001 Enumeration in Remote Aboriginal Australia, CAEPR Research Monograph No. 22 (reprinted 2004), ANU E Press, Canberra.

Martin, D. and Taylor, J. 1996, 'Ethnographic perspectives on the enumeration of Aboriginal people in remote Australia', *Journal of the Australian Population Association*, vol. 13, no. 1, pp. 17–33.

Martin D.F., Morphy, F., Sanders, W. and Taylor, J. 2002, *Making Sense of the Census: Observations of the 2001 Enumeration in Remote Aboriginal Australia*, CAEPR Research Monograph No. 22 (reprinted 2004), ANU E Press, Canberra.

Morice, R.D. 1976, 'Woman dancing Dreaming: Psychosocial benefits of the Aboriginal outstation movement', *Medical Journal of Australia*, vol. 2, pp. 939–42.

Morphy, F. 2002, 'When systems collide: the 2001 Census at a remote Northern Territory outstation', in D.F. Martin, F. Morphy, W.G. Sanders and J. Taylor, *Making Sense of the Census: Observations of the 2001 Enumeration in Remote Aboriginal Australia*, CAEPR Research Monograph No. 22 (reprinted 2004), ANU E Press, Canberra.

Morphy, F. 2003, Report to the Australian Bureau of Statistics on the Field Testing of Special Indigenous Form B at 'Community A', Arnhem Land, 10–14 November 2003, Confidential unpublished report to the ABS.

Morphy, F. 2004, 'Indigenous household structures and ABS definitions of the family: what happens when systems collide, and does it matter?' *CAEPR Working Paper No. 26*, CAEPR, ANU, Canberra.

Morphy, F, 2006, 'Lost in translation? Remote Indigenous households and definitions of the family', *Family Matters*, vol. 73, pp. 23–31.

Morphy, F. 2007, 'Uncontained subjects: "population" and "household" in remote Aboriginal Australia', *Journal of Population Research*, vol. 24, no. 2, pp. 163–84.

Morphy, H. 1984, *Journey to the Crocodile's Nest*, Australian Institute of Aboriginal Studies, Canberra.

PricewaterhouseCooper 2007, *Living in the Sunburnt Country. Indigenous Housing: Findings of the Review of the Community Housing and Infrastructure Program*, Final Report, February 2007, Department of Families, Community Services and Indigenous Affairs, Canberra.

Sanders, W. 2002, 'Adapting to circumstance: the 2001 Census in the Alice Springs town camps', in D.F. Martin, F. Morphy, W.G. Sanders and J. Taylor, *Making Sense of the Census: Observations of the 2001 Enumeration in Remote Aboriginal Australia*, CAEPR Research Monograph No. 22 (reprinted 2004), ANU E Press, Canberra.

Sanders, W. 2004, 'Indigenous people in the Alice Springs Town Camps: The 2001 Census data', *CAEPR Discussion Paper No. 26*, CAEPR, ANU, Canberra.

Scott, J.C. 1998, *Seeing Like a State: How Certain Schemes to Improve the Human Condition Have Failed*, Yale University Press, New Haven.

Smith, D.E. 1992, 'The cultural appropriateness of existing survey questions and concepts', in J.C. Altman (ed.), *A National Survey of Indigenous Australians: Options and Implications*, CAEPR Research Monograph No. 3, CAEPR, ANU, Canberra.

Szreter, S., Sholkamy, H. and Dharmalingam, A. (eds) 2004, *Categories and Contexts: Anthropological and Historical Studies in Critical Demography*, Oxford University Press, Oxford.

Taylor, J. 2002, 'The context for observation', in D. Martin, F. Morphy, W. Sanders and J. Taylor, *Making Sense of the Census: Observations of the 2001 Enumeration in Remote Aboriginal Australia*, CAEPR Research Monograph No. 22 (reprinted 2004), ANU E Press, Canberra.

Taylor, J. 2004, *Social Indicators for Aboriginal Governance: Insights from the Thamarrurr Region, Northern Territory*, CAEPR Research Monograph No. 24, ANU E Press, Canberra.

Taylor, J. 2005, 'Counting the cost: Stanner and demographic change in the Thamarrurr region', Paper presented at the two-day symposium, *W.E.H. Stanner: Anthropologist and Public Intellectual*, 24–25 November 2005, ANU, Canberra.

Taylor, J. 2006a, 'Indigenous people in the West Kimberley labour market', *CAEPR Working Paper No. 35*, CAEPR, ANU, Canberra.

Taylor, J. 2006b, 'Leaving the bush? Indigenous people and the mobility transition', CAEPR Seminar, 17 May, CAEPR, ANU, Canberra.

Taylor, J. 2007a, 'Indigenous peoples and indicators of well-being: Australian perspectives on United Nations global frameworks', *Social Indicators Research*, July 2007, available at http://www.springerlink.com/content/7r7035u2524q36n, accessed 26 July 2007.

Taylor, J. 2007b, 'Out of sight, out of mind, out of pocket', *National Indigenous Times*, 4 October 2007, pp. 18–19.

Taylor, J. and Stanley, O. 2005, 'The opportunity costs of the status quo in the Thamarrurr region, Northern Territory', *CAEPR Working Paper No. 28*, CAEPR, ANU, Canberra.

Villaveces-Izquierdo, S. 2004, 'Internal diaspora and state imagination: Colombia's failure to envision a nation', in S. Szreter, H. Sholkamy and A. Dharmalingam (eds), *Categories and Contexts: Anthropological Studies in Critical Demography*, Oxford University Press, Oxford.

Watson, N.L. 2007, 'Implications of land rights reform for Indigenous health', *Medical Journal of Australia*, vol. 186, no. 10, pp. 534–6.

Westbury, N. and Dillon, M.C. 2006, 'Australia's institutionalised second class', *Australian Financial Review*, 8 December 2006.

Wilson, T., Beneforti, M. and Barnes, T. 2005, 'Population statistics and the number of House of Representative seats for the Northern Territory', *People and Place*, vol. 13, no. 4, pp. 23–33.

CAEPR Research Monograph Series

1. *Aborigines in the Economy: A Select Annotated Bibliography of Policy Relevant Research 1985–90*, L. M. Allen, J. C. Altman, and E. Owen (with assistance from W. S. Arthur), 1991.

2. *Aboriginal Employment Equity by the Year 2000*, J. C. Altman (ed.), published for the Academy of Social Sciences in Australia, 1991.

3. *A National Survey of Indigenous Australians: Options and Implications*, J. C. Altman (ed.), 1992.

4. *Indigenous Australians in the Economy: Abstracts of Research, 1991–92*, L. M. Roach and K. A. Probst, 1993.

5. *The Relative Economic Status of Indigenous Australians, 1986–91*, J. Taylor, 1993.

6. *Regional Change in the Economic Status of Indigenous Australians, 1986–91*, J. Taylor, 1993.

7. *Mabo and Native Title: Origins and Institutional Implications*, W. Sanders (ed.), 1994.

8. *The Housing Need of Indigenous Australians, 1991*, R. Jones, 1994.

9. *Indigenous Australians in the Economy: Abstracts of Research, 1993–94*, L. M. Roach and H. J. Bek, 1995.

10. *The Native Title Era: Emerging Issues for Research, Policy, and Practice*, J. Finlayson and D. E. Smith (eds), 1995.

11. *The 1994 National Aboriginal and Torres Strait Islander Survey: Findings and Future Prospects*, J. C. Altman and J. Taylor (eds), 1996.

12. *Fighting Over Country: Anthropological Perspectives*, D. E. Smith and J. Finlayson (eds), 1997.

13. *Connections in Native Title: Genealogies, Kinship, and Groups*, J. D. Finlayson, B. Rigsby, and H. J. Bek (eds), 1999.

14. *Land Rights at Risk? Evaluations of the Reeves Report*, J. C. Altman, F. Morphy, and T. Rowse (eds), 1999.

15. *Unemployment Payments, the Activity Test, and Indigenous Australians: Understanding Breach Rates*, W. Sanders, 1999.

16. *Why Only One in Three? The Complex Reasons for Low Indigenous School Retention*, R. G. Schwab, 1999.

For information on CAEPR Discussion Papers, Working Papers and Research Monographs (Nos 1-19) please contact:

Publication Sales, Centre for Aboriginal Economic Policy Research, The Australian National University, Canberra, ACT, 0200

Telephone: 02–6125 8211
Facsimile: 02–6125 2789

Information on CAEPR abstracts and summaries of all CAEPR print publications and those published electronically can be found at the following WWW address:

http://www.anu.edu.au/caepr/

www.ingramcontent.com/pod-product-compliance
Lightning Source LLC
Chambersburg PA
CBHW061245270326
41928CB00041B/3436